CONCORDIA

Ralph David Gehrke

CONCORDIA PUBLISHING HOUSE

COMMENTARY

1 and 2 Samuel

ST. LOUIS   LONDON

The Bible text in this publication is from
the Revised Standard Version of the Bible,
copyright 1946 and 1952 by the Division
of Christian Education, National Council
of Churches, and used by permission.

Concordia Publishing House, St. Louis, Missouri
Concordia Publishing House Ltd., London, E. C. 1
© 1968 Concordia Publishing House
Library of Congress Catalog Card No. 68-19904
MANUFACTURED IN THE UNITED STATES OF AMERICA

CONTENTS

Preface   7

Introduction   11

Outline   23

Commentary on 1 and 2 Samuel   27

For Further Reading   393

Index of Special Subjects   395

Maps

     Palestine for 1 Sam. 1 – 15   26

     Palestine for 1 Sam. 16 – 31   134

     Palestine for 2 Samuel   230

PREFACE

The preparation of commentaries on the Bible is a continuing task of scholarship and faith, for the unchanging Word of God must speak to the varying needs of each age. Furthermore, new knowledge of ancient cultures and languages adds to the insight into the world and meaning of the Bible. A commentary is thus a means of listening to the text.

The Concordia Commentary offers its readers a running narrative interpretation of the Revised Standard Version of the Bible. Writers are free to criticize the translation since their work is based on the Hebrew, Aramaic, and Greek texts of the original Bible. Footnotes and foreign language expressions are generally omitted. Brief bibliographies provide direction for further study.

The writers of this series accept the Bible as the source of faith and the directive for life. They pursue their task in confessional commitment to Biblical revelation. Yet in their role as Biblical scholars it is their function to subordinate personal reflection and private or sectarian views to the unique and original direction of the text.

This commentary, therefore, is addressed to the devout who may often be mystified or frightened by the Bible's vastness and depth. The commentary attempts to provide a contemporary understanding of the ancient text rather than to develop practical implications for modern life. Theological, historical, and literary interests are uppermost. However, the writers are aware not only of the difference between the past and the present but also how little basic human problems have changed and how directly helpful the Biblical perspective and commitment remain.

The contributors (to this series) hope that their words may bear worthy witness to that Word which alone abides.

WALTER J. BARTLING AND ALBERT E. GLOCK

Editors

1 and 2 Samuel

INTRODUCTION

In this commentary, the author has aimed at assisting the general reader of the Biblical text by (1) removing, as much as possible, the obstacles present-day persons experience in reading about ancient events in an ancient document, (2) by pointing out the basic significance of the various narratives, (3) by illuminating the sacred narrative through such comment as will enable the Scriptural text to speak directly to him. It is hoped that the commentary's avoidance of the technicalities of Biblical scholarship and its extensive employment of the method of interpretative retelling will not disappoint the student who consults it for only occasional help on specific words or verses. Such help has in fact usually been incorporated in the general retelling.

Limitations of space have prevented the inclusion of many footnotes. For specific points the concerned student may consult the excellent studies included in the section "For Further Reading." The *Revised Standard Version* of the Scriptures incorporates many fruits of recent linguistic and textual research. The author has also taken into consideration not only the major discussions of the various types of subject matter involved but also the main versions of the text (Hebrew, Septuagint, Qumran fragments now available). The results of his research on such matters are ordinarily incorporated in the commentary without special comment or footnote. Above all, the author has tried to help Christians read this exciting account of the founding of Israelite kingship in the light of its fulfillment in the crucified and risen King from David's line, our Lord Jesus Christ!

Name and Content

The traditional names, "The First Book of Samuel" and "The Second Book of Samuel," fail to designate adequately either the content or the author of these "books." Their content is by no means limited to the life and activity of Samuel. Nor can Samuel be considered the author of these books. In fact, his death is reported (1 Sam. 25:1; 28:3) long before many of the events of these books occur. It was a mistake when Jewish and some Christian traditions identified these books with an entirely different document mentioned in 1 Chron. 29:29, the "Chronicles of Samuel the seer," and thus gave these books what comes close to being a misnomer.

At first these two Books of Samuel were themselves connected as one book; moreover, that one book was once an integral part of an extended account that stretched from Joshua through 2 Kings, a section that the Hebrew canon still significantly entitles "The Former Prophets." This traditional Hebrew title — contrasting with the title for the books Isaiah through Malachi, "The Latter Prophets" — should warn modern people against judging them by the alien standards of modern history writing, since they are truly "prophetic books," that is, books that convey the divine message of God rather than the sort of "historical information about Israel" that most modern people expect from what they call history.

Prophetic history employs a very excellent and legitimate history method; to appreciate it, we must first grasp the theological perspective from which it evaluates the events. Contemporary Biblical scholarship has designated the narrative Joshua through 2 Kings as "The Deuteronomic History." This name seeks to point out that their basic philosophy of history is the same as that of the Book of Deuteronomy and of King Josiah's "Deuteronomic Reformation" (2 Kings 23). The viewpoint of these reformers was that Israel suffered oppression and judgment at the hand of the Lord whenever it fell from His covenant but that whenever it repented, the Lord responded and raised up deliverance in fulfillment of His promises. (Cf. Judges 2:6-23)

The one-unit Book of Samuel was split into two books of almost equal length by the men who prepared the famous Greek translation of the Old Testament, the Septuagint. What could be put on a single roll in vowelless Hebrew script became much longer in the voweled Greek translation. The two books were called Books of Kingdoms, A and B, and what we call the Books of Kings was called Books of Kingdoms, C and D. Roman Catholic tradition has generally followed this lead, calling these books Books of Kings, 1, 2, 3, and 4.

The content of the Books of Samuel can be briefly outlined. The story of Samuel—his birth, call, and leadership of Israel—is told in Chs. 1—8, though Samuel

13

also appears in a minor role in some of the subsequent stories as prophet to the kings. In Chs. 9 – 15 the narrative concentrates on Saul, though he also appears occasionally in the subsequent narrative as David's persecutor, and his tragic end is recounted in Chs. 28 and 31. But from 1 Sam. 16 through the rest of 1 Samuel and all of 2 Samuel the story really concerns David: his rise to the throne (1 Sam. 16 – 2 Sam. 1), his great empire (2 Sam. 2 – 8), the famous narrative about the succession to his throne (2 Sam. 9 – 20), and an appendix. (2 Sam. 21 – 24)

Composition and Date

When he began the task of recounting the beginnings of kingship in Israel, the author of the Books of Samuel undoubtedly already had a lot of material at his disposal. Some was oral: songs originally sung by David (like the song of victory, 2 Sam. 22), tales that passed down from generation to generation (like the story of David and Goliath, 1 Sam. 17), stories that were told by various groups in various districts (like the story of deliverance remembered at the rock named Ebenezer, "Rock of Help," 1 Sam. 7). He also had available some written sources: official records kept at the king's court (archive material for 2 Sam. 8), lists (court officials, 2 Sam. 8 and 20; warriors, 23:8-39), the narrative of the succession to David's throne (2 Sam. 9 – 20 and 1 Kings 1 – 2), "The Book of Jashar," a source specifically referred to in the superscription to David's lament for Saul and Jonathan (2 Sam. 1:17). That superscription gives most illuminating insight into the path – typical in many respects – that this famous elegy traveled before it got into its present spot: (a) David sang it originally after hearing the tragic news of the death of the two

14

heroes; (b) it was taught to the people of Judah and presumably repeatedly sung by them; (c) it was written down in "The Book of Jashar," apparently an anthology of war poems that is no longer extant but is quoted also in Joshua 10:12 f.; (d) finally, in this written form it was transferred by the author-compiler of our present account to its present location in what we call the Second Book of Samuel.

A present-day historian shares with such an ancient historian the task of first gathering pertinent source materials (documents, articles, letters, reports, interviews). But standards of literary craftsmanship require of the modern historian that, as the second step in any retelling of events, he should offer a compact and chronologically consistent account that will reveal both his own interpretation and also its basis in the actual sources (usually quoting persons and documents or referring to written sources in footnotes). This second step in history-telling was, however, not required of the ancient narrator of the Books of Samuel. He was not bound by such present-day standards of literary continuity even though he did, to be sure, interpret his material as he made his selections and editorial comment. His audience, it seems, expected as comprehensive a story as possible, not only one view. Since the events surrounding the establishment of David's empire were remembered and reported with many different accents in different circles (just as "The New Deal" in recent American history received, and is still receiving, various interpretations in various circles of our nation), it is natural that various groups would foster and preserve various versions. At Ramah, for example, Samuel's prophet-disciples were likely to accent aspects of that tremendous development different from those accented by Saul's

Benjaminite followers, who were left high and dry in the defunct capital city of Gibeah, or by David's officials in the Jerusalem court circles, or, most interestingly, by the Benjaminite descendants of Jonathan, who lived in Jerusalem at the court — at David's express command. (2 Sam. 9)

Since our account is composite in nature as a result of this sort of literary activity, attempts have been made to isolate its various elements, especially "the written documents"; but with the exception of rather broad agreement that there is a compact and literarily consistent narrative about the succession to David's throne imbedded in 2 Sam. 9 – 20, it has not been possible to isolate clearly such written "sources"; certainly the early attempt to find in the Books of Samuel a continuation of the Pentateuchal documentary hypothesis' JEDP has failed. Present-day attempts to disentangle the various "traditions," often according to their supposed place of origin, have proved more fruitful; but it must be emphatically stated that there are limits to this sort of "detective work."

In any case, this brief commentary restricts itself to pointing out only obvious instances where clear evidence of local tradition is significant (1 Sam. 17:54; cf. p. 150); it does not set up any all-embracing theory. Realizing that the whole of our narrative is most likely compounded out of many separate parts whose origins can be only precariously conjectured, this commentary seeks rather to get at the point of each episode in its present form. It may well be that in the stage of oral tradition preceding our author's writing many of the traditions had already been interwoven; hence modern persons should avoid putting too much trust in modern criteria of "what the original must have been like" in attempting to reconstruct all the steps by which the book got into its present form. An informed guess (more cannot be offered!) suggests that much of the written account with its various strands already interwoven had appeared before 700 B. C., after the fall of the Northern Kingdom of Israel during the time of Hezekiah and Isaiah, and that final form was given to it subsequent to the Josianic Reformation, perhaps by adherents of that Reformation movement, most likely during the first years of the Exile.

Complicated and conjectural analysis concerning the composition, date, and authorship of the Books of Samuel need cause the believer no great perturbation. He realizes by faith that Scripture is no less inspired for having passed through such a process under the guidance of God. An adequate understanding of the doctrine of verbal inspiration does *not* necessitate that one posit that God dictated the account in a mechanical way to one person at one time. God spoke to the fathers of old in many and various ways (Heb. 1:1), and the Christian, who knows God as the one who spoke definitively in His Word Jesus Christ, puts himself underneath all that the divine Scriptures bring him, no matter what the human instrumentality happens to have been. He believes that it is God the Holy Spirit who brings him the divine message that focuses on Christ in the Scriptures in their present form, no matter what the process may have been by which they got into this their present form. In their oral form these stories were God's message for His people, even before they were written down in their present authoritative form. They are still God's Word when pastors, teachers, parents re-present them under the guidance of the Holy Spirit. Since the prophet Samuel is not a likely candidate for the unknown "author" of the Books of Samuel, and since the books themselves give us no real clues, the question of authorship may be answered with the words of Gregory the Great concerning the Book of Job, whose "author" is likewise unknown: "What difference does it make if we do not know who the author is, as long as by faith its author is believed to have been the Holy Ghost?"

Historical Background

In covering the period from the beginnings of Israelite kingship to the end of David's reign, the Books of Samuel do not give us a complete and logically organized picture of that history such as we expect in a modern history like John Bright's *History of Israel,* for, like the other Biblical books, these were written by believers for believers in ancient days and need not conform to conventions of modern historiography. But even the most critical modern historian would grant that this narrative is by no means fabricated fiction. It does fit into the general historical background of the time, and it may be helpful to review briefly how its account fits in with what is known from general history.

At first Israel consisted of 12 tribes held together in a loose confederacy by a common covenant. It was a confederacy that gathered for holy wars and for worship at the common sanctuary of the ark. At the end of the period of the Judges Israel had to face the grave threat of Philistine domination. These non-Semitic peoples had settled on the maritime coast about 1200 B. C. and in Samuel's day, 150 years later, were threatening the Hebrew tribes living in the central hill country with their efficient military organization. This threat, which the Israelites felt they could no longer meet in the previous manner of fighting holy wars, prompted them to demand a change in political organization, the formation of a national state headed by a permanent king such as the surrounding nations of Edom, Moab, Ammon, and many Canaanite city-states had.

The transition to this new political form was gradual, Saul first appearing as a "judge," that is, as a charismatic leader, winning his victory over the Ammonites in an old-fashioned holy war (1 Sam. 11). Gradually, however, the war of liberation from Philistine dominance (1 Sam. 14) helped prepare the way for a genuine national state along monarchical lines. This work was completed by David, who saved the disastrous situation caused by the defeat at Mount Gilboa and Saul's death. David not only defeated the Philistines decisively but became king of Judah by election, king of Israel by covenant, and king of a new capital city by conquest, making that city of Jerusalem also the religious center of a new united empire. Though plagued even in David's days by internal struggles and a fierce rivalry to determine the succession to his throne, the empire survived under Solomon. We cannot give precise dates for these events; but by synchronizing some chronological indications in the text with supplementary extra-Biblical information concerning surrounding nations, it is possible to suggest the following approximate dates: ca. 1050 B. C., fall of Shiloh; ca. 1020 – 1000 B. C., Saul king of Israel; ca. 1000 – 961 B. C., David king of Israel and an Israelite empire.

The Message of the Books of Samuel

What the books of Samuel bring us is not just information for reconstructing a history of Israel but a message central to the history of salvation: the establishment of God's own kingship on earth. The Lord's kingship was certainly not achieved by Saul, nor even by the man after His heart, David. His divine promises nevertheless still stood fast, and these books tell how God went about establishing what He had promised. Hence these books are essentially not about Samuel, Saul, and David but about their God, Yahweh, the Lord.

An Old Testament John the Baptist, Samuel prepares the way for the new era, the monarchy. Born of a previously barren woman, a forerunner of the great prophets, Samuel is faithful to the Mosaic covenant, even to the point of opposing the wish of the majority for a king, insisting that the Lord alone can be Israel's king. Even after the Lord graciously grants that desire of the people, Samuel establishes the Israelite monarchy on the basis of the Sinaitic covenant, keeping it from being an idolatrous divine kingship such as the pagan nations knew. When Saul proves unfaithful to his trust, Samuel regretfully proclaims his rejection.

Saul is the tragic king, chosen by the Lord to be Israel's first king but then rejected after he proves false to God's call. Despite his successes — perhaps even because of them — Saul prefers to hearken to the voice of the people. Hence he is finally abandoned by the Lord, and an evil spirit from the Lord comes upon him; he dies without having achieved national unity. In few other instances do the Scriptures picture the tragic course of an unfaithful servant of the Lord so vividly.

David is of course the chief character of these books, the "man after the Lord's heart," the one to whom the Lord entrusted the destiny of His people. After a fantastic, almost fairy-tale-like triumph over numerous obstacles, David becomes the Lord's representative on earth. An innovator and "modernizer" in the political realm, religiously David shares the ancient Israelite faith to the point of even respecting the sacrosanct person of his royal persecutor, the anointed of the Lord, also abasing himself before the Lord's prophet Nathan. David not only unites the nation and carves out an empire but brings the ancient ark to Jerusalem and makes "the city of David" "the holy city." He receives the great Messianic promise (2 Sam. 7) that he and his successors will be the adopted sons of the Lord, the ones by whom the Lord will establish His kingship on earth, a kingship which will never end.

In all these stories of the Books of Samuel it is the Lord, however, who remains the main actor. Through the events proclaimed by His Word, He manifests Himself as the Lord of Israel's history, of its past, present, and future. Hence these books are open-ended toward a future fulfillment of their great prophecies. Born at Bethlehem, a descendant of David, Jesus Christ is the Son of David. By His resurrection from the dead He entered upon an eternal kingship in a kingdom that embraces the entire universe for all eternity.

Text and Versions

The traditional Hebrew (Masoretic) text of the Books of Samuel is one of the least well-preserved of all Old Testament books. Hence, as even the RSV footnotes indicate, it must often be illuminated by references to the Greek version, the famous Septuagint, which often preserves helpful readings (e. g., 1 Sam. 13:1). Recently fragments of Hebrew manuscripts of the Books of Samuel came to light among the Dead Sea Scroll material in the famous Cave Four at Qumran; these fragments show that the Greek translation is dependent on a Hebrew version that also varies from the traditional

Masoretic form. Thus Qumran's version of 1 Sam. 17 is 27 verses shorter than that in the traditional Hebrew text. Several Hebrew versions of the Books of Samuel were once extant, and it is therefore not always possible for us to establish the text in detail; the publication of all the Dead Sea manuscript fragments of Samuel will enrich our understanding of the complicated history of the Masoretic text of Samuel. But such uncertainty of the reading of certain parts in no way undermines the trustworthiness of all that is preserved, nor does it undercut the message of the books. For God's Word still speaks clearly to us through what has been transmitted.

OUTLINE

I. Eli and Samuel   1 Samuel 1 – 3

  A. The Birth of Samuel   1 – 2:10

  B. Eli's Wicked Sons and God's Pronouncement of Judgment   2:11-36

  C. Samuel Is Established as the Lord's Prophet   3 – 4:1a

II. The Ark   1 Samuel 4:1b – 7:2

III. Samuel and Saul   1 Samuel 7:3 – 15:35

  A. Samuel Delivers Israel   7:3-17

  B. Negotiations Concerning the Establishment of Kingship in Israel   8

  C. The Secret Choice of the King   9:1 – 10:16

  D. Saul Chosen King and Publicly Acclaimed at Mizpah   10:17-27

  E. Saul Becomes Deliverer and King   11

  F. Saul Renews the Covenant for Monarchical Israel   12

23

G. The War of Liberation 13 – 14

H. Saul Rejected 15

IV. Saul and David 1 Samuel 16 – 2 Samuel 1

    A. The Lord Chooses David 16

    B. David and Goliath 17

    C. Saul Becomes Jealous of David's Success 18:6-30

    D. Saul Seeks to Kill David 19

    E. David and Jonathan 20

    F. David Flees to Philistine Territory 21

    G. David on the Borders of Judah 22

    H. In the Lord's Hand 23

    I. David Spares Saul's Life 24

    J. The Lord Keeps David from Polluting Himself with Blood and Reveals His Life's Secret – Through a Woman 25

    K. David Spares Saul's Life a Second Time 26

    L. David in Philistia 27

    M. Saul Visits the Witch at Endor 28

    N. David Sent Back from the Front 29

    O. A Campaign Against the Amalekites 30

    P. Saul's Tragic End 31

    Q. David Laments His Enemy's Fall 2 Samuel 1

V. David as King 2 Samuel 2 – 8

    A. David as King of Judah in Hebron 2

    B. Negotiations Toward Making David King Also of the North 3

    C. David Punishes the Murderers of Ishbosheth 4

D. A New Capital for an Incipient Empire   5

E. David Brings the Ark to Jerusalem   6

F. The Lord's Great Messianic Promise to David   7

G. David's Empire and Its Administration   8

VI. The Succession to David's Throne   2 Samuel 9 – 20

     A. Mephibosheth, Jonathan's Son   9

     B. Trans-Jordanian Campaigns   10 and 12:26-31

     C. David and Bathsheba   11

     D. David's Repentance   12:1-25

     E. The Beginning of an Avalanche of Evil
        13:1 – 14:3

     F. Joab Negotiates the Recall of Absalom   14:4-33

     G. David's Flight from Absalom   15:1 – 16:14

     H. The Great Debate Between Ahithophel and
        Hushai   16:15 – 17:23

     I. The Rebellion Crushed and Absalom Killed
        17:24 – 18:33

     J. David's Return from the Battle of Mahanaim   19

     K. Joab Crushes Sheba's Revolt   20

VII. The Appendix of the Book of Samuel
      2 Samuel 21 – 24

     A. Great Famine and Execution of Saul's De-
        scendants   21:1-14

     B. Exploits Against the Philistines   21:15-22

     C. The Lord's Rescue of His Royal Servant   22

     D. David's "Last Words"   23:1-7

     E. David's Warriors   23:8-39

     F. Mercy in the Midst of Judgment   24

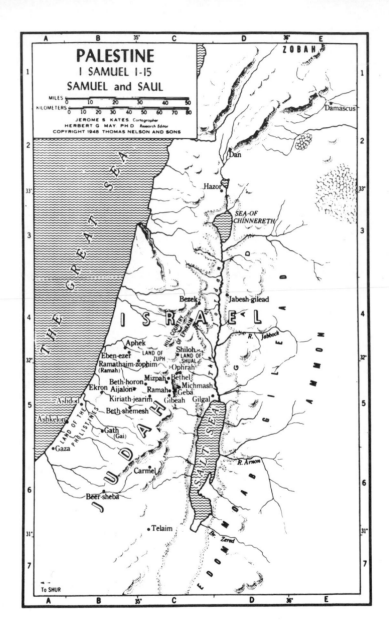

PALESTINE
I SAMUEL 1-15
SAMUEL and SAUL

MILES
0 10 20 30 40 50
KILOMETERS
0 10 20 30 40 50 60 70 80

JEROME S KATES Cartographer
HERBERT G MAY PH D Research Editor
COPYRIGHT 1948 THOMAS NELSON AND SONS

ZOBAH

Damascus

Dan

Hazor

SEA OF
CHINNERETH

THE GREAT SEA

Bezek

Jabesh-gilead

I S R A E L

R. Jabbock

AMMON

Aphek

HILL COUNTRY OF EPHRAIM

Eben-ezer

Shiloh

LAND OF ZUPH

LAND OF SHUAL

Ramathaim-zophim
(Ramah)

Ophrah

G I L E A D

Mizpah

Bethel

Beth-horon

Michmash

Ekron   Aijalon

Ramah   Geba

Ashdod

Kiriath-jearim

Gibeah   Gilgal

SALT SEA

Beth-shemesh

Ashkelon

LAND OF THE PHILISTINES

J U D A H

Gath
(Gai)

Gaza

M O A B

R. Arnon

Carmel

Beer-sheba

E D O M

Telaim

Br. Zered

To SHUR

Eli and Samuel

1 Samuel 1 – 3

The Birth of Samuel   1:1 — 2:10

Elkanah and His Household at Shiloh   *1:1-18*

¹ There was a certain man of Ramathaim-zophim of the hill country of Ephraim, whose name was Elkanah the son of Jeroham, son of Elihu, son of Tohu, son of Zuph, an Ephraimite. ² He had two wives; the name of the one was Hannah, and the name of the other Peninnah. And Peninnah had children, but Hannah had no children.

³ Now this man used to go up year by year from his city to worship and to sacrifice to the LORD of hosts at Shiloh, where the two sons of Eli, Hophni and Phinehas, were priests of the LORD. ⁴ On the day when Elkanah sacrificed, he would give portions to Peninnah his wife and to all her sons and daughters; ⁵ and, although *ᵃ* he loved Hannah, he would give Hannah only one portion, because the LORD had closed her womb. ⁶ And her rival used to provoke her sorely, to irritate her, because the LORD had

ᵃ Gk: Heb obscure

27

closed her womb. [7] So it went on year by year; as often as she went up to the house of the LORD, she used to provoke her. Therefore Hannah wept and would not eat. [8] And Elkanah, her husband, said to her, "Hannah, why do you weep? And why do you not eat? And why is your heart sad? Am I not more to you than ten sons?"

[9] After they had eaten and drunk in Shiloh, Hannah rose. Now Eli the priest was sitting on the seat beside the doorpost of the temple of the LORD. [10] She was deeply distressed and prayed to the LORD, and wept bitterly. [11] And she vowed a vow and said, "O LORD of hosts, if thou wilt indeed look on the affliction of thy maidservant, and remember me, and not forget thy maidservant, but wilt give to thy maidservant a son, then I will give him to the LORD all the days of his life, and no razor shall touch his head."

[12] As she continued praying before the LORD, Eli observed her mouth. [13] Hannah was speaking in her heart; only her lips moved, and her voice was not heard; therefore Eli took her to be a drunken woman. [14] And Eli said to her, "How long will you be drunken? Put away your wine from you." [15] But Hannah answered, "No, my lord, I am a woman sorely troubled; I have drunk neither wine nor strong drink, but I have been pouring out my soul before the LORD. [16] Do not regard your maidservant as a base woman, for all along I have been speaking out of my great anxiety and vexation." [17] Then Eli answered, "Go in peace, and the God of Israel grant your petition which you have made to him." [18] And she said, "Let your maidservant find favor in your eyes." Then the woman went her way and ate, and her countenance was no longer sad.

The important narrative concerning the beginning of the monarchy in Israel begins very simply with the story of a family. In the hill country of Ephraim at Ramah, Elkanah, a man of noble and well-known family, lives with two wives, Hannah and Peninnah. Elkanah should not be judged a bigamist; he had two wives because the first was barren and hence was thwarting the very purpose of marriage, continuity of the family (Deut. 21:15-17), to her great sorrow and shame (Gen. 30:1 f.). The conflict between Elkanah's two wives (one barren, the other the mother of many sons and daughters) always came to the fore at the pilgrimages Elkanah made with his entire family to the central sanctuary of Israel's tribal confederacy, Shiloh, at the precise moment when portions of the sacrificial meal were distributed. It seems that Hannah always received only one portion because, being alone, she deserved no more; this always provided her rival Peninnah with an opportunity for taunting her for her barrenness. On the present occasion Hannah therefore weeps and does not eat, even though Elkanah gives her touching assurance of his great love for her. Hannah leaves the meal as soon as she can in order to pour out her heart before the Lord at the entrance to the temple, where the high priest Eli is seated on his throne, available for consultation. Hannah's prayer culminates in a vow that if the Lord gives her a son, she will give him back to the Lord as a Nazirite. His long, unshorn hair will be the sign of his consecration to the Lord, and he will be the Lord's temple servant. Samuel, like Isaac, Samson, and John the Baptist, will be a son given by God to a previously barren mother. When the priest Eli observes the woman moving her lips so fervently and yet silently, he mistakenly imagines she is drunk in the Canaanite manner (cf. Amos 2:8; Is. 22:13) and therefore admonishes her for such disgraceful conduct; but when her soft answer convinces him of her sincerity, he dismisses her with his high-priestly promise and blessing, a truly divine word which cannot fail of fulfillment (cf. John 11:51). Hannah's response is touchingly modest, reminding us of Mary's "Let it be to me according to your word" (Luke 1:38). She believes, goes her way, partakes of the communion meal, and her face is no longer sad.

The Lord Fulfills His Promise, and Hannah Dedicates Samuel to the Lord   19-28

¹⁹ They rose early in the morning and worshiped before the LORD; then they went back to their house at Ramah. And Elkanah knew Hannah his wife, and the LORD remembered her; ²⁰ and in due time Hannah conceived and bore a son, and she called his name Samuel, for she said, "I have asked him of the LORD."

²¹ And the man Elkanah and all his house went up to offer to the LORD the yearly sacrifice, and to pay his vow. ²² But Hannah did not go up, for she said to her husband, "As soon as the child is weaned, I will bring him, that he may appear in the presence of the LORD, and abide there for ever." ²³ Elkanah her husband said to her, "Do what seems best to you, wait until you have weaned him; only, may the LORD establish his word." So the woman remained and nursed her son, until she weaned him. ²⁴ And when she had weaned him, she took him up with her, along with a three-year-old bull,^b an ephah of flour, and a skin of wine; and she brought him to the house of

^b Gk Syr: Heb three bulls

the **LORD** at Shiloh; and the child was young. [25] Then they slew the bull, and they brought the child to Eli. [26] And she said, "Oh, my lord! As you live, my lord, I am the woman who was standing here in your presence, praying to the **LORD**. [27] For this child I prayed; and the **LORD** has granted me my petition which I made to him. [28] Therefore I have lent him to the **LORD**; as long as he lives, he is lent to the **LORD**."

And they [x] worshiped the **LORD** there.

[x] Heb *he*

After worshiping the Lord at the sanctuary the next morning, the family returns home. In due time it becomes evident that the Lord has remembered and hearkened to Hannah's prayer, for she becomes the mother of the child whom she names Samuel. A modern etymology interprets the name as "the name of God," that is, "he over whom God's name is pronounced." But the narrator's explanation of the name in v. 20 shows that more is involved, namely, a play on the assonance of the name Samuel and the word *shaul* ("he who is asked") indicates, it seems, that this child Samuel will lead to the person Saul, Israel's first king, anointed by Samuel. Our story comes to its climax, however, in the consecration of the votive son at Shiloh. Another touching note shows that Elkanah, who shares the vow and purpose of his wife, wants to fulfill the vow promptly, perhaps at the very next annual festival, whereas the mother wishes to extend the time till the child is weaned, which could mean several years more (on vows, see Num. 30). Elkanah accedes to her wishes and prays that their lives may prosper until the vow may be fulfilled. The weaning is formally celebrated (cf. Gen. 21:8); then the child is taken on the pilgrimage together with significant offerings (a fully matured and therefore un- usually valuable bull, a skin of wine, and a bushel of flour) so that they might eat and drink and rejoice before the Lord on the occasion of the consecration of Samuel to the Lord's service. At Shiloh the child is given to the priest as the mother recalls the original occasion of her vow. Samuel will be a Nazirite. (Cf. 1:11 and Judg. 13:7)

Hannah's Magnificat   *2:1-10*

1 Hannah also prayed and said,
  "My heart exults in the LORD;
    my strength is exalted in the LORD.
  My mouth derides my enemies,
    because I rejoice in thy salvation.

2 "There is none holy like the LORD,
    there is none besides thee;
    there is no rock like our God.
3 Talk no more so very proudly,
    let not arrogance come from your mouth;
  for the LORD is a God of knowledge,
    and by him actions are weighed.
4 The bows of the mighty are broken,
    but the feeble gird on strength.
5 Those who were full have hired themselves out for
      bread,
    but those who were hungry have ceased to hunger.
  The barren has borne seven,
    but she who has many children is forlorn.
6 The LORD kills and brings to life;
    he brings down to Sheol and raises up.
7 The LORD makes poor and makes rich;
    he brings low, he also exalts.

⁸ He raises up the poor from the dust;
   he lifts the needy from the ash heap,
  to make them sit with princes
   and inherit a seat of honor.
 For the pillars of the earth are the LORD'S,
   and on them he has set the world.

⁹ "He will guard the feet of his faithful ones;
   but the wicked shall be cut off in darkness;
   for not by might shall a man prevail.
¹⁰ The adversaries of the LORD shall be broken to
     pieces;
   against them he will thunder in heaven.
 The LORD will judge the ends of the earth;
   he will give strength to his king,
   and exalt the power of his anointed."

Hannah's song of praise and thanksgiving at the festival is written in Hebrew poetic style, where one sentence parallels another. It follows the characteristic pattern of an Israelite hymn: an introductory summary (prayer element 1, vv. 1-3); the praise of the Lord, who is described as the majestic Ruler, who nevertheless in gracious compassion condescends to be the Lord of history and creation (prayer element 2, vv. 4-8); and, finally, a confession of confidence in Him who will judge the entire world and support His Messiah (prayer element 3, vv. 9-10).

(1) Hannah rejoices in the Lord, the mighty God, who, like a strong bullock, carries His head erect in a proud gesture of contempt for His foes, and these are warned not to rebel, because He has full knowledge of all actions. (2) But this Lord, who is so majestic in His holiness and power, intervenes, Hannah confesses, in

33

the world in the concrete events of daily life in order to redress wrongs. It does not avail a person to be strong, well fed, rich in children, healthy, wealthy, well born. God replaces people who take pride in such gifts with the feeble, the hungry, the barren, the dead, the poor, the lowly. Even the abode of the dead, Sheol, is not beyond His rulership, for He is the Creator, who has established order and justice in the universe. (3) The psalm ends with an expression of confidence that sees the Lord as the Judge of the universe and the Supporter of His Anointed. The reference to this Anointed points not only to the actual Davidic king who represented the Lord on Mount Zion (cf. Ps. 2) but to Him who alone fulfilled all the great promises attached to the Israelite kings, Jesus Christ. Thus the psalm places Samuel's life into the midst of God's activity, giving the theological key to the history of Samuel and Saul, which now follows. Mary's own Magnificat draws on this song of Hannah to celebrate the Incarnation of God. (Luke 1:46-55)

ELI'S WICKED SONS AND GOD'S PRONOUNCEMENT OF JUDGMENT   2:11-36

Eli's Corrupt Sons and Faithful Samuel   *11-21*

¹¹ Then Elkanah went home to Ramah. And the boy ministered to the LORD, in the presence of Eli the priest.

¹² Now the sons of Eli were worthless men; they had no regard for the LORD. ¹³ The custom of the priests with the people was that when any man offered sacrifice, the priest's servant would come, while the meat was boiling, with a three-pronged fork in his

hand, [14] and he would thrust it into the pan, or kettle, or caldron, or pot; all that the fork brought up the priest would take for himself. [c] So they did at Shiloh to all the Israelites who came there. [15] Moreover, before the fat was burned, the priest's servant would come and say to the man who was sacrificing, "Give meat for the priest to roast; for he will not accept boiled meat from you, but raw." [16] And if the man said to him, "Let them burn the fat first, and then take as much as you wish," he would say, "No, you must give it now; and if not, I will take it by force." [17] Thus the sin of the young men was very great in the sight of the LORD; for the men treated the offering of the LORD with contempt.

[18] Samuel was ministering before the LORD, a boy girded with a linen ephod. [19] And his mother used to make for him a little robe and take it to him each year, when she went up with her husband to offer the yearly sacrifice. [20] Then Eli would bless Elkanah and his wife, and say, "The LORD give you children by this woman for the loan which she lent to [d] the LORD"; so then they would return to their home.

[21] And the LORD visited Hannah, and she conceived and bore three sons and two daughters. And the boy Samuel grew in the presence of the LORD.

[c] Gk Syr Vg: Heb *with it*
[d] Or *for the petition which she asked of*

The account of Samuel's rising fortunes is now intertwined with a contrasting account of the decline and final rejection of Eli's wicked sons. The young Samuel ministers to the Lord under the tutelage of the old priest Eli, whereas the old priest's own undisciplined sons have, by contrast, no regard for the Lord or for the rights of the people over against the clergy. Although Mosaic law and sacred custom assigned certain portions of the communion sacrifices to the priests, these sons of Eli not only greedily appropriate the worshipers' rightful portion; they also arrogantly preempt the fresh meat even before the Lord's portion of the sacrifice has been offered on the altar. And if simple peasants and pious farmers voice their scruples about such violation of the sacred laws, these corrupt clergymen insultingly resort to threats of violence. Thus these priests despise the offerings of the Lord!

What these sons of Eli should be doing is being done by the young Samuel, who continues to minister before the Lord, girded for his sacred duties with a linen ephod, a light ceremonial garment, sometimes covering only the front of the body like an apron (1 Sam. 22:18; 2 Sam. 6:14). When worn by priests, it appears to have been more elaborate (cf. Ex. 28:28 f.). In any case, this ephod is different from the instrument of divination also so called (see 1 Sam. 10:20; cf. v. 28 and commentary on 1 Sam. 10:20, p. 86). An entirely different kind of garment is the little robe that Samuel's mother carefully prepares for each year's visit to Shiloh. Worn over the tunic, this proud gift is the mother's means of declaring her son's noble status. The family's pilgrimage is, we now hear, not merely a time of joyful reunion with Samuel. The parents return home each time with a new blessing from the Lord. As Eli puts it, the loan to the Lord is now paying good dividends: Hannah and Elkanah are blessed with five children. At the same time the Lord continues to bless Samuel's service at the sanctuary.

Eli Rebukes His Delinquent Sons   22-26

²² Now Eli was very old, and he heard all that his sons were doing to all Israel, and how they lay with the women who served at the entrance to the tent of meeting. ²³ And he said to them, "Why do you do such things? For I hear of your evil dealings from all the people. ²⁴ No, my sons; it is no good report that I hear the people of the **LORD** spreading abroad. ²⁵ If a man sins against a man, God will mediate for him; but if a man sins against the **LORD**, who can intercede for him?" But they would not listen to the voice of their father; for it was the will of the **LORD** to slay them.

²⁶ Now the boy Samuel continued to grow both in stature and in favor with the **LORD** and with men.

As the child Samuel continues to increase in wisdom and stature, the priest Eli grows older and more feeble. Despite his age, however, he does rebuke his sons most severely when he hears the widespread report of their immorality in the sanctuary. Eli's strongest argument to his sons is not that such action is offensive to the people but that no machinery of arbitration exists when a priest sins against the Lord. For settling ordinary cases arising between a human plaintiff and a human defendant the Lord is the umpire, speaking through His representatives, the judges or priests. If, however, as in the present case, the Lord becomes the plaintiff against His delinquent priests, there is no third party who is superior, to whom the Lord can appeal His case; as the offended party, He will simply take vengeance! Eli's sons disregard their father's admonition, for "it was the will of the Lord to slay them!" The hardening of their hearts is here traced back to the Lord as the primary cause (cf. Ex. 4:21; Joshua 11:20; 2 Sam. 24; Is. 6:9 f.; Mark 4:11 f.; John 12:37-43; Rom. 1:24, 26). This manner of speaking does not deny human freedom and responsibility, but it does point out the dire fact that after men have hardened their own hearts, God gives them up to their self-chosen lot and finally even sends them down the road to destruction.

Our attention is, however, soon drawn from the tragic situation in Eli's family to the one person who is able to take the place of these degenerate sons of Eli, one with whom God is well pleased and through whom He will carry on the true priesthood until it can be established anew. Samuel is therefore a type of Christ; and St. Luke (2:52) correctly takes the expressions of v. 26 ("the boy Samuel continued to grow both in stature and in favor with the Lord and with men") and applies them to the 12-year-old Jesus. He is the goal of the story begun here.

A Prophecy of Doom   27-36

²⁷ And there came a man of God to Eli, and said to him, "Thus the LORD has said, 'I revealed *ᵉ* myself to the house of your father when they were in Egypt subject to the house of Pharaoh. ²⁸ And I chose him out of all the tribes of Israel to be my priest, to go up to my altar, to burn incense, to wear an ephod before me; and I gave to the house of your father all my offerings by fire from the people of Israel. ²⁹ Why then look with greedy eye at *ᶠ* my sacrifices and my offerings which I commanded, and honor your sons above me by fattening yourselves upon the choicest parts of every offering of my people Israel?' ³⁰ Therefore the

ᵉGk Tg: Heb *Did I reveal*   ᶠOr *treat with scorn* Gk: Heb *kick at*

LORD the God of Israel declares: 'I promised that your house and the house of your father should go in and out before me for ever'; but now the **LORD** declares: 'Far be it from me; for those who honor me I will honor, and those who despise me shall be lightly esteemed. ³¹ Behold, the days are coming, when I will cut off your strength and the strength of your father's house, so that there will not be an old man in your house. ³² Then in distress you will look with envious eye on all the prosperity which shall be bestowed upon Israel; and there shall not be an old man in your house for ever. ³³ The man of you whom I shall not cut off from my altar shall be spared to weep out his *ᵍ* eyes and grieve his *ᵍ* heart; and all the increase of your house shall die by the sword of men.*ʰ* ³⁴ And this which shall befall your two sons, Hophni and Phinehas, shall be the sign to you: both of them shall die on the same day. ³⁵ And I will raise up for myself a faithful priest, who shall do according to what is in my heart and in my mind; and I will build him a sure house, and he shall go in and out before my anointed for ever. ³⁶ And every one who is left in your house shall come to implore him for a piece of silver or a loaf of bread, and shall say, "Put me, I pray you, in one of the priest's places, that I may eat a morsel of bread."'"

ᵍ Gk: Heb *your*   *ʰ* Gk: Heb *die as men*

The Israelites had raised their voices against the corruption at Shiloh, but seemingly in vain. Old Eli had also rebuked his sons, also seemingly in vain. Now the Lord speaks doom upon them through a "man of God," that is, a man who, in contrast to ordinary men, was

God's messenger, a prophet. References to the Lord's rejection of the delinquent priesthood of Eli's house, the substitution of the rival Zadokite line, and the humiliating situation of these rejected country priests after Josiah's reform reflect a rather common Old Testament feature — a continual refocusing of an original prophecy to the ever unfolding situation, a refocusing that ends with the spotlight shining on the true fulfillment: the true King-Priest, Christ Jesus. The speech of the "man of God" follows the well-known pattern of a prophetic pronouncement of doom — element 1: accusation of the culprits (vv. 27b-29); element 2: the messenger formula (v. 30a, "Therefore the Lord . . . declares"); element 3: the announcement of the divine verdict (vv. 30b-36). The prophet's accusation (1) is all the more cutting because it is prefaced with a reminder that it was the Lord who graciously called the house of Eli to serve Him (a) in the open-air court of the sanctuary, where the altar stood, (b) inside the temple, where the incense altar stood, and (c) in the giving of oracles. Why then, the prophet scolds, have they greedily taken the best of the portions that belonged to the Lord and fattened themselves with them? And why has Eli, the responsible head of the priestly family, failed to restrain them? Therefore the messenger formula (2) announces the verdict (3). The original promise given to this priestly family is abrogated; the living God is no idol bound to comply with the whims of unfaithful people who dishonor Him and think they can manipulate Him with "earlier promises." God's promises are not subject to a sort of magic by which He can be controlled! He is therefore changing His policy toward them. But instead of completely rejecting them from all priestly service or completely annihilating them, the Lord will still preserve their house — so that their survivors may see how God blesses the rivals who will take their place. Old and respected men will be lacking in their house; the only survivor of Saul's extermination of the Elides at Nob, Abiathar, will escape to live on, but only in misery, disappointment, and vexation, especially when he, too, is finally put out of office, banished to Anathoth to weep out his eyes there while the Jerusalem priests, the Zadokites, enjoy what once belonged to his family. A sign that will guarantee, already now, the eventual fulfillment of the judgment is that Hophni and Phineas will soon both die on the same day.

On the heels of this withering judgment we next hear, surprisingly enough, the famous promise of "a faithful priest," that is, a priest who is established and can be depended on (cf. 25:28; 2 Sam. 7:12 ff.). He will serve in closest connection with the Lord's anointed ("Messiah" in Hebrew; "Christ" in Greek). In v. 10 we heard that the Lord's anointed will be the Lord's instrument in the establishment of the age of salvation. And so we ask, "Who is this established priest?" In view of the immediate context, we may answer, "Samuel" but it will soon become clear that Samuel's house and priesthood is not established forever; in fact, he and his sons are soon pushed aside at the establishment of the monarchy. We may answer, "*Zadok* is the established priest who will work in closest contact with the king." It is true, there is a partial fulfillment of this prophecy when Zadok and his family supplant Abiathar, son of Eli, under Solomon (1 Kings 2:27) and in the days thereafter. Yet the prophecy was not really fulfilled by Zadok either. His descendants in the New Testament era are the Sadducees, and they lose out completely when the temple is destroyed by Titus A. D. 70. The focus must be reset if the prophecy concerning the office of the faith-

41

ful priest is to be fully explained. And the focus must be ultimately centered on Christ Jesus, the eternal High Priest, who by His death and resurrection fulfilled 1 Sam. 2:35 as well as 2 Sam. 7:1 ff. For all the promises of God "find their Yes in him." (2 Cor. 1:20)

SAMUEL IS ESTABLISHED
AS THE LORD'S PROPHET   3:1 — 4:1A

The Lord Speaks to Samuel   *3:1-14*

¹ Now the boy Samuel was ministering to the **LORD** under Eli. And the word of the **LORD** was rare in those days; there was no frequent vision.

² At that time Eli, whose eyesight had begun to grow dim, so that he could not see, was lying down in his own place; ³ the lamp of God had not yet gone out, and Samuel was lying down within the temple of the **LORD**, where the ark of God was. ⁴ Then the **LORD** called, "Samuel! Samuel!" *ⁱ* and he said, "Here I am!" ⁵ and ran to Eli, and said, "Here I am, for you called me." But he said, "I did not call; lie down again." So he went and lay down. ⁶ And the **LORD** called again, "Samuel!" And Samuel arose and went to Eli, and said, "Here I am, for you called me." But he said, "I did not call, my son; lie down again." ⁷ Now Samuel did not yet know the **LORD**, and the word of the **LORD** had not yet been revealed to him. ⁸ And the **LORD** called Samuel again the third time. And he arose and went to Eli, and said, "Here I am, for you called me." Then Eli perceived that the **LORD** was calling the boy. ⁹ Therefore Eli said to Samuel, "Go, lie down; and if he calls you, you shall say,

ⁱ Gk See 3. 10: Heb *the* LORD *called Samuel*

42

'Speak, **LORD**, for thy servant hears.'" So Samuel
went and lay down in his place.

¹⁰ And the **LORD** came and stood forth, calling
as at other times, "Samuel! Samuel!" And Samuel
said, "Speak, for thy servant hears." ¹¹ Then the
LORD said to Samuel, "Behold, I am about to do a
thing in Israel, at which the two ears of every one that
hears it will tingle. ¹² On that day I will fulfil against
Eli all that I have spoken concerning his house, from
beginning to end. ¹³ And I tell him that I am about to
punish his house for ever, for the iniquity which he
knew, because his sons were blaspheming God,ʲ
and he did not restrain them. ¹⁴ Therefore I swear to
the house of Eli that the iniquity of Eli's house shall
not be expiated by sacrifice or offering for ever."

ʲ Another reading is *for themselves*

Just as the frame of a picture helps us in viewing
the picture, so the framework of this story, its introductory and concluding verses (v. 1 and vv. 19-21), help us
to see that much more is involved in this chapter than
Samuel's pronouncement of judgment on Eli's house.
These bracketing verses help us see that Samuel is
hereby being called and established as the Lord's accredited prophet. At first Samuel is pictured as an
apprentice, aiding the aged priest in the traditional
priestly activities, such as sacrificing, praying, watching
the ark at night, opening the temple doors at dawn. One
aspect of normal priestly activity, however, is missing:
the word of the Lord is rare; visions are infrequent. That
means that the Lord is silent; and the inference from the
context seems to be that this is because of the hardness
of the hearts of Eli's sons. Samuel is as yet only Eli's

helper; God's direct revelation is still foreign to him. As it turns out, even Eli does not count on such a possibility — only after three false starts does he begin to realize that the young Samuel has heard the word of the Lord and that a new prophetic era has been inaugurated.

The old priest, seemingly too feeble to watch all night in the sanctuary, has appointed the young Samuel to attend the Lord, that is, to be on hand before His lamp throughout the night, much as a dutiful servant waits on his master (cf. Ex. 27:20 f; 30:7 f.). Just enough olive oil had been measured out into the shell-like pottery lamp to last through the night; at the very end of the night, just before the flame would burn itself out at the coming of dawn, the Lord calls out from above the ark (cf. Ex. 25:22) to the young man. Utterly inexperienced in the reception of divine oracles, Samuel misunderstands and dutifully rises and runs — three times — to be at Eli's service. Finally the old priest recognizes the once-familiar pattern of revelation and teaches his apprentice correct procedure in obtaining the divine oracle, using the formula, "Speak, Lord, for thy servant hears."

The Lord speaks again from His position above the ark (Ex. 25:22) and, upon hearing the traditional response from Samuel, announces His own imminent interference in Israel's history. The Lord will fulfill the word of judgment He had earlier spoken against Eli's delinquent house because his sons cursed God without Eli having effectively restrained them. With an oath the Lord swears that no amount of offerings, animal or cereal, will wipe out the debt of guilt for Eli's house, since by their blasphemies they have desecrated their holy office and the worship of the holy God.

44

Samuel Speaks the Lord's Message   *15-18*

¹⁵ **Samuel lay until morning; then he opened the doors of the house of the LORD. And Samuel was afraid to tell the vision to Eli.** ¹⁶ **But Eli called Samuel and said, "Samuel, my son." And he said, "Here I am."** ¹⁷ **And Eli said, "What was it that he told you? Do not hide it from me. May God do so to you and more also, if you hide anything from me of all that he told you."** ¹⁸ **So Samuel told him everything and hid nothing from him. And he said, "It is the LORD; let him do what seems good to him."**

The modest young apprentice's fear of proclaiming such a frightful message to his master is understandable. After all, Eli was his superior, and this message meant ruin for him as well as catastrophe for a nation without a priesthood. Therefore Samuel tries to go about his daily tasks without making the harsh words of judgment known. Eli, however, instructs his apprentice in the necessity of faithfully proclaiming even harsh words of woe (cf. Ezek. 2:10 f.; Jer. 17:16; 20:8 f.). Eli's solemn adjuration is, however, carefully phrased with a vague formula that refrains from stating the exact evil that should come to Samuel if he does not oblige; Eli also refrains from mentioning the name "LORD," lest he inadvertently blaspheme (cf. Amos 6:10). It is the duty of those who receive the Lord's word to transmit it to those to whom it is addressed, and so Samuel finally tells everything. As for Eli's response ("It is the LORD; let him do what seems good to him"), it is difficult to decide whether this is hypocritical blasphemy (amounting to "Well, we can't change that; but I'm happy it will not come in my day") or whether the old priest is humbly bowing to God's judgment. If the latter alternative is true — and it seems more likely — Eli is a person who believes in the midst of judgment, still mindful of his responsibility to the young prophet-in-the-making. In any case, Eli speaks without reproaching the Lord. Like Hannah, he knows that God will fulfill His plans.

Samuel Is Accredited as the Lord's Prophet
in Shiloh   *3:19 — 4:1a*

¹⁹ And Samuel grew, and the LORD was with him and let none of his words fall to the ground. ²⁰ And all Israel from Dan to Beer-sheba knew that Samuel was established as a prophet of the LORD. ²¹ And the LORD appeared again at Shiloh, for the LORD revealed himself to Samuel at Shiloh by the word of the LORD.

¹ And the word of Samuel came to all Israel.

The final verses act as a closing framework, corresponding to the introductory framework of the story in v. 1. They emphasize the fact that Israel's communication with the Lord has now been restored through Samuel. God acknowledges and accredits Samuel as a true prophet, confirming whatever prophecies he makes (Deut. 18:22). And so the extraordinary thing happens that in Shiloh (the sanctuary that had been despised by the people because of Eli's wicked sons, where no word of God appeared) a new era of prophetic activity has now been inaugurated, one that is recognized by all people in the entire territory of Israel from border to border.

The Ark

1 Samuel 4:1b — 7:2

The ark of the Lord plays an important role in these three chapters as well as throughout the Books of Samuel. Already in Israel's previous history it had been important; all Israelites knew the story of how at Mount Sinai the Lord had condescended to come down and dwell in the midst of His new covenant people, invisibly sitting on His ark-throne as their King, traveling with them through the wilderness as "the LORD of hosts, who is enthroned on the cherubim." Israelites also knew how the ark had played a key role in the conquest of the Holy Land: how the Jordan river had opened before it and the walls of Jericho had toppled before it. After their settlement in the Promised Land the ark had been stationed in the central sanctuary at Shiloh, and from His invisible seat above it the Lord had revealed His will for His people through His priests and prophets, recently, as we heard in the previous chapter (Ch. 3), through the young prophet Samuel.

The ark was to remain the symbol of the Lord's covenant presence until the very end of Israel's history

as a nation, especially after David brought it to Mount
Zion, where it served as the most holy object in his new
religious and political capital city (2 Sam. 6). In the
present three chapters we learn that although His ark
is captured by the enemy, the Lord of the ark conquers
that enemy all by Himself and returns the ark to the
borders of Judah.

Though Defeated, Israel Still Remains Impenitent 4:1b-4

**Now Israel went out to battle against the Phi-
listines; they encamped at Ebenezer, and the Philistines encamped at Aphek. ² The Philistines drew up
in line against Israel, and when the battle spread,
Israel was defeated by the Philistines, who slew about
four thousand men on the field of battle. ³ And when
the troops came to the camp, the elders of Israel said,
"Why has the LORD put us to rout today before the
Philistines? Let us bring the ark of the covenant of
the LORD here from Shiloh, that he may come among
us and save us from the power of our enemies." ⁴ So
the people sent to Shiloh, and brought from there
the ark of the covenant of the LORD of hosts, who is
enthroned on the cherubim; and the two sons of Eli,
Hophni and Phinehas, were there with the ark of
the covenant of God.**

This account presupposes on the part of its hearers
an appreciation for the ritual of a holy war that we who
live 3,000 years later can unfortunately acquire only
after a bit of study. A holy war was usually a defensive
war, a fact which would fit in well with the Septuagint's
introduction to our story, "It came to pass in those days
that the Philistines mobilized for war against Israel,
and the Israelites, in turn, came out to meet them at

Aphek." The entire procedure of initiating a holy war (proclaiming an emergency, summoning the tribes, mustering as the host of the Lord, receiving the Lord's oracle assurance, "The LORD has delivered the enemy into your hand," etc.) is not explicitly detailed here, though it is taken for granted (cf. pp. 105 f., item 5). What is noteworthy here is that after Israel is defeated in an initial skirmish, the warriors return to the camp, and the tribal elders consult concerning the reasons for the defeat, or, as they dare to put it, the reasons for the Lord's having routed them. They do not, however, find the fault in the sin they harbor within their midst (cf. 7:6 ff.); rather, they say their fault has been their failure to harness the Lord's power and to exploit His presence by taking His ark into the battle to guarantee the victory, as once at Jericho (Joshua 6:6) or earlier in the wilderness (Num. 10:35-36), though it seems that since Israel's settlement in Palestine the ark only rarely left the Shiloh sanctuary and accompanied the army (cf. v. 7b). It is entirely clear from the story that even after the initial defeat there is no genuine repentance. In fact, now the archdefilers of God's people, the wicked priests Hophni and Phinehas, stand in the forefront of the story as prime witnesses to the fact that no real change of heart has occurred. But since a holy war cannot be fought unless there is wholehearted confidence in the Lord (cf. Judg. 7:3), this attempt at exploiting the Lord's worship paraphernalia is not successful either. After all, the ark was not a magic box to which the Lord was bound and which might be manipulated in such a way as to force the Lord to fight a holy war and grant victory. It is not the external ark indeed that wins the victory in the holy war; it is the Lord, who is in and with the ark, and faith which trusts the Lord above the ark,

49

for without the Lord the ark is a bare box and no saving instrument of God's activity!

The Capture of the Ark 5-11

⁵ When the ark of the covenant of the LORD came into the camp, all Israel gave a mighty shout, so that the earth resounded. ⁶ And when the Philistines heard the noise of the shouting, they said, "What does this great shouting in the camp of the Hebrews mean?" And when they learned that the ark of the LORD had come to the camp, ⁷ the Philistines were afraid; for they said, "A god has come into the camp." And they said, "Woe to us! For nothing like this has happened before. ⁸ Woe to us! Who can deliver us from the power of these mighty gods? These are the gods who smote the Egyptians with every sort of plague in the wilderness. ⁹ Take courage, and acquit yourselves like men, O Philistines, lest you become slaves to the Hebrews as they have been to you; acquit yourselves like men and fight."

¹⁰ So the Philistines fought, and Israel was defeated, and they fled, every man to his home; and there was a very great slaughter, for there fell of Israel thirty thousand foot soldiers. ¹¹ And the ark of God was captured; and the two sons of Eli, Hophni and Phinehas, were slain.

The greatness of the ark is underscored by the great religious acclamation that greets its arrival in the Israelite camp (cf. 2 Sam. 6:15; Lev. 23:24; Num. 29:1; Num. 10:35 f.). The Philistines rightly understand the meaning of the shout: Israel's God has come into camp, and they are afraid that they will suffer the fate of the vanquished in ancient warfare: enslavement by the victors, in this case by the "Hebrews," a term which conveys the worthlessness of the Israelites (in sharp contrast to the greatness of their God, against whom effective resistance is impossible). The Philistines exhort one another to fight with the courage of despair, since their existence as free men is at stake.

But the Lord is not with Israel! The presence of Hophni and Phinehas brings disaster! The Israelites are defeated most ruinously (on the numbers cf. p. 93). The ark of God is taken, and the wicked priest-custodians are slain.

The Effect of the News in Shiloh   *12-22*

[12] A man of Benjamin ran from the battle line, and came to Shiloh the same day, with his clothes rent and with earth upon his head. [13] When he arrived, Eli was sitting upon his seat by the road watching, for his heart trembled for the ark of God. And when the man came into the city and told the news, all the city cried out. [14] When Eli heard the sound of the outcry, he said, "What is this uproar?" Then the man hastened and came and told Eli. [15] Now Eli was ninety-eight years old and his eyes were set, so that he could not see. [16] And the man said to Eli, "I am he who has come from the battle; I fled from the battle today." And he said, "How did it go, my son?" [17] He who brought the tidings answered and said, "Israel has fled before the Philistines, and there has also been a great slaughter among the people; your two sons also, Hophni and Phinehas, are dead, and the ark of God has been captured." [18] When he mentioned the ark of God, Eli fell over backward from his seat by the side of the gate; and his neck was broken and

51

he died, for he was an old man, and heavy. He had judged Israel forty years.

¹⁹ Now his daughter-in-law, the wife of Phinehas, was with child, about to give birth. And when she heard the tidings that the ark of God was captured, and that her father-in-law and her husband were dead, she bowed and gave birth; for her pains came upon her. ²⁰ And about the time of her death the women attending her said to her, "Fear not, for you have borne a son." But she did not answer or give heed. ²¹ And she named the child Ichabod, saying, "The glory has departed from Israel!" because the ark of God had been captured and because of her father-in-law and her husband. ²² And she said, "The glory has departed from Israel, for the ark of God has been captured."

The relaying of the news back to Shiloh is described in a most vivid manner: the messenger foreshadows his disastrous news by his very appearance; the high priest sits at the side of the sanctuary gate in his accustomed seat and, though blind, is still on the lookout for the sound of those who come from the direction of the battle, his heart trembling in fear for the ark of God. He hears first the cry in the city and subsequently the messenger's report of four items of news, the last and climactic of which is the capture of the ark. It seems that Eli might have endured his private sorrow, but his realization of the full implications of the loss of the ark, which his sons had carried into the battle with unclean hands, is something he cannot bear; it causes the old man's collapse. Eli is here (18b) accounted one of the judges of Israel, one of the so-called minor judges (cf. Judg. 10: 1-5; 12:8-15). There is no reference to the Philistines' subsequent sack of the Israelite central sanctuary at Shiloh, though that is referred to in Jer. 7:12 f. and Ps. 78: 60, 64 and corroborated by recent Danish archaeological excavations on the site. This account stresses the immensity of the Lord's judgment on the house of Eli.

Another episode also illuminates the significance of the capture of the ark: news of the birth of a son is ordinarily the most joyous news a mother can hear, but now it causes no joy for the woman whose birth pangs come suddenly as a result of the shocking news. For this mother even the birth of a son cannot compensate for the loss of the cultic presence of the Lord, which is what the loss of the ark meant for her. The child is given the inglorious name Ichabod, "Where Is the Glory?" She does not lament the loss of her father-in-law or of her husband, but she laments the Lord's judgment on the house of Eli and His abandoning of His people. This is indeed the lowest point in the ark story; but Chs. 5 and 6 will tell what still must be told: how the God of the ark avenges Himself on His enemies and returns to dwell among His people.

Dagon Does Obeisance to the Lord 5:1-5

¹ When the Philistines captured the ark of God, they carried it from Ebenezer to Ashdod; ² then the Philistines took the ark of God and brought it into the house of Dagon and set it up beside Dagon. ³ And when the people of Ashdod rose early the next day, behold, Dagon had fallen face downward on the ground before the ark of the LORD. So they took Dagon and put him back in his place. ⁴ But when they rose early on the next morning, behold, Dagon had fallen face downward on the ground before the ark of the LORD, and the head of Dagon and both

his hands were lying cut off upon the threshold; only the trunk of Dagon was left to him. ⁵ This is why the priests of Dagon and all who enter the house of Dagon do not tread on the threshold of Dagon in Ashdod to this day.

After there is no possibility of human assistance, then He who stood idly by when His ark was wrested from His delinquent people by the archenemy steps forth to manifest His power. The story of the Lord's taking the offensive is told in a manner calculated to make the Israelite hearers break out again and again in hearty laughter at the foolish Philistines, who imagine that they can set up the Lord's ark as the trophy of a conquered god in the temple of their god Dagon, intending perhaps to bring the god of Israel under their god's suzerainty, so that they might control him and count on his support. First, the rival deity piously bows down before the Lord, and the surprised Philistines find him in that position the next morning. Next, even after having propped him up again, though still not realizing the dangerous power they have introduced into their midst, they see on the following morning that their god has been so vigorous in his prostration before his Superior that his head and hands have been broken off and lie on the threshold—a threshold so "consecrated" by contact with his shattered remains that ever after they must leap over it!

The Lord Troubles the Philistines   *6-12*

⁶ The hand of the LORD was heavy upon the people of Ashdod, and he terrified and afflicted them with tumors, both Ashdod and its territory. ⁷ And when the men of Ashdod saw how things were, they

said, "The ark of the God of Israel must not remain with us; for his hand is heavy upon us and upon Dagon our god." ⁸ So they sent and gathered together all the lords of the Philistines, and said, "What shall we do with the ark of the God of Israel?" They answered, "Let the ark of the God of Israel be brought around to Gath." So they brought the ark of the God of Israel there. ⁹ But after they had brought it around, the hand of the LORD was against the city, causing a very great panic, and he afflicted the men of the city, both young and old, so that tumors broke out upon them. ¹⁰ So they sent the ark of God to Ekron. But when the ark of God came to Ekron, the people of Ekron cried out, "They have brought around to us the ark of the God of Israel to slay us and our people." ¹¹ They sent therefore and gathered together all the lords of the Philistines, and said, "Send away the ark of the God of Israel, and let it return to its own place, that it may not slay us and our people." For there was a deathly panic throughout the whole city. The hand of God was very heavy there; ¹² the men who did not die were stricken with tumors, and the cry of the city went up to heaven.

The lively humor of the account is increased when the Lord's next attack becomes even more devastating and not only afflicts the Philistines with a plague of mice but smites them in the rear with "tumors," or "hemorrhoidal boils," effecting a complete collapse of their human dignity. This is surely vigorous humor! When the people of Ashdod see "how they are" and realize why the hand of the Israelite God is heavy against them, they call an emergency meeting of the five princes of the Philistine pentapolis. According to a reading preserved in the Septuagint version, it would seem that the people of Gath suggested that they would be able to handle the ark. In any case, the Lord's advent there causes a great panic among them, the sort of confusion which He always sent upon the enemy when He was intervening in a holy war. There, too, an outbreak of piles brings about as complete a collapse of any semblance of respectability as the Egyptian magicians experienced when they tried to compete with Moses (Ex. 9:11). Consequently the ark is sent to the northernmost of the Philistine cities, the one nearest to Israel, Ekron. This time it is received with a cry of terror evoked by the deadly "panic." All persons not actually killed by what seems to have been a kind of bubonic plague are stricken with tumors, and the cry of the city goes up to heaven. The Philistine offensive has now been turned into a complete rout! The "god" of the conquered people has not been conquered!

The Advice of the Diviners 6:1-11

¹ The ark of the LORD was in the country of the Philistines seven months. ² And the Philistines called for the priests and the diviners and said, "What shall we do with the ark of the LORD? Tell us with what we shall send it to its place." ³ They said, "If you send away the ark of the God of Israel, do not send it empty, but by all means return him a guilt offering. Then you will be healed, and it will be known to you why his hand does not turn away from you." ⁴ And they said, "What is the guilt offering that we shall return to him?" They answered, "Five golden tumors and five golden mice, according to the number of the lords of the Philistines; for the same plague was upon all of you and upon your lords. ⁵ So you must

make images of your tumors and images of your mice that ravage the land, and give glory to the God of Israel; perhaps he will lighten his hand from off you and your gods and your land. ⁶ Why should you harden your hearts as the Egyptians and Pharaoh hardened their hearts? After he had made sport of them, did not they let the people go, and they departed? ⁷ Now then, take and prepare a new cart and two milch cows upon which there has never come a yoke, and yoke the cows to the cart, but take their calves home, away from them. ⁸ And take the ark of the LORD and place it on the cart, and put in a box at its side the figures of gold, which you are returning to him as a guilt offering. Then send it off, and let it go its way. ⁹ And watch; if it goes up on the way to its own land, to Beth-shemesh, then it is he who has done us this great harm; but if not, then we shall know that it is not his hand that struck us, it happened to us by chance."

¹⁰ The men did so, and took two milch cows and yoked them to the cart, and shut up their calves at home. ¹¹ And they put the ark of the LORD on the cart, and the box with the golden mice and the images of their tumors.

After the ark of the Lord has been in the country of the Philistines seven months, the Philistine leaders summon their religious professionals. These diviners also realize that they must send it back "to its own place," but they are uncertain as to how to do this; after all, the danger of a false move is great, and they can easily call new plagues down upon themselves. At the same time they must keep up the front of respectability and avoid acknowledging the superiority of the

Lord. The diviners are therefore most cautious in giving
their advice. They begin their suggestions with a con-
ditional clause that puts the responsibility for the decision on the leaders ("If you send away the ark . . ."),
and they conclude with a shrewd suggestion for a delicate situation, "Do not send it empty, but by all means
return him a guilt offering," a reparation gift to the
angry God of Israel for having laid violent hands on
His property. "Then you will be healed." By casting
the gold of the guilt offering in the form of the trouble-
some tumors and plague-spreading mice and by sending
them beyond their borders it would appear that the
Philistines hope to rid their land, by a process of sympathetic magic, of the unbearable terror and at the same
time to conciliate the angry God of Israel with guilt
offerings. The diviners sound almost like Israelite priests
when they warn the leaders against hardening their
hearts as foolish Pharaoh once did. "If you do that,"
they say in effect, "He (you know who!) will make sport
also of you, and the ark will still go free!"

The manner in which the guilt offering is to be
conveyed to the God of Israel is also well thought out.
On the one hand, these Philistine diviners are most
scrupulous in their prescription that this be done with
all respect for holy ritual: a new cart, cows which have
never been used for servile purposes. On the other hand,
the diviners put as many obstacles in the Lord's way
as possible — so that all obscurities will be cleared up
and it will be entirely clear that the return was not due
to chance. Thus it is only with the utmost reluctance
that they will concede any superior power to the God
of Israel: the cows, separated from their calves, their
udders bursting, will then with their lowing proclaim
that the Lord has in fact intervened. The crucial test,

the diviners say, will be whether or not the cows take the route straight into the hill country of Israel, to Beth-shemesh, the Israelite town nearest Philistine territory. If they do, "then it is he who has done us this great harm; but if not, then . . . it happened to us by chance." The Philistine leaders accept these suggestions, and everything is readied for the experiment.

The Ark Returns from Philistia   *12-18*

¹² And the cows went straight in the direction of Beth-shemesh along one highway, lowing as they went; they turned neither to the right nor to the left, and the lords of the Philistines went after them as far as the border of Beth-shemesh. ¹³ Now the people of Beth-shemesh were reaping their wheat harvest in the valley; and when they lifted up their eyes and saw the ark, they rejoiced to see it. ¹⁴ The cart came into the field of Joshua of Beth-shemesh, and stopped there. A great stone was there; and they split up the wood of the cart and offered the cows as a burnt offering to the LORD. ¹⁵ And the Levites took down the ark of the LORD and the box that was beside it, in which were the golden figures, and set them upon the great stone; and the men of Beth-shemesh offered burnt offerings and sacrificed sacrifices on that day to the LORD. ¹⁶ And when the five lords of the Philistines saw it, they returned that day to Ekron.

¹⁷ These are the golden tumors, which the Philistines returned as a guilt offering to the LORD: one for Ashdod, one for Gaza, one for Ashkelon, one for Gath, one for Ekron; ¹⁸ also the golden mice, according to the number of all the cities of the Philistines belonging to the five lords, both fortified cities and un-

walled villages. **The great stone, beside which they
set down the ark of the LORD, is a witness to this day
in the field of Joshua of Beth-shemesh.**

The test proves the superior power of the God of
Israel. The oxen head directly toward Beth-shemesh,
and their goal at that place is the first place in Israelite
territory suitable for a sacrifice, a large stone that is
to serve as an altar (cf. 14:33). The fact that the oxen
halt there is a sign that the Lord desires a sacrifice
at that spot. Accordingly, the people of Beth-shemesh
offer a burnt offering with great joy, using the materials
that the Lord Himself has given them for the offering:
the wood of the cart and the oxen. The golden mice
are the guilt offering given by the heathen; the whole
burnt offering is the Israelite sacrifice.

The five Philistine princes wait to see that the experiment suggested by their diviners is completed and
the danger of a continued plague has been successfully
removed from Philistine territory; then they return.

*The Ark Punishes Those Who
Do Not Respect It*   *6:19−7:2*

**19 And he slew some of the men of Beth-shemesh,
because they looked into the ark of the LORD; he
slew seventy men of them,*k* and the people mourned
because the LORD had made a great slaughter among
the people. 20 Then the men of Beth-shemesh said,
"Who is able to stand before the LORD, this holy
God? And to whom shall he go up away from us?"
21 So they sent messengers to the inhabitants of
Kiriath-jearim, saying, "The Philistines have re-**

k Cn: Heb *of the people seventy men, fifty thousand men*

turned the ark of the **LORD**. Come down and take it up to you."

¹ And the men of Kiriath-jearim came and took up the ark of the **LORD**, and brought it to the house of Abinadab on the hill; and they consecrated his son, Eleazar, to have charge of the ark of the **LORD**. ² From the day that the ark was lodged at Kiriath-jearim, a long time passed, some twenty years, and all the house of Israel lamented after the **LORD**.

At v. 19 a variant reading preserved in the Septuagint states that "the sons of Jeconiah did not participate in the joy of the men of Beth-shemesh" and that they therefore receive the same judgment the Philistines had received (on numbers cf. p. 93). The Israelites must also realize that the Lord is holy and that men cannot approach Him without danger unless they have first been cleansed (cf. Is. 6:1-8; 2 Sam. 6:6-11). Hence the ark must travel further northeastward to the city on a neighboring height, Kiriath-jearim, one of the Gibeonite tetrapolis (Joshua 9:17), a city therefore that was Israelite only by adoption, situated in a no-man's-land between specific Israelite and pagan territory. There on a height, perhaps at the ancient town sanctuary, the ark will remain in "neutral territory" between the Philistines and Israelites, who had both experienced its terrible power, until David will bring it to his new capital city, Jerusalem (2 Sam. 6), after his decisive victory over the Philistines (2 Sam. 5:15-25). Then the Lord will set up His throne in the city of David, to be worshiped there in Old Testament times. From there the Lord will one day go forward in the mighty movement that began with Christ Jesus' resurrection from the dead.

Samuel and Saul

1 Samuel 7:3 – 15:35

SAMUEL DELIVERS ISRAEL   7:3-17

Samuel Renews the Covenant   3-6

[3] Then Samuel said to all the house of Israel, "If you are returning to the LORD with all your heart, then put away the foreign gods and the Ashtaroth from among you, and direct your heart to the LORD, and serve him only, and he will deliver you out of the hand of the Philistines." [4] So Israel put away the Baals and the Ashtaroth, and they served the LORD only.

[5] Then Samuel said, "Gather all Israel at Mizpah, and I will pray to the LORD for you." [6] So they gathered at Mizpah, and drew water and poured it out before the LORD, and fasted on that day, and said there, "We have sinned against the LORD." And Samuel judged the people of Israel at Mizpah.

Since the ark has not actually been restored to Israel but still remains in a Canaanite border city under Philistine control and since the people are still subjugated to the Philistines, we hear that the Israelites lament, seemingly for the lost ark and for what was equivalent, the lost leadership of the Lord. In this crisis (which threatens the very existence of the Israelite confederacy and their faith in the Lord) it is Samuel who steps forward and in a covenant renewal preceded by a ritual purification of the people (cf. Gen. 35:2 and Joshua 24:23) calls on them to put away the Baalim and Ashtaroth (that is, the idols, earrings, and magical amulets that represented the male and female Canaanite fertility deities), so that the Lord may again act and deliver them out of the hands of the Philistines. When the ceremonial purification has been completed, the way is open for calling a general assembly of all Israel at Mizpah. What then takes place there is a penitential liturgy of covenant renewal. By it Samuel restores Israel's covenant relation to the Lord. The people's fasting and pouring out of water are symbolic of their confession ("We have sinned!"). Samuel "judges" the people of Israel at Mizpah, which means more than that he hears law cases that have been appealed to him from the lower village-elder courts; it means that at the central sanctuary of the sacred confederacy he acts as the mediator of the covenant, interceding for them as Moses once did and proclaiming the sacred law to them.

Samuel Brings Victory over the Philistines　　　　　*7-14*

7 Now when the Philistines heard that the people of Israel had gathered at Mizpah, the lords of the Philistines went up against Israel. And when the people of Israel heard of it they were afraid of the Philistines. 8 And the people of Israel said to Samuel, "Do not cease to cry to the LORD our God for us,

that he may save us from the hand of the Philistines."
⁹ So Samuel took a sucking lamb and offered it as
a whole burnt offering to the LORD; and Samuel
cried to the LORD for Israel, and the LORD answered
him. ¹⁰ As Samuel was offering up the burnt offering,
the Philistines drew near to attack Israel; but the
LORD thundered with a mighty voice that day against
the Philistines and threw them into confusion; and
they were routed before Israel. ¹¹ And the men of
Israel went out of Mizpah and pursued the Philistines, and smote them, as far as below Beth-car.
¹² Then Samuel took a stone and set it up between
Mizpah and Jeshanah,ˡ and called its name Ebenezer; ᵐ for he said, "Hitherto the LORD has helped
us." ¹³ So the Philistines were subdued and did not
again enter the territory of Israel. And the hand of
the LORD was against the Philistines all the days
of Samuel. ¹⁴ The cities which the Philistines had
taken from Israel were restored to Israel, from Ekron
to Gath; and Israel rescued their territory from the
hand of the Philistines. There was peace also between Israel and the Amorites.

ˡ Gk Syr: Heb *Shen*   ᵐ That is *Stone of help*

When the Philistines realize that a conspiracy
against their leadership is afoot, they send a detachment to investigate. Catching wind of this Philistine
advance, the Israelites call on Samuel to take the role
of Moses in ceaseless intercession for them (cf. Ex.
17:8-13). Samuel's response to their desperate cries is
twofold: he sacrifices a sucking lamb and cries aloud
to the Lord on Israel's behalf. Then we are told, "And
the LORD answered him." Just what the Lord's answer
was is, however, difficult to determine, since our ac-

count of it is told in the religious language of a holy war, according to which, on the one hand, the Lord alone discomfits and terrifies the enemy (cf. pp. 105 f.), but, on the other hand, the men of Israel actually do go forth from Mizpah and pursue the Philistines in some sort of military engagement.

In attempting to understand exactly what really happened, some scholars imagine (1) that the Philistine investigators saw that only a harmless religious service was being carried on and therefore left when the Israelites maintained their composure and continued with the service. There is, however, little in the text to substantiate such an explanation. Other interpreters imagine (2) that some sort of military action took place, in which the Philistines were driven off, though by no means annihilated. According to these interpreters any indication of complete victory is due to the holy war imagery, which is, however, not meant to be taken in modern military terms. Though more likely, this explanation does not do justice to many features of the story. Still other interpreters (3) go further along this line, imagining that the real skirmish fought here was only the first, anticipatory step toward the help that was promised in the worship service, since it was only Saul and David who later did what is referred to in vv. 13 f.: drive them completely from Israelite territory, take away the Israelite territory they had annexed, and make a treaty with the original inhabitants of the land, the Amorites. Such an interpretation fails, however, to square with the text's claim that Samuel did these things. At best it can be considered only a probable explanation. An additional interpretation (4) adds some illumination to this passage — though it, too, is not absolutely conclusive in establishing what actually happened.

65

This explanation views what is here described not as a military exploit but as the literary dramatization of an actual cultic covenant lawsuit like the one recorded in Deut. 32, in which the Lord not only indicts faithless Israel for its unbelief in the face of His mighty acts but calls on them to repent and renew the covenant, promising them His judgment on their enemies. According to this interpretation, at the tribal confederacy's meeting Samuel, as the chief prophet and priest, not only indicts faithless Israel for its unbelief but effectively proclaims the Lord's judgment on the Philistines. Such an explanation, perhaps also combined with the third one, may help us more in our attempt to get back to what actually happened. For it is clear, in any case, that the Philistines did continue to dominate Israel (9:16; 10:5; 13) and that a war of liberation had to be taken up by Saul (Ch. 14) and won by David (2 Sam. 5:17-25). Here, however, the fight against the Philistines is not described in purely military language but in theological language that confesses that the real victories in God's kingdom are won by God. That finally has always been faith's view of history, even in the midst of unresolved crises. And Samuel refers to that when he consecrates the memorial stone as a witness to the fact that it was the Lord who had helped them (Eben-ezer: "Stone of help").

Samuel Judges Israel   15-17

¹⁵ **Samuel judged Israel all the days of his life. ¹⁶ And he went on a circuit year by year to Bethel, Gilgal, and Mizpah; and he judged Israel in all these places. ¹⁷ Then he would come back to Ramah, for his home was there, and there also he administered justice to Israel. And he built there an altar to the LORD.**

These verses speak of Samuel not as a major judge, that is, as a military and political liberator like Gideon, nor merely as a sort of arbiter who hears cases of conflict between individuals and clans, as a modern judge does, but as a legal officer of Israel's tribal confederacy, an administrator of the Lord's covenant law like the so-called minor judges (Judg. 10:1-5; 12:8-15). He exercises his judicial duties at holy times (festivals) in holy places (the sanctuaries of Bethel, Gilgal, Mizpah, and Ramah), officiating beside the Lord's altar. Thus Samuel steps forth, when the tribal confederacy threatens to collapse, in order to salvage what can be salvaged and to renew Israel's life under the Lord's covenant. And when the demand for a monarchy becomes irresistible, it is Samuel who will arrange for this new institution to be inserted into the framework of the ancient covenant.

NEGOTIATIONS CONCERNING THE ESTABLISHMENT OF KINGSHIP IN ISRAEL 8

This chapter deals with the negotiations that eventually lead to the establishment of the monarchy in Israel. It is most interesting to note that the initial demand of the people's representatives is referred by the Lord's piqued human representative to the Lord Himself. And it is the Lord Himself who then calls for a continuation of the negotiations so that the pitfalls of the original demand can be pointed out before the request is finally allowed!

The Conference at Ramah   *8:1-9*

¹ When Samuel became old, he made his sons judges over Israel. ² The name of his first-born son

67

was Joel, and the name of his second, Abijah; they were judges in Beer-sheba. [3] Yet his sons did not walk in his ways, but turned aside after gain; they took bribes and perverted justice.

[4] Then all the elders of Israel gathered together and came to Samuel at Ramah, [5] and said to him, "Behold, you are old and your sons do not walk in your ways; now appoint for us a king to govern us like all the nations." [6] But the thing displeased Samuel when they said, "Give us a king to govern us." And Samuel prayed to the LORD. [7] And the LORD said to Samuel, "Hearken to the voice of the people in all that they say to you; for they have not rejected you, but they have rejected me from being king over them. [8] According to all the deeds which they have done to me,[n] from the day I brought them up out of Egypt even to this day, forsaking me and serving other gods, so they are also doing to you. [9] Now then, hearken to their voice; only, you shall solemnly warn them, and show them the ways of the king who shall reign over them."

[n] Gk: Heb lacks *to me*

The immediate reason for the demand for a king is that Samuel's sons have, by their perversion of justice, discredited the office of judgeship to which, it seems, their father had appointed them. It is natural that all the clan and tribal heads should come to Samuel at Ramah with their demand. After all, he is the one who, ever since his convocation of the tribes at Mizpah in the wake of the catastrophe of Shiloh, functioned as the leader of the tribes and as a sort of mediator of the covenant (cf. Ch. 7). Negotiations with him would be natural. The elders are cognizant of the critical situation in which Israel has now been placed: robbed of her freedom to act, a prey for her neighbors since her humiliating defeat by the Philistines, her religious and political institutions in decay and disorder now that her central sanctuary has been lost. What is needed, they say, is a strong man, a king who will judge them among the nations, that is, provide them with effective leadership in a hostile world. As it is, Israel's organization has nothing to compare with that of the well-organized neighbors whose resources are consolidated behind a king. The former practice of waiting for a deliverer to gather some tribes only temporarily is no longer sufficient for the situation they now must face.

Samuel's initial reaction to the request is somewhat surprising, since he injects, first of all, his own personal feelings into the midst of the deliberations. He assumes that the request is directed against himself personally and is therefore much displeased. However, the Lord, to whom this priest-prophet turns in prayer, does not permit him to reject the entire affair out of personal pique as something entirely undebatable; rather, the Lord urges him to hear them out, so that what is involved in their proposal can be exposed — the danger of rejecting the Lord, the King who is enthroned in their midst and who reveals Himself to them through His prophets and priests. Human logic would expect the Lord to have responded to Samuel in somewhat the following manner: "Do not give in one bit to them, for earthly kingship abrogates My royal rule over Israel!" But God's "logic" accepts the insult — without, however, really retreating from His real position as sovereign Lord of this people.

The great danger of apostasy, the Lord explains, has been the temptation to which they have continually been succumbing ever since the exodus from Egypt —

apostasy from the Lord their God. To be sure, the elders had tried to maintain a continuity with the ancient tribal confederacy setup by saying that the new king shall "judge" them (v. 5), but the reprehensible novelty of their plan is that they are imitating pagan nations. Israel is forgetting that it is a special people that has no king but the Lord (cf. Judg. 8:23). Its present delinquency, which threatens Samuel's life's work of restoring the faith and worship of the Lord, is only a continuation of its longtime delinquency. "According to all the deeds which they have done to me," the Lord says, ". . . so they are also doing to you." Hence—and here God's unique logic of love breaks through—listen to their voice; enter into negotiations with them; however, as you discuss this, warn them about the dangerous aspect of their demand and show them the end toward which their demand for a king "to govern us like all the nations" will lead: their abandonment of their unique position as the Lord's people and their capitulation to pagan royal ideology. Instead of nursing personal grievances, Samuel has a positive task to perform.

Samuel Warns Against a Monarchy
on a Worldly Pattern   *10-18*

¹⁰ So Samuel told all the words of the LORD to the people who were asking a king from him. ¹¹ He said, "These will be the ways of the king who will reign over you: he will take your sons and appoint them to his chariots and to be his horsemen, and to run before his chariots; ¹² and he will appoint for himself commanders of thousands and commanders of fifties, and some to plow his ground and to reap his harvest, and to make his implements of war and the equipment of his chariots. ¹³ He will take your

daughters to be perfumers and cooks and bakers.
¹⁴ He will take the best of your fields and vineyards
and olive orchards and give them to his servants.
¹⁵ He will take the tenth of your grain and of your
vineyards and give it to his officers and to his servants. ¹⁶ He will take your menservants and maid-
servants, and the best of your cattle ⁰ and your asses,
and put them to his work. ¹⁷ He will take the tenth of
your flocks, and you shall be his slaves. ¹⁸ And in that
day you will cry out because of your king, whom you
have chosen for yourselves; but the LORD will not
answer you in that day."

⁰ Gk: Heb *young men*

Samuel, as the Lord's spokesman, "told all the
words of the LORD to the people who were asking a king
from him." And then as a warning, to discourage them
from their intention, Samuel proclaims "the ways of
the king" who will reign over them, underlining especially the tyrannical arbitrariness of such a monarch.
Samuel's repeated use of the phrase "he will take . . . he
will take" describes just what the petty kings of Canaan
did in the semifeudal Canaanite system at the time of
Saul: they maintained their small armies of picked
foot soldiers and aristocratic professional charioteers
as a privileged class by rewarding them for their services with crown land (8:14) and movable property such
as sheep, oxen, asses, and slaves (v. 17), which the king
had acquired by purchase, confiscation, or, most often,
by taxation on all fields, vineyards, and flocks. The
common people were called on to provide conscript
labor for building roads, fortifications, buildings (12b-13,
16). The climax of Samuel's warning is to the effect that
if they get their way and obtain a king, they will get

more than they had bargained for. "You shall be his slaves," says Samuel. "And in that day you will cry out because of your king, whom you have chosen for yourselves; but the LORD will not answer you in that day."

Samuel's Advice Refused   *19-22*

¹⁹ **But the people refused to listen to the voice of Samuel; and they said, "No! but we will have a king over us, ²⁰ that we also may be like all the nations, and that our king may govern us and go out before us and fight our battles." ²¹ And when Samuel had heard all the words of the people, he repeated them in the ears of the LORD. ²² And the LORD said to Samuel, "Hearken to their voice, and make them a king." Samuel then said to the men of Israel, "Go every man to his city."**

The response of the people to Samuel's warning is not only refusal ("No!") but a renewed demand bolstered by what they consider the most cogent reason: the Philistine crisis, they say, demands the leadership of a king. Otherwise they cannot continue to exist in a world where other nations have kings and they do not.

It is interesting to note that Samuel now repeats all the words of the people "in the ears of the LORD," and then the Lord grants the request! The apparent contradiction between the Lord's earlier criticism of the people's request for a king and His final grant of that request ceases to be a contradiction as soon as we distinguish between a kingship according to the pattern of the pagan nations such as the people wanted and the Israelite kingship as it finally, under God's most gracious blessing, came to be — a kingship transformed to express God's will. Samuel's final dismissal of the elders seems to leave the possibility open that negotiations will continue until Samuel will be in a position to establish a kingship in accordance with the will of the Lord. The problem has been opened for discussion and negotiation, but it has not yet been solved. In fact, now the question is raised, "Who will be the king who will not ruin God's people but rule over them according to God's good pleasure?" That question, once raised, is solved neither by Saul nor by David nor by any of the royal sons of David, of whom the question was in a way asked each time at his coronation: "Art thou he that should come, or do we look for another?" That question is solved only in Him from the house and lineage of David who was the real King (John 18:36), who truly fulfilled all that is promised here, and who established God's reign over all men.

The Secret Choice of the "King" 9:1 — 10:16

Saul Seeks His Father's Lost Asses   *9:1-10*

¹ There was a man of Benjamin whose name was Kish, the son of Abiel, son of Zeror, son of Becorath, son of Aphiah, a Benjaminite, a man of wealth; ² and he had a son whose name was Saul, a handsome young man. There was not a man among the people of Israel more handsome than he; from his shoulders upward he was taller than any of the people.

³ Now the asses of Kish, Saul's father, were lost. So Kish said to Saul his son, "Take one of the servants with you, and arise, go and look for the asses." ⁴ And they *ᵖ* passed through the hill country of Eph-

ᵖ Gk Vg: Heb *he*

73

raim and passed through the land of Shalishah, but they did not find them. And they passed through the land of Shaalim, but they were not there. Then they passed through the land of Benjamin, but did not find them.

⁵ When they came to the land of Zuph, Saul said to his servant who was with him, "Come, let us go back, lest my father cease to care about the asses and become anxious about us." ⁶ But he said to him, "Behold, there is a man of God in this city, and he is a man that is held in honor; all that he says comes true. Let us go there; perhaps he can tell us about the journey on which we have set out." ⁷ Then Saul said to his servant, "But if we go, what can we bring the man? For the bread in our sacks is gone, and there is no present to bring to the man of God. What have we?" ⁸ The servant answered Saul again, "Here, I have with me the fourth part of a shekel of silver, and I will give it to the man of God, to tell us our way." ⁹ (Formerly in Israel, when a man went to inquire of God, he said, "Come, let us go to the seer"; for he who is now called a prophet was formerly called a seer.) ¹⁰ And Saul said to his servant, "Well said; come, let us go." So they went to the city where the man of God was.

H. Gressmann described this section in a classic manner when he said that it tells how the handsome young farmer boy Saul went out in search of his father's lost she-asses and found a royal crown. The story begins in a very matter-of-fact manner, but as it continues, one mysterious surprise after another increases our interest until we finally realize at the climax that God has been at work preparing the way for the first Israelite king. At first we hear only that the handsome and sturdy young Benjaminite Saul is sent by his respected and well-to-do father to find the valuable she-asses that had wandered off and disappeared. As the search through the Ephraimite hill country proves increasingly hopeless and exasperating, Saul proposes that the search be abandoned. But his servant-companion suggests that they consult the famous man of God who lives in the city they are just passing, the seer Samuel. Perhaps he can reveal the object of their search to Saul. Little does Saul — or for that matter the servant — know that the seer will reveal, as the real goal of his journey, something of which Saul has as yet no inkling. Fortunately the prudent servant even has the customary gift with which to pay the seer for his services. So the two hasten toward the seer's city.

Saul and the Maidens at the Spring　　　　　*11-13*

¹¹ As they went up the hill to the city, they met young maidens coming out to draw water, and said to them, "Is the seer here?" ¹² They answered, "He is; behold, he is just ahead of you. Make haste; he has come just now to the city, because the people have a sacrifice today on the high place. ¹³ As soon as you enter the city, you will find him, before he goes up to the high place to eat; for the people will not eat till he comes, since he must bless the sacrifice; afterward those eat who are invited. Now go up, for you will meet him immediately."

Outside this city (which is apparently a small walled town with only one gate, situated on the side of a hill) they meet young maidens going forth to draw water

at the spring that lies a bit below the city. The travelers'
simple question for information, "Is the seer here?"
receives a very full answer from the talkative and seemingly highly impressed young women, for they tell the
handsome young man that the seer has fortunately just
returned to the city and is indeed about to proceed from
the city up the hill to the high place, where he will preside over a special sacrificial meal. When the maidens
stress the fact that Saul has arrived just in time, they
are, in a way, telling the readers what the explanatory
editorial note in v. 9 also intimates: though Saul imagines
he is coming to consult a "seer," he is actually dealing
with a "prophet," who is in on God's secret counsels
for the young farmer lad. The maidens imply also that
if Saul and his servant hurry, they may yet catch the
prophet before he sets out for the high place.

The First Confrontation of Prophet
and King-Designate   14-17

[14] So they went up to the city. As they were entering
the city, they saw Samuel coming out toward them on
his way up to the high place.
    [15] Now the day before Saul came, the LORD had
revealed to Samuel: [16] "Tomorrow about this time
I will send to you a man from the land of Benjamin,
and you shall anoint him to be prince over my people
Israel. He shall save my people from the hand of the
Philistines; for I have seen the affliction of [q] my people, because their cry has come to me." [17] When
Samuel saw Saul, the LORD told him, "Here is the
man of whom I spoke to you! He it is who shall rule
over my people."

    [q] Gk: Heb lacks *the affliction of*

The village maidens had prepared the sturdy farmer boy for his confrontation with the prophet. The prophet, in turn, had also been prepared for this encounter by a special revelation given to him the day before. Moreover, the prophet had already made special preparations for the reception of this special guest at the sacrifice that was to be held on the high place, for on the previous day the Lord had "opened Samuel's ear" to the secret that the next day He was sending him a man from Benjamin whom he should anoint to be prince, the one designated to save Israel from the Philistines. The word "king" is purposely not used throughout this account because it is a word still freighted with false and offensive pagan associations of divine kingship; instead of it the word "prince," or "leader," is used whenever this new office is spoken of in any positive way. It is still too early to speak of a king. Oppressed Israel's cry to the Lord has been heard. And now, when Samuel first confronts the divinely designated young man face to face, the Lord says to him, "Here is the man of whom I spoke to you. He it is who shall rule over my people." So it happens that when they first meet, Samuel is already in on God's secret, whereas Saul has as yet no idea of what he is getting into.

A Surprising Greeting for the Farmer Boy　　　*18-21*

18 Then Saul approached Samuel in the gate, and said, "Tell me where is the house of the seer?" 19 Samuel answered Saul, "I am the seer; go up before me to the high place, for today you shall eat with me, and in the morning I will let you go and will tell you all that is on your mind. 20 As for your asses that were lost three days ago, do not set your mind on them, for they have been found. And for whom is all that is

desirable in Israel? Is it not for you and for all your father's house?" [21] Saul answered, "Am I not a Benjaminite, from the least of the tribes of Israel? And is not my family the humblest of all the families of the tribe of Benjamin? Why then have you spoken to me in this way?"

The question the young man puts to the aged man whom he meets at the gate ("Where is the house of the seer?") receives a surprising answer. The aged man not only replies, "I am the seer," but he enthusiastically urges the young stranger to come along to the high place to participate in the sacrifice, then to stay overnight with him. He promises him a full revelation of the secret of his heart and life. Only in a sort of parenthetical remark does he get rid of Saul's as yet unexpressed query about the lost she-asses, saying that the asses have been found. Then — to make sure that the finding of the asses becomes secondary — he goes on to his principal concern and all but reveals to him the secret. He asks, "And for whom is all that is desirable in Israel? Is it not for you and for all your father's house?" As far as Saul is concerned, he does of course understand that something great is being promised, but he cannot begin to understand this fully. He can only puzzle at the prospect of his insignificant tribe and family being chosen, "Why then have you spoken to me in this way?"

The Guest of Honor at the Sacrificial Meal   *22-24b*

[22] Then Samuel took Saul and his servant and brought them into the hall and gave them a place at the head of those who had been invited, who were about thirty persons. [23] And Samuel said to the cook, "Bring the portion I gave you, of which I said to you,

'Put it aside.'" [24] So the cook took up the leg and the upper portion [r] and set them before Saul; and Samuel said, "See, what was kept is set before you. Eat; because it was kept for you until the hour appointed, that you might eat with the guests." [s]

[r] Heb obscure   [s] Cn: Heb *saying, I have invited the people*

At the banquet on the high place, attended by a select company of guests, puzzling things continue to happen to Saul, things that point in the direction of the secret of his life. The guests at this special meeting are waiting for him, it seems, almost in answer to the deliberations of Ch. 8. He is seated at the head of the table of representatives of the people, who may be meeting in secret (seemingly in order to avoid Philistine countermoves). Surprisingly enough, he receives, as the choice piece specially reserved for him, the short fat tail, and the prophet says to him: See what was kept for you until the set feast that you might eat with the guests. Saul must begin the meal; only then may the others follow. Though the precise nature of the relationship established by the communion meal between God, the representatives of the people, and the new king-designate is kept vague, it seems that Samuel is also here attempting to build the new Israelite kingship into the existing covenant forms by means of a covenant meal and to bind it to the Lord's ultimate claim of kingship over Israel. (Cf. Ex. 24:11)

The Secret Negotiations Between Saul and Samuel   *9:24c — 10:1b*

So Saul ate with Samuel that day. [25] And when they came down from the high place into the city,

79

a bed was spread for Saul *t* upon the roof, and he lay down to sleep. [26] Then at the break of dawn *u* Samuel called to Saul upon the roof, "Up, that I may send you on your way." So Saul arose, and both he and Samuel went out into the street.

[27] As they were going down to the outskirts of the city, Samuel said to Saul, "Tell the servant to pass on before us, and when he has passed on stop here yourself for a while, that I may make known to you the word of God."

[1] Then Samuel took a vial of oil and poured it on his head, and kissed him and said, "Has not the LORD anointed you to be prince over his people Israel? And you shall reign over the people of the LORD and you will save them from the hand of their enemies round about.

t Gk: Heb *and he spoke with Saul*
u Gk: Heb *and they arose early and at break of dawn*

Further mysteries follow those at the meal when Samuel and Saul return to the city. Saul not only sleeps on the flat roof of Samuel's house; a significant conversation also takes place between them. But again we are mysteriously not told what they talked about. All Samuel had promised him earlier (9:19c) was to tell him all that was on his mind. "But what was that?" we ask, "Problems of state? Plans of action?" No answers are given. Early the next morning, after the servant has been sent ahead so that the prophet can be alone with Saul, Saul is anointed "prince" over God's heritage and deliverer in Israel. At this point already Saul becomes the "anointed" of the Lord (Hebrew: "Messiah"; Greek: "Christ") and receives a special sacred character.

Signs to Corroborate the Anointment   *10:1c-13*

And this shall be the sign to you that the **LORD** has anointed you to be prince [w] over his heritage. [2] When you depart from me today you will meet two men by Rachel's tomb in the territory of Benjamin at Zelzah, and they will say to you, 'The asses which you went to seek are found, and now your father has ceased to care about the asses and is anxious about you, saying, "What shall I do about my son?"' [3] Then you shall go on from there further and come to the oak of Tabor; three men going up to God at Bethel will meet you there, one carrying three kids, another carrying three loaves of bread, and another carrying a skin of wine. [4] And they will greet you and give you two loaves of bread, which you shall accept from their hand. [5] After that you shall come to Gibeathelohim, [x] where there is a garrison of the Philistines; and there, as you come to the city, you will meet a band of prophets coming down from the high place with harp, tambourine, flute, and lyre before them, prophesying. [6] Then the spirit of the **LORD** will come mightily upon you, and you shall prophesy with them and be turned into another man. [7] Now when these signs meet you, do whatever your hand finds to do, for God is with you. [8] And you shall go down before me to Gilgal; and behold, I am coming to you to offer burnt offerings and to sacrifice peace offerings. Seven days you shall wait, until I come to you and show you what you shall do."

[9] When he turned his back to leave Samuel, God gave him another heart; and all these signs came to

[w] Gk: Heb lacks *over his people Israel? And you shall . . . to be prince*
[x] Or *the hill of God*

pass that day. ¹⁰ When they came to Gibeah, ᶻ behold, a band of prophets met him; and the spirit of God came mightily upon him, and he prophesied among them. ¹¹ And when all who knew him before saw how he prophesied with the prophets, the people said to one another, "What has come over the son of Kish? Is Saul also among the prophets?" ¹² And a man of the place answered, "And who is their father?" Therefore it became a proverb, "Is Saul also among the prophets?" ¹³ When he had finished prophesying, he came to the high place.

ᶻ Or *the hill*

The signs that will confront Saul on his road home from Ramah foreshadow the future and confirm the divine significance of his consecration. For the young man Saul they must have been also somewhat puzzling. The first one concerns a meeting at the border of Benjaminite territory with the menservants sent out to seek him, who will conclude their report to Saul rather significantly with the double-meaning question of his father Kish, "What shall I do about my son?" The second sign (at the holy oak Saul encounters worshipers on their way to the sanctuary at Bethel) is also puzzling. Why should Saul receive offerings meant for God? Is he to represent God in some way? Are taxes being paid to him already now? The third sign will occur when Saul will be met, in sight of the Philistine garrison, by a band of prophets engaged in religious exercises as they come down from the holy heights with music, in prophetic ecstasy. Then Saul himself will be seized by the contagious Spirit and become a different man. The actualization of this third sign (vv. 11-13) ends up with the uncomprehending neighbors' puzzling question,

"Is Saul also among the prophets?" that is, "How can such a respectable young man get into such disreputable company?" The man who responds to them asks, "Why not? The son of Kish is as much to be expected among them as anyone else; prophetic inspiration does not depend on parentage." (It is also possible to interpret this to mean that the man who responded meant to join in their criticism, asking, "How can such a well-born young man get into the company of people who have no father, that is, who come from nowhere, from outside normal society?" In any case, the question "Is Saul also among the prophets?" became a proverb that was appealed to whenever a person acted out of character.) We may also ask: Is this mysterious prophetic activity that takes hold of Saul perhaps connected with a prophetic underground movement that is preparing for the approaching war of liberation against the Philistines? No matter how we answer that question, one thing is entirely clear: Samuel had already received (9:16) the divine promise concerning Saul, "He shall save my people from the hand of the Philistines, for I have seen the affliction of my people." And Samuel now concludes his instructions to Saul by saying, "Now when these signs meet you, do whatever your hand finds to do, for God is with you." When these signs do actually come to pass, soon after, Saul knows that he has been charismatically called and equipped by the LORD. This certainty contrasts, however, with the vagueness of Samuel's instructions (v. 8) that he go to Gilgal — all adding again to a sense of mysterious anticipation.

Saul Interrogated by His Uncle About His Secret 14—16

14 Saul's uncle said to him and to his servant, "Where did you go?" And he said, "To seek the asses;

and when we saw they were not to be found, we went to Samuel." ¹⁵ And Saul's uncle said, "Pray, tell me what Samuel said to you." ¹⁶ And Saul said to his uncle, "He told us plainly that the asses had been found." But about the matter of the kingdom, of which Samuel had spoken, he did not tell him anything.

The fullness with which Saul understands the secret of his life, his calling, becomes very clear in the last episode. On returning home from Ramah, Saul goes to the high place, where his uncle interrogates him, trying to find out what he has learned from the prophet Samuel during his stay with him. But now it is Saul's turn to know the secret (the matter of the kingship) but not to reveal it. Perhaps he did this out of fear of being considered a megalomaniac; more likely, he is waiting for God's own action to call him to further activity.

SAUL CHOSEN KING AND PUBLICLY ACCLAIMED AT MIZPAH   10:17-27

The Assembly of the Tribal Confederacy   *17-19*

¹⁷ Now Samuel called the people together to the LORD at Mizpah; ¹⁸ and he said to the people of Israel, "Thus says the LORD, the God of Israel, 'I brought up Israel out of Egypt, and I delivered you from the hand of the Egyptians and from the hand of all the kingdoms that were oppressing you.' ¹⁹ But you have this day rejected your God, who saves you from all your calamities and your distresses; and you have said, 'No! but set a king over us.' Now therefore present yourselves before the LORD by your tribes and by your thousands."

The meeting to which aged Samuel gathers the people should not be compared to a modern political convention or election-day assembly; it is, rather, like the gathering of the people mentioned in the Song of Deborah (Judg. 5), a gathering of free citizen-soldiers who muster according to their tribes, clans, families — every male 20 years of age and over. It is at one and the same time a religious and a military gathering. The act of determining who the new king is to be is preceded by an announcement in which Samuel addresses the tribal confederacy of Israel in the manner customary for a mediator of the covenant, speaking therefore in the name of the Lord. A historical review of Israel's past relations with the Lord shows that we are here dealing with the same sort of covenant formulations as in the Introduction to the Commandments (Ex. 20:2), where the announcement, "I am the LORD your God" is followed by the historical review "who brought you out of the land of Egypt, out of the house of bondage." (For the constituent elements of a covenant see pp. 97 f.) The Lord's deeds on Israel's behalf in the exodus and during the conquest and settlement of the Promised Land are the foundation of her response to Him.

This basic relationship has, however, been ungratefully rejected and lightly esteemed by a people who want a kingship like that of the heathen nations round about. "You have this day rejected your God, who saves you from all your calamities and your distresses." Samuel does not mince words, because he wants Israel to know that even if the Lord is about to grant their desire for a king, this does not by any means indicate that He is capitulating to their sinful conception of the kingship. Despite their rejection of Him and His kingship, the Lord still is "staying in office" as their

85

real suzerain and lord. It is only on the basis of such a preliminary statement that Samuel then calls on the people ("now therefore," v. 19) to present themselves before the Lord, that is, to approach in worship by their tribes, clans, families.

The Lord Chooses the New King   *20-23*

²⁰ Then Samuel brought all the tribes of Israel near, and the tribe of Benjamin was taken by lot. ²¹ He brought the tribe of Benjamin near by its families, and the family of the Matrites was taken by lot; finally he brought the family of the Matrites near man by man,ᵃ and Saul the son of Kish was taken by lot. But when they sought him, he could not be found. ²² So they inquired again of the LORD, "Did the man come hither?" ᵇ and the LORD said, "Behold, he has hidden himself among the baggage." ²³ Then they ran and fetched him from there; and when he stood among the people, he was taller than any of the people from his shoulders upward.

ᵃ Gk: Heb lacks *finally . . . man by man*
ᵇ Gk: Heb *Is there yet a man to come hither?*

The choice by sacred lot (cf. pp. 121 f. and Joshua 7:16-18) was made, it seems, by means of the Urim and Thummim drawn from the oracle pocket in the priest's ephod. Each tribe appeared before the Lord as a group or by its representatives and received the answer "Yes" or "No," until finally the proper tribe, clan, family, and person was chosen. In any case, the procedure makes it entirely clear that not Israel but the Lord is choosing the new king. Human influence is ruled out. Each tribe, each clan, each family, each person has an equal chance before the Lord. But at the end we are in for a surprise—the person who is taken by the Lord's lot has hidden himself! Only a new oracle pronouncement enables the people to bring him forth from an odd sort of company, the baggage servants. But even then the modestly shy young man makes an overwhelming impression as he steps forth among the astonished folk army: he is every inch a king, standing head and shoulders above every one else. Does the story hereby wish us to indicate that in Israel all natural endowments for kingship can really make a person a king only if they are coupled with true humility? It seems so; and as we hear it, we also begin to ask, "Will Saul remain so humble and noble?"

How the New King Is Presented and Acclaimed 24-27

[24] And Samuel said to all the people, "Do you see him whom the LORD has chosen? There is none like him among all the people." And all the people shouted, "Long live the king!"

[25] Then Samuel told the people the rights and duties of the kingship; and he wrote them in a book and laid it up before the LORD. Then Samuel sent all the people away, each one to his home. [26] Saul also went to his home at Gibeah, and with him went men of valor whose hearts God had touched. [27] But some worthless fellows said, "How can this man save us?" And they despised him, and brought him no present. But he held his peace.

The people joyfully accept Saul as the one chosen by the Lord, respectfully greeting him with the acclamation that subsequently became a standard part of the coronation ritual, "Long live the king!" Next in the ritual comes the proclamation of "the rights and duties of the kingship." The kingship which the Lord is granting is not to be one like that of the heathen (who had an idolatrous concept of sacred kingship attached to their human kings) but a kingship in keeping with the great Sinaitic covenant, according to which both king and people live under the lord of the covenant, the Lord. It becomes evident that the Lord is transforming the nation's desires for a king in such a way that the new institution of Israelite kingship is to be subsumed under Israel's ancient covenant faith in the Lord. This so-called "way of the king" with its stipulation of the reciprocal relations between king, people, and the Lord is so important that an official copy is not only formally drawn up in writing but also deposited, as were treaties in the ancient world, "before the LORD," that is, at the sanctuary, presumably to be reread at important occasions and festivals. (Cf. Joshua 24:26; Ex. 34:1; Deut. 17:14-17; 2 Kings 11:12)

After the service Samuel dismisses the people. The king-elect Saul returns home! He is accompanied, however, by a group of "men of valor whose hearts God had touched," that is, filled with the Spirit, as was Saul. An atmosphere of conspiracy seems to surround this military host of volunteers who seem to be planning the next move (a war of liberation from Philistine oppression?). By contrast, some worthless fellows, "sons of Belial," represent an opposition party of sorts. They despise Saul, show him no respect, and ask, "How can this awkward farmer boy save us?" So the people are split into various factions, the largest, central group seemingly remaining uncommitted, waiting to see what will happen. A special event will in fact be necessary if the king-designate is to really command the respect of the entire nation. For the technical and organizational superiority of the Philistines is so great that when Israel confronts their army (13:6), it ends up crawling into caves, many even deserting to the enemy (cf. 14:21). To raise an army for a campaign against the Philistines is out of the question. But soon by means of the Ammonite crisis the Lord will begin to bring about a change. Then Saul, who now prudently acts as if he did not even notice the criticisms aimed at him, will act. And then even a formal coronation of the king-designate will take place.

SAUL BECOMES DELIVERER AND KING! 11

When commentators have compared this story of Saul's victory over the Ammonites and his coronation at Gilgal with the preceding stories of his secret consecration at Ramah (10:1 ff.) and his public choice by lot at Mizpah (10:17 ff.), they have usually either tried to harmonize them into one connected history, or they have designated them as various originally separate literary sources; and in the latter case they have usually said that this last account in Ch. 11 is the only historically trustworthy version of the "real origin" of the monarchy. Such harmonizing and such literary criticism have, however, not proved fruitful in appreciating the unique contributions of each version. It is better to assume that before these various sacred accounts concerning God's establishing Saul as king were put down in their final written form as we now have them, they were each told, retold, and nurtured in certain specific circles (in Mizpah, the central sanctuary that seems to have taken plundered Shiloh's place; in Gilgal, the ancient Benjami-

89

nite sanctuary that seems to have become important after the Philistines captured Mizpah; in Gibeah, Saul's hometown and later his capital). After the loss of the ark there was, it seems, no truly central sanctuary to cultivate one single tradition, and so it seems natural that the events were told with various local emphases. (Cf. Introduction, pp. 13 f.) The person who gave final shape to our story did not attempt to create a historical account such as we can get from John Bright's *A History of Israel,* but he carefully respected the various sacred traditions of the various sanctuaries, preserving them and including them. His purpose, however, was not to set before his readers a comprehensively chronological account of the origin of kingship in Israel but rather to help the Lord's people understand the manifold roots of their kingship. God's action and initiative is primary in his account, shaping and sometimes overriding the deeds of His human servants. This is sacred history, written by believers for believers!

Nahash of Ammon Besieges Israelite
Jabesh-Gilead   *11:1-4*

[1] **Then Nahash the Ammonite went up and besieged Jabesh-gilead; and all the men of Jabesh said to Nahash, "Make a treaty with us, and we will serve you."** [2] **But Nahash the Ammonite said to them, "On this condition I will make a treaty with you, that I gouge out all your right eyes, and thus put disgrace upon all Israel."** [3] **The elders of Jabesh said to him, "Give us seven days respite that we may send messengers through all the territory of Israel. Then, if there is no one to save us, we will give ourselves up to you."** [4] **When the messengers came to Gibeah of**

Saul, they reported the matter in the ears of the people; and all the people wept aloud.

The account of Saul's exploit in our chapter is closely related in form and content to the accounts of the judges' exploits in the Book of Judges. This puts Saul on a plane with the deliverers Ehud, Barak, and Gideon. As is always the case in those stories, so also here God's people are in danger of enslavement at the hands of foreign oppressors. The situation of the Israelite town of Jabesh-gilead is hopeless, once the Ammonite bedouin chief has moved against it and laid siege to it. No permanent, all-embracing political organization exists to unite the Israelite tribes for defensive action against the aggressor. Hence there is no attempt at resisting Nahash's invasion; the best the city elders can do is to attempt to mask their political capitulation under the terms of a formal treaty. But the Ammonite king scornfully offers them a treaty that includes the outrageous condition that he is to receive the right eye of every male, thus making the men of Jabesh-gilead not only militarily incapable of future resistance but "putting disgrace on all Israel." Nahash is so convinced of Israel's inability to resist that he "magnanimously" even grants the hesitant elders of the city a 7-day truce, pursuing his aim of disgracing Israel and its God, the Lord, to the farthest extreme imaginable. Apparently Nahash had sized up the situation correctly—this was the lowest point of Israel's political fortunes—for even in Gibeah, the most likely source of aid, there is only helpless weeping when the news of the impending atrocity arrives. After all, Gibeah is the home of the king-designate, a Benjaminite town closely related to the people of Jabesh-gilead ever since their daughters had been "given" to those Benjaminites who survived the earlier civil war. (Judg. 21:8-14)

Saul Delivers Israel from Nahash 5-11

⁵ Now Saul was coming from the field behind the oxen; and Saul said, "What ails the people, that they are weeping?" So they told him the tidings of the men of Jabesh. ⁶ And the spirit of God came mightily upon Saul when he heard these words, and his anger was greatly kindled. ⁷ He took a yoke of oxen, and cut them in pieces and sent them throughout all the territory of Israel by the hand of messengers, saying, "Whoever does not come out after Saul and Samuel, so shall it be done to his oxen!" Then the dread of the LORD fell upon the people, and they came out as one man. ⁸ When he mustered them at Bezek, the men of Israel were three hundred thousand, and the men of Judah thirty thousand. ⁹ And they said to the messengers who had come, "Thus shall you say to the men of Jabesh-gilead: 'Tomorrow, by the time the sun is hot, you shall have deliverance.'" When the messengers came and told the men of Jabesh, they were glad. ¹⁰ Therefore the men of Jabesh said, "Tomorrow we will give ourselves up to you, and you may do to us whatever seems good to you." ¹¹ And on the morrow Saul put the people in three companies; and they came into the midst of the camp in the morning watch, and cut down the Ammonites until the heat of the day; and those who survived were scattered, so that no two of them were left together.

In a desperate situation Saul now steps forth from obscurity, coming from the fields with his oxen to investigate the ill-boding lamentations in the village.

Though he had been king-designate ever since Samuel's secret anointing of him, up to this time Saul had lived a normal life as an obedient farmer lad — even his public designation at Mizpah does not seem to have changed that. But when Saul hears the news from Jabesh-gilead, the Spirit of God leaps down upon him, crashing in like lightning that rends the very air, granting Saul the Lord's divine power (such as once strengthened Samson, Judg. 14:19; 15:14). It is not clear whether the anger kindled within him is directed against the cruel plan and outrageous blasphemy of Nahash or against the faithless lament of the people; but what is clear is that God is again intervening to deliver His people through His specially endowed servant. By cutting up the oxen and sending pieces as tokens to the tribes (much as the fiery cross was sent to the clans in early Scottish history; cf. also Judg. 19:29) he is declaring himself the divinely chosen charismatic leader of the Israelite tribes and summoning them for a holy war on pain of a curse on those who do not comply ("Whoever does not come out, so shall it be done to his oxen"). No wonder the "dread of the LORD" falls upon the people; they are afraid to disobey, and the once-splintered groups come to the mustering place at Bezek "as one man." There the one-time farmer lad reviews an army that is ready for action!

We are again surprised by the large numbers; since what we know about the logistics of ancient warfare precludes even Alexander's having nearly this large an army. Assyrian armies, 250 years later, seem to have numbered barely 8,000. As often, the Septuagint text has a numerical variant; in this case its versions present the even larger numbers: 600,000 and 70,000. Some scholars have suggested that the word "thousand" has been added to the original number by a later hand; others translate the word *'eleph* not as a numerical term ("thousand") but as a social term ("clan unit"), pointing to the sense this makes in the Gideon story, Judg. 7:2-6, and particularly in Joshua's initial attack on Ai, Joshua 7:3-5. Other scholars assert that this use of large military numbers is typical of popular ancient Near Eastern military communiques. Still others suggest that numbers of a later census, say, of the time of David, were used in this account, so that what proved true only later is in a way prophetic here. Be that as it may, the separate mention of the tribe of Judah — which is otherwise seldom mentioned in concerted action with the other tribes — is surprising. A few commentators have felt that this is an unauthentic note, which should be removed from the regular text to a footnote. Since, however, the proportion of the numbers here is 10 to 1 in favor of the North, this note may well be very early and may reflect the fact that the more powerful components of Israel's tribal confederacy were from the North. Hence the interpreter must be cautious; certainly he ought not ridicule ancient peoples for failing to employ modern methods of calculation; on the other hand, he ought not fail to notice the problem which these ancient numbers present to modern readers.

The military action itself is reported in brief but bold strokes. A typical war stratagem hoodwinks the Ammonites into false security. They are told by the Jabesites, "Tomorrow we will go forth to you," a play on the phrase "go forth," which means going forth not in surrender, but in attack, "and then you may do to us whatever you please." (At this point the Israelite hearers of this story must have broken out in hearty laughter!) Then comes Saul's sudden attack in the last of the three night watches. He employs a strategy similar to that used by Gideon (Judg. 7:16), Abimelech (Judg. 9:43), the Philistines (1 Sam. 13:17), David (2 Sam. 18:2). Saul seems to have marched all night, dividing his troops into the traditional three columns, attacking on three different fronts at the same time. The Ammonites do not seem to notice the Israelites until they have broken into their camp.

Saul's Prudent Domestic Politics 12-15

12 Then the people said to Samuel, "Who is it that said, 'Shall Saul reign over us?' Bring the men, that we may put them to death." 13 But Saul said, "Not a man shall be put to death this day, for today the LORD has wrought deliverance in Israel." 14 Then Samuel said to the people, "Come, let us go to Gilgal and there renew the kingdom." 15 So all the people went to Gilgal, and there they made Saul king before the LORD in Gilgal. There they sacrificed peace offerings before the LORD, and there Saul and all the men of Israel rejoiced greatly.

The purpose of our account is not to describe the battle but to answer the question raised at the beginning of the chapter as to whether this nation, with only a king-designate available, can meet the challenge of external threats. That question receives a remarkably positive answer in the final verses of our chapter. The army looks upon this victory as a clear refutation of the "anti-Saul party," which had earlier expressed its doubts as to Saul's ability to deliver them from the threat of Philistine expansion (10:27). That group of dissenters had doubted that Saul was the right man, perhaps because he did not measure up to the pagan royal ideal. Apparently Samuel's solution of the monarchy question had not been accepted by such people. Indeed Samuel's designation of Saul and the Mizpah assembly's acclamation of Saul apparently had not really caught the imagination of the entire nation. Now, however, this clear-cut victory convinces them that the Lord has wrought deliverance in Israel through Saul; he has successfully followed the pattern of the judges of old, leading the people's army in a successful holy war! So strong is the enthusiasm of the people for Saul that a sort of lynch justice attempts to exploit this opportunity to root out the anti-Saul adherents of the pagan royal ideal. It is Saul who steps forward to protect these opponents of his and prevents what might easily have become a bloody quarrel, facing the would-be lynchers with a religious objection, "Not a man shall be put to death this day, for today the LORD has wrought deliverance in Israel." In this way the entire matter of instituting the monarchy in Israel is advanced to a more sure footing. Saul has proved to be the Lord's man. Now nothing stands in the way of elevating him—in a manner more complete than had been done secretly at Ramah and rather unsurely at Mizpah—to genuine kingship. Samuel is able to call on the people to proceed down the Jordan valley to Gilgal in order to officially anoint the Benjaminite Saul king there at the ancient and respected Benjaminite sanctuary. Gilgal was a good choice also because, situated near Jericho in the Jordan valley, it was less exposed to possible Philistine attack, and besides, it was connected in Israelite tradition with Joshua's glorious campaigns of conquest.

The actual "coronation" at Gilgal is described with a few brief but significant sentences. It is no secular ceremony; rather, it is a religious feast in which the Lord,

His victorious king, and Israel are united in worship and communion. It involves more than the final thanksgiving service at the end of a holy war; in a real sense, Israelite kingship is thereby "renewed" (v. 14). What we now see emerging is a new situation: Israel is no longer to be a loosely connected, temporary tribal confederacy that comes together for worship and defensive holy wars; Israel now has a king at its head, and it has been readied for what was impossible before this: a frontal attack on the Philistines. Soon Saul can gather special troops about himself at his new capital city Gibeah. We dare never forget that Saul is the anointed of the Lord. It is the Lord who has used the Ammonite crisis to modify Israel's originally mistaken plans for a kingship like that of the nations, so that it is to become genuinely Israelite and not pagan and so that in its fulfillment He may reveal the King after His own heart.

SAMUEL RENEWS THE COVENANT
FOR MONARCHICAL ISRAEL   12

At this juncture in Israel's history when the new institution of kingship is to be inserted into the old setup of a tribal confederacy and when the new relationship of king and people has to be fixed, the prophet Samuel steps forth to confirm Israel's ancient covenant with the Lord as the basis for the new setup. In this chapter, therefore, we are not dealing with a sort of "coronation sermon," in which Samuel is to be thought of as expressing his personal views about the new developments; rather, we are dealing with a religious gathering in which Samuel functions as a covenant mediator, calling on Israel at this critical juncture to confirm the covenant it had long ago made with the Lord at Sinai. Since the fundamental elements of Israel's covenant with the Lord are here confirmed, it is wise to take note of them briefly, so that we may more easily understand the nature of the assembly at Gilgal and its activities. The covenant usually included the following five elements (here each is illustrated by its Sinaitic formulation from Ex. 20): (1) the preamble ("I am the LORD your God"); (2) the historical prolog ("who brought you out of the land of Egypt, out of the house of bondage"); (3) the fundamental stipulation ("You shall have no other gods before me"); (4) specific stipulations (applying to various aspects of life, as in the specific commandments and laws, e. g., "You shall not take the name of the LORD your God in vain"); (5) the curses and blessings ("I the LORD your God am a jealous God, visiting the iniquity . . . of those who hate me, but showing steadfast love to thousands of those who love me and keep my commandments"). These elements were accordingly basic to any ceremony of covenant renewal, such as is described here in Ch. 12. The elements need not always come in this order or be expressed in this phraseology; but they are, as we shall see, present.

Samuel Insures His Own Position
as Legitimate Covenant Mediator 12:1-6

¹ **And Samuel said to all Israel, "Behold, I have hearkened to your voice in all that you have said to me, and have made a king over you. ² And now, behold, the king walks before you; and I am old and gray, and behold, my sons are with you; and I have walked before you from my youth until this day. ³ Here I am; testify against me before the LORD and before his anointed. Whose ox have I taken? Or whose ass have**

I taken? Or whom have I defrauded? Whom have I oppressed? Or from whose hand have I taken a bribe to blind my eyes with it? Testify against me *c* and I will restore it to you." ⁴ They said, "You have not defrauded us or oppressed us or taken anything from any man's hand." ⁵ And he said to them, "The LORD is witness against you, and his anointed is witness this day, that you have not found anything in my hand." And they said, "He is witness."

⁶ And Samuel said to the people, "The LORD is witness,*d* who appointed Moses and Aaron and brought your fathers up out of the land of Egypt.

c Gk: Heb lacks *Testify against me*   *d* Gk: Heb lacks *is witness*

Before undertaking the actual covenant renewal itself, Samuel first insures his own position as covenant mediator over against both the people and the king (who now, after the Ammonite victory and his subsequent formal coronation, "walks before" them). If Samuel is to stand before them as the legitimate and lawful representative of the Lord and of His covenant, to confirm it in the new situation, then he wishes first to have the king and the people formally confirm the fact that his life has been blameless in respect to stipulations of the covenant. Hence he refers to obtaining someone else's property, like an ox or ass (cf. Ex. 20:17; 23:4), to defrauding and oppressing (cf. Ex. 22:21-24), to accepting bribes to acquit a murderer (cf. Ex. 23:8). These are all references to Element 4 of the covenant, its specific stipulations. This initial speech is therefore not, as has sometimes been imagined, the act of a weary old man who is about to resign but first seeks an acknowledgment of his faithful service from the people; rather, this is a great man's wise step forward, a step that is necessary if he is to have a position of trust from which he can then move to outline the shape the new institution of Israelite kingship should take inside of the old framework of the Sinaitic covenant. Hence Samuel first wants the people's acknowledgment that he has been a faithful servant of the covenant. Like every judicial act, this had to be sworn to before witnesses.

The Present Enterprise in the Light
of the Covenant and of God's Past Deeds   *7-15*

[7] Now therefore stand still, that I may plead with you before the LORD concerning all the saving deeds of the LORD, which he performed for you and for your fathers. [8] When Jacob went into Egypt and the Egyptians oppressed them,[e] then your fathers cried to the LORD and the LORD sent Moses and Aaron, who brought forth your fathers out of Egypt, and made them dwell in this place. [9] But they forgot the LORD their God; and he sold them into the hand of Sisera, commander of the army of Jabin king of[f] Hazor, and into the hand of the Philistines, and into the hand of the king of Moab; and they fought against them. [10] And they cried to the LORD, and said, 'We have sinned, because we have forsaken the LORD, and have served the Baals and the Ashtaroth; but now deliver us out of the hand of our enemies, and we will serve thee.' [11] And the LORD sent Jerubbaal and Barak,[g] and Jephthah, and Samuel, and delivered you out of the hand of your enemies on every side; and you dwelt in safety. [12] And when you saw that Nahash the king of the Ammonites came against you, you said to me, 'No, but a king shall reign over us,'

[e] Gk: Heb lacks *and the Egyptians oppressed them*
[f] Gk: Heb lacks *Jabin king of*   [g] Gk Syr: Heb *Bedan*

when the **LORD** your God was your king. [13] And now behold the king whom you have chosen, for whom you have asked; behold, the **LORD** has set a king over you. [14] If you will fear the **LORD** and serve him and hearken to his voice and not rebel against the commandment of the **LORD**, and if both you and the king who reigns over you will follow the **LORD** your God, it will be well; [15] but if you will not hearken to the voice of the **LORD**, but rebel against the commandment of the **LORD**, then the hand of the **LORD** will be against you and your king.[h]

[h] Gk: Heb *fathers*

Following the traditional pattern for covenant renewal, Samuel calls on the people to take their stand before the Lord so that he may plead with them as in a legal proceeding "concerning all the saving deeds of the LORD which he performed for you and for your fathers." A historical prolog (Element 2 of the covenant, vv. 8-13) then places before the people the Lord's deeds on their behalf from the times of the patriarch Jacob to the present. All the basic "articles of Israel's faith" are included in what can be seen as two cycles of events that lead to the present. Cycle 1 includes the following: They were oppressed in Egypt, they cried to the Lord, the Lord sent the deliverers, they came to the Promised Land. Cycle 2 includes: They forgot the Lord, He sold them into the hand of oppressors, they cried to the Lord (their prayer is neatly summarized), the Lord sent the deliverers, or judges, they dwelt in safety. Samuel's liturgical recital of God's deeds proclaims both His anger against the people's sin (Law) and His steadfast love, which remained loyal to the covenant despite Israel's disloyalty (Gospel).

101

But the recital of the Lord's dealing with Israel does not end with some past event; rather, Samuel brings things up to the present crisis by showing how Israel's present desire for a king like those of the other nations has been rebellion and sin in view of the fact that "the LORD your God was your king." The Lord's claim to His own sovereign and royal lordship is still in force, Samuel insists, even now after the people have chosen an earthly king. His continued lordship, Samuel emphasizes, is the basis even of the new situation and is binding on both the earthly king and the people. Samuel therefore presents the king with a twofold "Behold," (v. 13) as both the one "whom you have chosen" and as the one whom "the LORD has set over you."

On this basis, then, as in every covenant-renewal ceremony, blessing and curse (Element 5 of the covenant) are pronounced: blessing for people and king if they keep the covenant; curses if they are disobedient.

In the Presence of the Lord   16-19

¹⁶ Now therefore stand still and see this great thing, which the LORD will do before your eyes. ¹⁷ Is it not wheat harvest today? I will call upon the LORD, that he may send thunder and rain; and you shall know and see that your wickedness is great, which you have done in the sight of the LORD, in asking for yourselves a king." ¹⁸ So Samuel called upon the LORD, and the LORD sent thunder and rain that day; and all the people greatly feared the LORD and Samuel.

¹⁹ And all the people said to Samuel, "Pray for your servants to the LORD your God, that we may

not die; for we have added to all our sins this evil, to ask for ourselves a king."

The sacred ceremony is, however, by no means complete now that Samuel has opened up the view into the present and the future. The unatoned guilt of the people who have rebelled against the Lord's rulership by asking for a king like those of the other nations still stands in the way of the realization of the Lord's promise. Hence this sin, this temptation to apostasy, has to be removed. At Samuel's word a theophany occurs before the worshiping congregation, as the Lord manifests His presence in their midst, sending forth lightning and rain from the cloudless blue sky of the Palestinian harvest season, revealing Himself as once at Sinai (Ex. 19:7 ff.). The people, scared to death by the Lord's holy presence (cf. Ex. 20:18 f.), acknowledge and confess their sin, saying, "We have added to all our sins this evil, to ask for ourselves a king."

The Covenant Renewed   *20-25*

[20] And Samuel said to the people, "Fear not; you have done all this evil, yet do not turn aside from following the LORD, but serve the LORD with all your heart; [21] and do not turn aside after [i] **vain things which cannot profit or save, for they are vain. [22] For the LORD will not cast away his people, for his great name's sake, because it has pleased the LORD to make you a people for himself. [23] Moreover as for me, far be it from me that I should sin against the LORD by ceasing to pray for you; and I will instruct you in the good and the right way. [24] Only fear the LORD, and**

[i] Gk Syr Tg Vg: Heb *because after*

serve him faithfully with all your heart; for consider what great things he has done for you. 25 But if you still do wickedly, you shall be swept away, both you and your king."

The people's confession of sins opens the way for the absolution-like assurance of salvation Samuel then proclaims as mediator of the covenant: "Fear not. . . . The LORD will not cast away his people, for his great name's sake, because it has pleased the LORD to make you a people for himself." Then the fundamental stipulation (Element 3 of the covenant, vv. 20 f.) is referred to in the admonition, "Do not turn aside from following the LORD . . . after vain things which cannot profit or save."

In his response to the people Samuel also outlines the task the Lord has given him in the new situation. He will be both an intercessor for them and an instructor in the good and right way (both explaining the fundamental stipulation of the covenant and applying it most specifically to all areas of life in specific stipulations). In fact, Samuel says, he would sin against the Lord if he would fail to continue as such an intercessor and teacher. In some respects this speech is a farewell like those made by other great figures of sacred history as they renewed the covenant before their passing from the scene (Moses, Deut. 29–31; Joshua, Joshua 24). Samuel, however, is by no means resigning. He is not ready for that. He must continue as prophet-priest. In fact, his last words (vv. 24 f.) are proclamations of blessing and curse, the very fundamental points of the message of the prophets. Samuel appears here as a type of all the intercessors among the priests and prophets of Israel who pleaded for God's people, mediated God's Word to them until finally that One appeared who was at one and the same time the Mediator and Intercessor for His people. (Rom. 8:34; 1 John 2:1)

THE WAR OF LIBERATION   13—14

If we of the 20th century wish to understand the next three chapters in all their original vividness, we must be aware of the hallowed conventions and customary procedures of Israel's sacred wars, procedures that were self-evident to the ancient tellers and hearers of these stories. We moderns can ignore these only at the risk of misunderstanding much of what is told. A sacred war usually began with (1) a prophet's official announcement of a crisis (the Philistine attack here). (2) Usually some daring exploit by a specially-gifted (charismatic) hero (deliverer or "judge") was hailed by a man of God as the sign that such a war was to be fought (in these chapters the deliverer is not so much Saul as it is Jonathan, whose acts of slaying the Gibeah garrison commander and of attacking the Michmash outpost show that he is the divinely chosen hero). Then (3) the summons was sent (in this case by trumpet) for the tribes to assemble. After the elders of each tribe had deliberated, (4) all men 20 years and over gathered at the mustering place (in this instance, at Gilgal). (5) There in the sacred camp, in which only those who were ritually pure and who had proved loyal to the Lord's covenant were allowed, special sacrifices were offered and finally the priest or prophet announced the divine oracle, "The Lord has given the enemy into your hands" (in 13:3 Saul foolishly does not wait for Samuel to do this; later, however, 14:18-20, 37, he does seek the Lord's oracle before going into battle). Then (6) "the people of

105

the Lord" (the official name of the Lord's army) went forth. But the battle was not considered merely a military campaign (though military combat most certainly took place, and the soldiers fought as hard as they could, calling out the watchword and raising a special war cry as they hurled themselves into the fray); rather, the battle was one in which the Lord did the real fighting (cf. 14:23). (7) Hence it could be engaged in only by soldiers who were ritually pure (cf. the command 14:24 to avoid unclean food; also 14:31 ff.) and who had wholehearted confidence in the Lord (such as Jonathan displayed here, 13:3 and especially 14:6; cf. Judg. 7:3). (8) The Lord's attack was usually accompanied by supernatural phenomena, such as thunder, hailstones, or panic which utterly confused the overwhelmed enemy (here the very earth trembles, 14:15, 23). (9) Since the booty belonged to the Lord, no private person could claim any part of it (cf. Saul's mistake in Ch. 15). (10) A victory celebration in which blessings and curses were pronounced was usually held at the end of the war. In the period of the judges, holy wars were fought in this classic form; though a standing army of professionals replaced the institution with the rise of the monarchy, the tradition with its rich imagery remained alive in Israel's imagination into New Testament times.

Chapters 13 and 14 describe the war of liberation. It is described, however, not in modern military terms, but in the religious and theological terms of an ancient holy war. Hence the present story centers in Jonathan's exploits, even though it is clear from the outset (13:7-14) that the hero Jonathan will not receive the throne as Saul's successor, but that the Lord has already sought a man after His own heart. For that reason a sense of tragedy hangs over the entire story from the outset:

106

king Saul is himself responsible for his brilliant son's failure to succeed him on the throne of Israel.

*An Initial Israelite Revolt Crushed
by the Philistine Counterattack*　　　　　　　1-7

¹ Saul was . . .ʲ years old when he began to reign; and he reigned . . . and two ᵏ years over Israel.

² Saul chose three thousand men of Israel; two thousand were with Saul in Michmash and the hill country of Bethel, and a thousand were with Jonathan in Gibeah of Benjamin; the rest of the people he sent home, every man to his tent. ³ Jonathan defeated the garrison of the Philistines which was at Geba; and the Philistines heard of it. And Saul blew the trumpet throughout all the land, saying, "Let the Hebrews hear." ⁴ And all Israel heard it said that Saul had defeated the garrison of the Philistines, and also that Israel had become odious to the Philistines. And the people were called out to join Saul at Gilgal.

⁵ And the Philistines mustered to fight with Israel, thirty thousand chariots, and six thousand horsemen, and troops like the sand on the seashore in multitude; they came up and encamped in Michmash, to the east of Beth-aven. ⁶ When the men of Israel saw that they were in straits (for the people were hard pressed), the people hid themselves in caves and in holes and in rocks and in tombs and in cisterns, ⁷ or crossed the fords of the Jordan ˡ to the land of Gad and Gilead. Saul was still at Gilgal, and all the people followed him trembling.

ʲ The number is lacking in Heb
ᵏ *Two* is not the entire number. Something has dropped out.
ˡ Cn: Heb *Hebrews crossed the Jordan*

It is impossible to reckon the interval of time between the Ammonite war and the beginning of this war, which secured independence from the Philistines. As the RSV notes indicate, the numbers have been disarranged (perhaps 2 should be emended to 22).

After the Ammonite victory Saul had begun to organize a standing army, laying the foundation for a sort of military monarchy; but it is Jonathan who begins the actual war of liberation by smiting either an official of the Philistines or a pillar meant to symbolize the Philistine claim on the country. Such an act of rebellion at Saul's hometown, Gibeah, challenges the Philistine claims and is an act of faith, one which the Israelites understand and to which they respond as soon as Saul's trumpet signal summons them to muster for a holy war at Gilgal.

The Philistines also rightly understand that "the Hebrews have rebelled." They respond by overwhelming the land with an army "as sand on the seashore for number" (on numbers see pp. 93 f.). The immediate effect of the Philistine countermove is disastrous for the defenseless Israelites. Saul, to judge from the following, has to abandon the territory north of the ravine, so that Michmash falls to the Philistines, becoming the center of their operations in the area. Saul is forced to muster his army in the distant Jordan valley at Gilgal, though Jonathan still holds Geba and the territory south of the ravine. North of that ravine raiders from the Philistine camp go forth, burning, pillaging, murdering throughout the countryside, with little or no opposition from the Israelites, who had either hidden in caves or had tremblingly deserted the Promised Land and had fled across the Jordan in a sort of conquest in reverse!

Saul's Unsuccessful Attempts at a Counterattack   8-23

⁸ He waited seven days, the time appointed by Samuel; but Samuel did not come to Gilgal, and the people were scattering from him. ⁹ So Saul said, "Bring the burnt offering here to me, and the peace offerings." And he offered the burnt offering. ¹⁰ As soon as he had finished offering the burnt offering, behold, Samuel came; and Saul went out to meet him and salute him. ¹¹ Samuel said, "What have you done?" And Saul said, "When I saw that the people were scattering from me, and that you did not come within the days appointed, and that the Philistines had mustered at Michmash, ¹² I said, 'Now the Philistines will come down upon me at Gilgal, and I have not entreated the favor of the LORD'; so I forced myself, and offered the burnt offering." ¹³ And Samuel said to Saul, "You have done foolishly; you have not kept the commandment of the LORD your God, which he commanded you; for now the LORD would have established your kingdom over Israel for ever. ¹⁴ But now your kingdom shall not continue; the LORD has sought out a man after his own heart; and the LORD has appointed him to be prince over his people, because you have not kept what the LORD commanded you." ¹⁵ And Samuel arose, and went up from Gilgal to Gibeah of Benjamin.

And Saul numbered the people who were present with him, about six hundred men. ¹⁶ And Saul, and Jonathan his son, and the people who were present with them, stayed in Geba of Benjamin; but the Philistines encamped in Michmash. ¹⁷ And raiders came out of the camp of the Philistines in three companies; one company turned toward Ophrah, to the land of

Shual, [18] another company turned toward Beth-horon, and another company turned toward the border that looks down upon the valley of Zeboim toward the wilderness.

[19] Now there was no smith to be found throughout all the land of Israel; for the Philistines said, "Lest the Hebrews make themselves swords or spears"; [20] but every one of the Israelites went down to the Philistines to sharpen his plowshare, his mattock, his axe, or his sickle; [m] [21] and the charge was a pim for the plowshares and for the mattocks, and a third of a shekel for sharpening the axes and for setting the goads. [n] [22] So on the day of the battle there was neither sword nor spear found in the hand of any of the people with Saul and Jonathan; but Saul and Jonathan his son had them. [23] And the garrison of the Philistines went out to the pass of Michmash.

[m] Gk: Heb *plowshare*   [n] The Heb of this verse is obscure

Meanwhile things go badly also at the mustering place of Saul's army in the ancient sanctuary of Gilgal, a historic place hallowed by the events of the conquest, when it was Joshua's camp. Saul's situation becomes hopeless while he waits for Samuel—who does not come! The people seemingly look upon this as a sign that there is no blessing in this campaign, and they leave the encampment in droves. In desperation Saul (who does not want to begin the campaign without entreating the favor of God) does what should have been reserved for the Lord's prophet or priest: he braces himself and performs the priestly functions in this emergency himself. At the very instant that he concludes the sacrifice Samuel suddenly appears, and Saul soon hears the condemnation, "You have done foolishly." Despite his piety, Saul had not, Samuel points out, kept the command of the Lord his God (v. 13), who is not dependent on a certain number of warriors to win His wars for Him, and whose possibilities and capabilities far transcend human calculation. In violating the sacred rites of the holy war Saul has acted like a pagan king of a heathen nation, not like the Lord's anointed, who should have believed in the midst of the crisis: the Lord will not abandon His people. That is why Saul's kingdom will not be established. The Lord's choice of Saul was an act of pure grace; but unbelieving Saul proved unfaithful to His call.

The Greek version of v. 15 gives a fuller view (here inserted in parentheses) of the ensuing action: "Samuel arose and went up from Gilgal (and went his way. What was left of the people went up after Saul against the enemy force. And they came from Gilgal) to Geba of Benjamin." A copyist's eye seems to have slipped from the first occurance of the word "Gilgal" to the second. Since the place-names "Geba" and "Gibeah" were so much alike in Hebrew script, which did not write out the vowels, it has not always been clear to later generations which place was meant: Saul's hometown, Gibeah (modern *Tell-el Ful*, 3 miles north of Jerusalem), or Geba (modern *Jeba*, 3 miles northeast of Gibeah on the south side of the ravine, or pass, of Michmash. However, on the basis of geographical probability we can with some plausibility depart from the RSV and Hebrew reading of Gibeah at this point and adopt the Greek version's Geba, since Geba lay just south across the very deep ravine opposite the captured city of Michmash. Grollenberg's *Atlas of the Bible* (p. 68) has aerial photos of the area.

In other words, as a result of various countermoves,

the Philistines have taken over Michmash, where part of Saul's army had originally been stationed (v. 2), whereas Saul now must move up with his small army to Geba, where Jonathan still holds his original position. The Philistines now send out their raiders from Michmash toward the north, west, and east; and in a southward direction they even move an outpost to the very northern edge of the ravine on the immediate boundary line facing Geba. This sets the stage for the next part of the story: Jonathan's great exploit, told in most vivid popular style in the next chapter. The enslavement of the Israelite farmers has been so complete that any possible move toward rebellion is hampered by the Philistine monopoly on iron. Even agricultural implements have to be bought from, and blacksmithed by the Philistines at an exorbitantly high price. By this "economic warfare" Israel has been kept in such a state of disarmament that only the king and the crown prince have genuine weapons.

Jonathan's One-Man Holy War Against the Philistines
14:1-15

¹ One day Jonathan the son of Saul said to the young man who bore his armor, "Come, let us go over to the Philistine garrison on yonder side." But he did not tell his father. ² Saul was staying in the outskirts of Gibeah under the pomegranate tree which is at Migron; the people who were with him were about six hundred men, ³ and Ahijah the son of Ahitub, Ichabod's brother, son of Phinehas, son of Eli, the priest of the LORD in Shiloh, wearing an ephod. And the people did not know that Jonathan had gone. ⁴ In the pass,ᵒ by which Jonathan sought

ᵒ Heb *between the passes*

**to go over to the Philistine garrison, there was a
rocky crag on the one side and a rocky crag on the
other side; the name of the one was Bozez, and the
name of the other Seneh. 5 The one crag rose on the
north in front of Michmash, and the other on the
south in front of Geba.**

**6 And Jonathan said to the young man who bore
his armor, "Come, let us go over to the garrison of
these uncircumcised; it may be that the LORD will
work for us; for nothing can hinder the LORD from
saving by many or by few." 7 And his armor-bearer
said to him, "Do all that your mind inclines to;[p]
behold, I am with you, as is your mind so is mine."[q]
8 Then said Jonathan, "Behold, we will cross over
to the men, and we will show ourselves to them. 9 If
they say to us, 'Wait until we come to you,' then we
will stand still in our place, and we will not go up
to them. 10 But if they say, 'Come up to us,' then we
will go up; for the LORD has given them into our
hand. And this shall be the sign to us." 11 So both
of them showed themselves to the garrison of the
Philistines; and the Philistines said, "Look, Hebrews
are coming out of the holes where they have hid themselves." 12 And the men of the garrison hailed Jonathan and his armor-bearer, and said, "Come up to
us, and we will show you a thing." And Jonathan
said to his armor-bearer, "Come up after me; for the
LORD has given them into the hand of Israel."
13 Then Jonathan climbed up on his hands and feet,
and his armor-bearer after him. And they fell before
Jonathan, and his armor-bearer killed them after
him; 14 and that first slaughter, which Jonathan and**

[p] Gk: Heb *Do all that is in your mind. Turn*
[q] Gk: Heb lacks *so is mine*

his armor-bearer made, was of about twenty men within as it were half a furrow's length in an acre [r] of land. [15] And there was a panic in the camp, in the field, and among all the people; the garrison and even the raiders trembled; the earth quaked; and it became a very great panic.

[r] Heb *yoke*

When Jonathan suggests to his armor-bearer that they go over to the Philistine outpost on the other side of the ravine, he leaves the Geba camp without telling his father, embarking on an enterprise in which the Lord is to give him the command to proceed or to halt, removing all possibility of his being hindered by his father, the king, who is, it seems, delaying with his army on the outskirts of the city of Geba at a pomegranate tree later pointed out as "Saul's tree." Saul's priest Ahijah, of Eli's line, is mentioned because he carries the ephod, here seemingly the receptacle from which the sacred lots are drawn to determine the will of the Lord. The sharpness of two crags on either side of the deep ravine ("Slippery" and "Thorny") is mentioned because this will help the hearer visualize Jonathan's daring exploit in the no-man's-land between the two forces. It is, however, not foolhardiness but faith that moves Jonathan to embark single-handedly on a holy war against the uncircumcised; he does not have to be repeatedly compelled to join battle, as was the case with Gideon (Judg. 6 and 7). For Jonathan is convinced that the Lord has no difficulty in saving by many or by few. Unlike his father, who first sets out to calculate the number and size of his army, Jonathan puts his trust in God, knowing that Israel's battles are

114

the Lord's battles (cf. 18:17) and that He is able to save. But even this venture must, he feels, be based on a clear revelation from God. This will be announced, surprisingly enough, by the Philistines themselves. Their call to the Hebrews to come to their campsite will serve as the Lord's sign that He has given them into Jonathan's hand. (For the holy war imagery cf. pp. 105 f., item 5, and 23:4; 24:4; Joshua 6:2; Judg. 3:28; 5:14.) The self-confident Philistines' derisive summons to the slaves who had crawled out of their holes to come up "and we will show you a thing!" is, it seems, mockery, since they think such a daring deed impossible. By means of the enemy's ridicule, however, the Lord has revealed His will to Jonathan. And so the two Israelites disappear from enemy sight—only, however, to reappear suddenly in front of them! What is then described is not merely the military detail of how Jonathan presumably smites the enemy with the sword and his armor-bearer then dispatches them, but, more important, how the Lord's terror accompanies Jonathan and overwhelms not only the detachment at the outpost but also those in the camp at Michmash, at the lookout, and even in the midst of the hated "raiders." The Lord Himself intervenes, as He had done in Deborah's time at the Battle of Esdraelon (Judg. 4 and 5), in Joshua's time at Aijalon (Joshua 10), and at the Red Sea. (Ex. 14)

Repercussions in the Israelite Camp   *16-23*

16 And the watchmen of Saul in Gibeah of Benjamin looked; and behold, the multitude was surging hither and thither.[s] 17 Then Saul said to the people who were with him, "Number and see who has gone from us." And when they had numbered, behold,

[s] Gk: Heb *they went and thither*

Jonathan and his armor-bearer were not there. [18] And Saul said to Ahijah, "Bring hither the ark of God." For the ark of God went at that time with the people of Israel. [19] And while Saul was talking to the priest, the tumult in the camp of the Philistines increased more and more; and Saul said to the priest, "Withdraw your hand." [20] Then Saul and all the people who were with him rallied and went into the battle; and behold, every man's sword was against his fellow, and there was very great confusion. [21] Now the Hebrews who had been with the Philistines before that time and who had gone up with them into the camp, even they also turned to be with [f] the Israelites who were with Saul and Jonathan. [22] Likewise, when all the men of Israel who had hid themselves in the hill country of Ephraim heard that the Philistines were fleeing, they too followed hard after them in the battle. [23] So the LORD delivered Israel that day; and the battle passed beyond Beth-aven.

[f] Gk Syr Vg Tg: Heb *round about, they also, to be with*

Next, Saul's army is drawn into Jonathan's raid. A clear-sighted watchman can see the surging beyond the ravine. As time goes on, Saul and his army can hear the tumult become louder and louder, and they become more and more aware of the growing confusion which the Lord is striking into the enemy. With an inkling of what is up, Saul quickly inspects his forces. Yes, Jonathan and his armor-bearer are not present! Faced with a new situation and a new decision, Saul wishes to consult the Lord's holy oracle. Seemingly in the sacred ceremony of the sacred lot the priest put forth his hands into the ephod to draw out and in some way handle the lots, but it took time to ascertain an answer, for which a "perfect lot" seems to have been necessary. At the moment, however, there is no time left for such ceremony, since the increasing tumult beyond the ravine demands immediate intervention. Saul therefore tells the priest to stop and, without waiting for the verdict of the Lord, rallies his troops and marches across the ravine posthaste. There he finds the Philistines in complete disarray, the Lord's panic having so thoroughly confused them that they are fighting one another. Moreover, Israelites who had been sold into Philistine slavery and others who had been in hiding have now risen up in revolt and are fighting against the Philistines. As the text says, "The LORD delivered Israel that day."

Saul's Tragic Oath 24-30

²⁴ And the men of Israel were distressed that day; for Saul laid an oath on the people, saying, "Cursed be the man who eats food until it is evening and I am avenged on my enemies." So none of the people tasted food. ²⁵ And all the people ᵘ came into the forest; and there was honey on the ground. ²⁶ And when the people entered the forest, behold, the honey was dropping, but no man put his hand to his mouth; for the people feared the oath. ²⁷ But Jonathan had not heard his father charge the people with the oath; so he put forth the tip of the staff that was in his hand, and dipped it in the honeycomb, and put his hand to his mouth; and his eyes became bright. ²⁸ Then one of the people said, "Your father strictly charged the people with an oath, saying, 'Cursed be the man who eats food this day.'" And the people were faint. ²⁹ Then Jonathan said, "My

ᵘ Heb *land*

117

father has troubled the land; see how my eyes have become bright, because I tasted a little of this honey. ³⁰ How much better if the people had eaten freely today of the spoil of their enemies which they found; for now the slaughter among the Philistines has not been great."

Saul considers the battle a truly crucial one, as is clear from the fact that he imposes a fast on his army, seemingly having pronounced his solemn curse at the time when they left their camp and he had to break off consultation of the oracle. What makes this move tragic is that the measure by which Saul intends to gain the favor of the Lord turns out to be a mistake; after all, "an army travels on its stomach." The Israelites, without food and drink, naturally become less and less effective, as is shown by the episode of Jonathan and the honey. When the people find honeycomb on the ground inviting them to refresh themselves, they indeed run up to it, their mouths watering, but Saul's curse keeps them from eating. But Jonathan does eat (after all, he knew nothing of his father's curse), and his eyes are brightened as his strength is renewed. When apprised of the royal command, Jonathan expresses the paradox of Saul's action very well: by this well-meant measure his father has actually brought disaster on the land, since the Israelites cannot follow up their victory now, as would have been possible had they been permitted to eat during the pursuit.

Saul Sets Up an Altar   *31-35*

³¹ They struck down the Philistines that day from Michmash to Aijalon. And the people were very faint; ³² the people flew upon the spoil, and took sheep

118

and oxen and calves, and slew them on the ground; and the people ate them with the blood. ³³ Then they told Saul, "Behold, the people are sinning against the LORD, by eating with the blood." And he said, "You have dealt treacherously; roll a great stone to me here." *v* ³⁴ And Saul said, "Disperse yourselves among the people, and say to them, 'Let every man bring his ox or his sheep, and slay them here, and eat; and do not sin against the LORD by eating with the blood.'" So every one of the people brought his ox with him that night, and slew them there. ³⁵ And Saul built an altar to the LORD; it was the first altar that he built to the LORD.

v Gk: Heb *this day*

The victory Saul's son has won is nevertheless a substantial one, driving the enemy some 20 miles out of the central ridge hill country back down the invasion route up which they had come. Meanwhile, when evening comes and the fast can end, the famished people fly upon the spoil, even disregarding the cultic regulation against eating flesh with blood in it, so that Saul again has to intervene in order to uphold the stipulations of the covenant that life belongs to the Lord and that therefore the lifeblood must first be offered to the Lord (Gen. 9:4; Lev. 17:10-12). Saul provides a large altar where the victims can be consecrated and the victims' lives (and blood) can first be offered to the Lord, so that the flesh might then be eaten without offense.

The Verdict by Lot 36-46

³⁶ Then Saul said, "Let us go down after the Philistines by night and despoil them until the morning

119

light; let us not leave a man of them." And they said, "Do whatever seems good to you." But the priest said, "Let us draw near hither to God." ³⁷ And Saul inquired of God, "Shall I go down after the Philistines? Wilt thou give them into the hand of Israel?" But he did not answer him that day. ³⁸ And Saul said, "Come hither, all you leaders of the people; and know and see how this sin has arisen today. ³⁹ For as the LORD lives who saves Israel, though it be in Jonathan my son, he shall surely die." But there was not a man among all the people that answered him. ⁴⁰ Then he said to all Israel, "You shall be on one side, and I and Jonathan my son will be on the other side." And the people said to Saul, "Do what seems good to you." ⁴¹ Therefore Saul said, "O LORD God of Israel, why hast thou not answered thy servant this day? If this guilt is in me or in Jonathan my son, O LORD, God of Israel, give Urim; but if this guilt is in thy people Israel,ʷ give Thummim." And Jonathan and Saul were taken, but the people escaped. ⁴² Then Saul said, "Cast the lot between me and my son Jonathan." And Jonathan was taken.

⁴³ Then Saul said to Jonathan, "Tell me what you have done." And Jonathan told him, "I tasted a little honey with the tip of the staff that was in my hand; here I am, I will die." ⁴⁴ And Saul said, "God do so to me and more also; you shall surely die, Jonathan." ⁴⁵ Then the people said to Saul, "Shall Jonathan die, who has wrought this great victory in Israel? Far from it! As the LORD lives, there shall not one hair of his head fall to the ground; for he has wrought with God this day." So the people ran-

ʷ Vg Compare Gk: Heb *Saul said to the* LORD, *the God of Israel*

somed Jonathan, that he did not die. **46** Then Saul
went up from pursuing the Philistines; and the Philistines went to their own place.

After the delay Saul wishes to continue the pursuit.
He can do this, however, only after consulting the Lord
through His priest Ahijah. But Ahijah is unable to obtain an answer for Saul. Though the exact technique
employed in using the ephod is not certain, it seems that
answers to yes-or-no questions were given by means of
two objects (sticks, or some sort of dice) called Urim
and Thummim, which were drawn out of some sort of
pocket. The ritual sometimes consumed a lot of time
(cf. v. 19); in the present instance, when the oracle does
not respond, it seems that either no objects come out
of the pocket or that even when they come out, the response is still indefinite. In any case, Saul obtains no
answer. God is silent! That can only mean that something
has called forth His wrath (as at the time of Achan's
deed, Joshua 7). So a different question is presented:
"Who is responsible for the Lord's anger, the people
or the royal family?" The result, surprisingly enough,
is that not the people (who had eaten blood!) but the
royal house is responsible. And then, in answer to Saul's
earnest prayer and his insistent question, "Who, Saul
or Jonathan," the lot of Thummim ("yes") falls on
Jonathan! Because of the honey episode Jonathan
knows that he is guilty of violating the fast and that his
father's solemn curse of the Lord is now falling on him.
He is ready to die, though it is clear from his "confession" that he does not consider his "error" grievous
("I tasted a little honey," he says!). The father, however,
utters another oath, keeping it purposely rather vague,
since the curse that accompanies it, once definitely

121

spoken, will be irrevocable. The people, however, refuse to let the father, who has so hampered their campaign, kill the son, who had that day wrought a deed of salvation as the Lord's man. Jonathan's victory, they maintain, is the guarantee that God does not want him to die. When Saul now breaks off the campaign and returns homeward, it might seem that he agrees with the people that the Lord is with Jonathan; but we may well imagine that Saul is also perplexed, feeling that somehow Jonathan is still under the curse he uttered and that what the prophet Samuel had already told him (13:7 f.) will come true: Jonathan will not be his successor! Jonathan, it turns out then, is an admirable person, but he is not the one whom the Lord has chosen. We will still have to wait for him to whom this episode points (David) and, more important, for Him to whom this entire history of salvation points, Christ Jesus.

Notes Concerning Saul's Kingdom   47-52

[47] When Saul had taken the kingship over Israel, he fought against all his enemies on every side, against Moab, against the Ammonites, against Edom, against the kings of Zobah, and against the Philistines; wherever he turned he put them to the worse. [48] And he did valiantly, and smote the Amalekites, and delivered Israel out of the hands of those who plundered them.

[49] Now the sons of Saul were Jonathan, Ishvi, and Malchishua; and the names of his two daughters were these: the name of the first-born was Merab, and the name of the younger Michal; [50] and the name of Saul's wife was Ahinoam the daughter of Ahimaaz. And the name of the commander of his army was Abner the son of Ner, Saul's uncle; [51] Kish was

the father of Saul, and Ner the father of Abner was the son of Abiel.

52 There was hard fighting against the Philistines all the days of Saul; and when Saul saw any strong man, or any valiant man, he attached him to himself.

In the Books of Kings the account of a king's reign usually ends with the well-known reference to other information about the events of his reign which may be obtained from the archives. We do not have exactly that same formula about Saul here, but we do have something very similar: a summary of Saul's reign. The compiler of the final form of our book rightly realized that Saul gave the various tribes of Israel a unity that led to the united empire under David. His was a reign of fighting; he was the one who established a professional army (of which his cousin Abner was general) to replace the tribal militia. But above all, we are to see Saul's reign as part of the history of salvation. The final notice about his family is important, especially since these are to be the very people who will be involved in the story about David. The final verdict will be that Saul's dynasty is not the chosen one — the sons are killed and the daughters die without significant issue.

SAUL REJECTED   15

The battle against the Philistines (Ch. 14) was broken off before it could conclude in what was normally the final step in a holy war: the ritual annihilation of the enemy, with an accompanying ban on the booty. In Ch. 15, however, that particular aspect of a holy war becomes the main point of the narrative. That such a custom as utter destruction of the enemy was current in Israel is an offense to many modern readers of the Bible, despite the fact that such atrocities as saturation bombings, explosions of atomic bombs over populous cities, and the liquidation of millions of persons in gas chambers have taken place in our own time — with but relatively small protest. Israel's procedure remains an offense to moderns even after historical research has made it clear that many ancient peoples conducted this sort of religious war (cf. the Moabite Stone). Before we go too far, however, in making comparisons with ancient and modern "parallels" and thus apply value judgments of our later age to ancient peoples who lived in different conditions with different conceptions, we should try to understand this custom in the rich Biblical context that our chapter provides.

The Lord Initiates a Holy-War Campaign
Against Amalek   *15:1-3*

¹ And Samuel said to Saul, "The LORD sent me to anoint you king over his people Israel; now therefore hearken to the words of the LORD. ² Thus says the LORD of hosts, 'I will punish what Amalek did to Israel in opposing them on the way, when they came up out of Egypt. ³ Now go and smite Amalek, and utterly destroy all that they have; do not spare them, but kill both man and woman, infant and suckling, ox and sheep, camel and ass.'"

The campaign against the Amalekites is a campaign ordered by the Lord as another step in establishing His lordship on earth in the midst of that people with whom He had made His covenant. No nation dare set itself up against the Lord's great kingship. And this was precisely what the nomadic tribe of Amalek had always been doing in attacking Israel. These war-loving desert raiders, who had attacked feeble Israel in the desert after the Exodus, were typical and traditional opponents of the Lord, hence the saying, "The LORD will have war with Amalek from generation to generation" (Ex. 17:16). This helps us understand that, once Israel has attained a hitherto unknown power in its war of independence, the newly anointed king is called on by the Lord's prophet, Samuel, to settle this unsettled business.

The consecration of persons and property as "holy" to the Lord meant that all precious objects were put into His sanctuary-treasury and all living creatures were put to the edge of the sword. This ban was applied not only against external enemies — usually in defensive warfare — but also against disloyal Israelites; cf. Judg. 19 and 20. Hence it should not be characterized as a bloodthirsty, sadistic orgy but as a ritual marked by the fear of the Lord both on the part of those on whom this frightful judgment descended and on the part of those who were called to execute it. The anointed king accepted the role of executioner when he undertook this campaign. On this score, at least, there is no difference of opinion between him and the Lord (or, for that matter, the Lord's prophet, Samuel).

Saul's Conduct of the Amalek Campaign   4-9

⁴ So Saul summoned the people, and numbered them in Telaim, two hundred thousand men on foot, and ten thousand men of Judah. ⁵ And Saul came to the city of Amalek, and lay in wait in the valley. ⁶ And Saul said to the Kenites, "Go, depart, go down from among the Amalekites, lest I destroy you with them; for you showed kindness to all the people of Israel

when they came up out of Egypt." So the Kenites departed from among the Amalekites. [7] And Saul defeated the Amalekites, from Havilah as far as Shur, which is east of Egypt. [8] And he took Agag the king of the Amalekites alive, and utterly destroyed all the people with the edge of the sword. [9] But Saul and the people spared Agag, and the best of the sheep and of the oxen and of the fatlings, and the lambs, and all that was good, and would not utterly destroy them; all that was despised and worthless they utterly destroyed.

The troops muster for this campaign at Telaim, south of Judah, deep in the Negeb. The Amalekites are trapped by means of an ambush in their home valley, only, however, after Israel's traditional nomadic allies, the Kenites, have first been moved out of harm's way. The actual military aspect of the campaign is only briefly alluded to; the account must hasten on to depict the important result: Saul executes the ban only partially! Only the cattle that are worthless are utterly destroyed. "Saul and the people spared Agag and the best" of the livestock. In other words, Saul does not conduct this campaign as he had been directed by the Lord, as a holy war, but as a secular battle. Thus he feels, it seems, that he is at liberty to dispense with the ban and to satisfy both the Lord and the people with the sacrifice of the booty he has captured. To Saul the difference between such a sacrifice of the booty and the ban apparently does not seem great; God is still being honored. Moreover, it seems the much more expedient course of action since the people also wish to have their cake and eat it, that is, offer the best to the Lord and enjoy the sacrificial meal to celebrate the victory. Saul feels he has

126

discovered a way to obey both the Lord, who had chosen him, and the people, who had acclaimed him. This becomes more apparent from the ensuing altercation between prophet and king.

The Lord Sends His Messenger
to the Disobedient King   *10-12*

10 The word of the LORD came to Samuel: 11 "I repent that I have made Saul king; for he has turned back from following me, and has not performed my commandments." And Samuel was angry; and he cried to the LORD all night. 12 And Samuel rose early to meet Saul in the morning; and it was told Samuel, "Saul came to Carmel, and behold, he set up a monument for himself and turned, and passed on, and went down to Gilgal."

It is not Samuel who initiates the altercation between prophet and king; rather, it is the Lord Himself who at night reveals His will to His prophet, to a prophet who is, surprisingly, angry with the Lord for upsetting all his personal hopes by rejecting the newly successful king. The aged prophet intercedes for Saul all night long, hoping to avert the impending judgment, in much the same way that Moses interceded for Israel at Mount Sinai after the Golden Calf incident (Ex. 32 – 34); but in this case the Lord does not budge, and Samuel is obliged to set out the next morning to find the disobedient king. He is told that Saul has been making a triumphal return to the sanctuary at Gilgal and that he has at Carmel set up a monument to his victory. So Samuel must head for Gilgal, where the concluding thanksgiving service of the holy war is about to take place.

127

Samuel Challenges the Victorious King   *13-21*

¹³ And Samuel came to Saul, and Saul said to him, "Blessed be you to the LORD; I have performed the commandment of the LORD." ¹⁴ And Samuel said, "What then is this bleating of the sheep in my ears, and the lowing of the oxen which I hear?" ¹⁵ Saul said, "They have brought them from the Amalekites; for the people spared the best of the sheep and of the oxen, to sacrifice to the LORD your God; and the rest we have utterly destroyed." ¹⁶ Then Samuel said to Saul, "Stop! I will tell you what the LORD said to me this night." And he said to him, "Say on."

¹⁷ And Samuel said, "Though you are little in your own eyes, are you not the head of the tribes of Israel? The LORD anointed you king over Israel. ¹⁸ And the LORD sent you on a mission, and said, 'Go, utterly destroy the sinners, the Amalekites, and fight against them until they are consumed.' ¹⁹ Why then did you not obey the voice of the LORD? Why did you swoop on the spoil, and do what was evil in the sight of the LORD?" ²⁰ And Saul said to Samuel, "I have obeyed the voice of the LORD, I have gone on the mission on which the LORD sent me, I have brought Agag the king of Amalek, and I have utterly destroyed the Amalekites. ²¹ But the people took of the spoil, sheep and oxen, the best of the things devoted to destruction, to sacrifice to the LORD your God in Gilgal."

When king Saul greets the aged prophet with a blessing, he does this apparently with feelings of joy and exultation at the victory and also with a good conscience, that is, with a conscience that is as yet unaroused. He is apparently also genuinely sincere in

128

his report, "I have performed the commandment of the LORD." But the prophet can barely hear what the king is saying because of the bleating and lowing of the livestock that fills his ears. Saul explains very coolly and objectively that this is the booty of the war against Amalek, that the people spared the finest animals, that these are about to be sacrificed to the Lord here at His sanctuary, and that the ban was executed on all the rest at the site of the battle. The prophet Samuel now interrupts the king's pious recital to proclaim the Lord's personal message to him: "Unimpressive and self-deprecating as you once were, God chose you to be king over Israel, a choice of pure grace, but one which called on you to act with responsibility. You were sent on a mission to restore His honor and lordship against a rebellious nation (a summons to bring forth the fruits of faith!). Why did you not obey the word of the Lord? Did the booty blind you to your duty?" Saul tries to justify himself and to nullify the charges against him by marshaling his deeds ("I have obeyed . . . I have gone . . . I have destroyed"), but unfortunately his own testimony breaks down when he must say, "I have brought Agag the king," and when he reports, "But the people took of the spoil, sheep and oxen, the best of the things devoted to destruction, to sacrifice to the LORD your God in Gilgal."

Saul Is Rejected by the Lord   22-29

²² And Samuel said,

"**Has the LORD as great delight in burnt offerings
    and sacrifices,
    as in obeying the voice of the LORD?
Behold, to obey is better than sacrifice,
    and to hearken than the fat of rams.**

129

²³ For rebellion is as the sin of divination,
      and stubbornness is as iniquity and idolatry.
   Because you have rejected the word of the LORD,
      he has also rejected you from being king."
²⁴ And Saul said to Samuel, "I have sinned; for I have transgressed the commandment of the LORD and your words, because I feared the people and obeyed their voice. ²⁵ Now therefore, I pray, pardon my sin, and return with me, that I may worship the LORD." ²⁶ And Samuel said to Saul, "I will not return with you; for you have rejected the word of the LORD, and the LORD has rejected you from being king over Israel." ²⁷ As Samuel turned to go away, Saul laid hold upon the skirt of his robe, and it tore. ²⁸ And Samuel said to him, "The LORD has torn the kingdom of Israel from you this day, and has given it to a neighbor of yours, who is better than you. ²⁹ And also the Glory of Israel will not lie or repent; for he is not a man, that he should repent."

Samuel's famous response (22 f.), couched in poetic rhythm, simply means: Sacrificing all sorts of victims, even whole burnt offerings, to the Lord can never compensate for failing to hearken to His voice. Saul wants to worship God while transgressing His Word! To disobey God, to fail to hearken to His Word, is to fall into idolatry, to violate the first and fundamental stipulation of His covenant, and is as wicked as overt superstitious witchcraft and sorcery. Stubbornness and passive resistance to God is as bad as outright worship of idols. And then comes the pronouncement of doom: "Because you have rejected the word of the LORD, he has also rejected you from being king."

At this the king's composure breaks. The Word of God has punctured his pretensions. He confesses his sin. Though he does, to a certain extent, take the same stance that David later took after Nathan exposed his sin (2 Sam. 12:13), it is noteworthy that David's reply is devoid of alibi, whereas Saul here makes excuses and seeks to obviate the consequences of a break with the prophet by an atoning sacrifice. In fact, that seems to be the reason why the prophet will not at first accept Saul's "confession" and his suggestion that they both now go back to the interrupted routine and present a solid front before the people at the sacrifice, as if nothing of major importance had happened between them. Faced with the prophet's "No," the desperate king tries to force him to come with him, grasping the skirts of his robe. The resulting rent in the garment is, the prophet explains, only a significant sign that the Lord has torn the kingdom from him and given it to a neighbor of his who is better than he. God's rejection is not an overhasty word that He will change; what He says is true. Saul will not remain in His royal office; it will be given to one who is better. If we ask, "How will Saul's successor be better? In obedience, in faith, or in some other respect?" the rest of the Books of Samuel will answer: "Better because God chose him and gave to him the Promise."

The End of the Affair   30-33

30 Then he said, "I have sinned; yet honor me now before the elders of my people and before Israel, and return with me, that I may worship the LORD your God." 31 So Samuel turned back after Saul; and Saul worshiped the LORD.

32 Then Samuel said, "Bring here to me Agag

131

the king of the Amalekites." And Agag came to him cheerfully. Agag said, "Surely the bitterness of death is past." ³³ And Samuel said, "As your sword has made women childless, so shall your mother be childless among women." And Samuel hewed Agag in pieces before the LORD in Gilgal.

It surprises us to hear that when Saul confesses his sin a second time (this time without alibi) and asks Samuel to accompany him and honor him before the people, Samuel agrees. And it is expressly stated that Saul worships the Lord. This does not necessarily imply hypocrisy; it is clear, however, that Samuel first has to complete the ritual of the ban by hewing the Amalekite king in pieces "before the LORD."

The Split Between Prophet and King   34-35

³⁴ Then Samuel went to Ramah; and Saul went up to his house in Gibeah of Saul. ³⁵ And Samuel did not see Saul again until the day of his death, but Samuel grieved over Saul. And the LORD repented that he had made Saul king over Israel.

The chapter ends with the sad picture of the permanent split between the once united prophet and king. Both sadly go their separate ways. What had come between them was God's judgment; they are both broken by it. The prophet Samuel wends his lonely way to Ramah, contrary to his own personal wishes; the king returns to Gibeah, undoubtedly even surrounded by a victorious army, but he is a tragic figure, a broken man. This famous story mirrors not only the conflict between the ancient, old-fashioned Israelite faith and the new kingship when the conflict first broke out in connection with the regulations of a holy war; it mirrors also a conflict that will continue to shape the relationship of kings and prophets throughout Israel's history until the Lord has truly set up the King after His heart, "great David's greater Son."

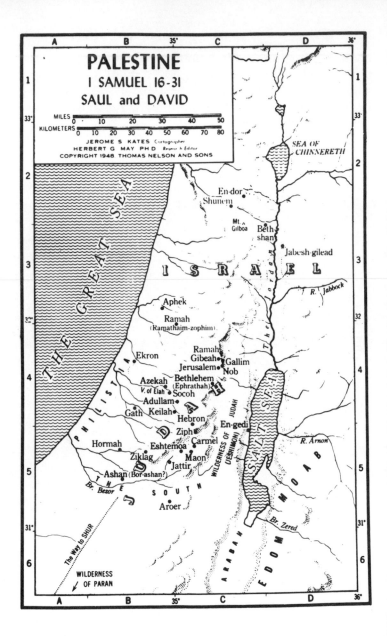

PALESTINE
I SAMUEL 16-31
SAUL and DAVID

MILES
0 10 20 30 40 50

KILOMETERS
0 10 20 30 40 50 60 70 80

JEROME S KATES Cartographer
HERBERT G MAY PH D Research Editor
COPYRIGHT 1948 THOMAS NELSON AND SONS

THE GREAT SEA

SEA OF CHINNERETH

En-dor
Shunem

Mt. Gilboa
Beth-shan

Jabesh-gilead

I S R A E L

R. Jabbock

Aphek

Ramah
(Ramathaim-zophim)

Ekron

Ramah
Gibeah
Jerusalem
Gallim
Nob

Azekah
Bethlehem
(Ephrathah)
V. of Elah
Socoh

Adullam

Gath
Keilah

Hebron

Ziph

En-gedi

Hormah

Eshtemoa
Carmel

Ziklag

Maon

Jattir

Ashan (Bor-ashan?)

Aroer

Br. Bezor

T H E   S O U T H

WILDERNESS OF JUDAH

JESHIMON

SALT SEA

R. Arnon

M O A B

A R A B A H

Br. Zered

E D O M

The Way to SHUR

WILDERNESS OF PARAN

PHILISTIA

Saul and David

1 Samuel 16 — 2 Samuel 1

THE LORD CHOOSES DAVID   16

What now begins is the long account of David's
rise from obscurity to his becoming the greatest king
Israel ever had (1 Sam. 16 — 2 Sam. 5). While David is
still serving at Saul's court, his story is intertwined with
the story of Saul and his family (Chs. 16 — 20); once he
is forced to flee that court, we follow his adventurous
life as a freebooter who successfully meets the challenges of a precarious existence on the borders of the
Holy Land (Chs. 21 — 31); finally, after Saul's death,
we see him reigning as king in Hebron, gaining one
success after another until finally he captures the Jebusite city of Jerusalem and makes it the capital of his
united empire (2 Sam. 1 — 5). This fascinating account
of David's rise to greatness clearly indicates that he is
God's shining gift to His people. Never again did Israel
experience such a bright epoch. No wonder that thereafter they always looked back to it, even picturing the
end-time Messiah as David Returned.

Samuel Anoints the Unknown Shepherd Boy   *16:1-13*

¹ The **LORD** said to Samuel, "How long will you grieve over Saul, seeing I have rejected him from being king over Israel? Fill your horn with oil, and go; I will send you to Jesse the Bethlehemite, for I have provided for myself a king among his sons." ² And Samuel said, "How can I go? If Saul hears it, he will kill me." And the **LORD** said, "Take a heifer with you, and say, 'I have come to sacrifice to the **LORD.**' ³ And invite Jesse to the sacrifice, and I will show you what you shall do; and you shall anoint for me him whom I name to you." ⁴ Samuel did what the **LORD** commanded, and came to Bethlehem. The elders of the city came to meet him trembling, and said, "Do you come peaceably?" ⁵ And he said, "Peaceably; I have come to sacrifice to the **LORD;** consecrate yourselves, and come with me to the sacrifice." And he consecrated Jesse and his sons, and invited them to the sacrifice.

⁶ When they came, he looked on Eliab and thought, "Surely the **LORD'S** anointed is before him." ⁷ But the **LORD** said to Samuel, "Do not look on his appearance or on the height of his stature, because I have rejected him; for the **LORD** sees not as man sees; man looks on the outward appearance, but the **LORD** looks on the heart." ⁸ Then Jesse called Abinadab, and made him pass before Samuel. And he said, "Neither has the **LORD** chosen this one." ⁹ Then Jesse made Shammah pass by. And he said, "Neither has the **LORD** chosen this one." ¹⁰ And Jesse made seven of his sons pass before Samuel. And Samuel said to Jesse, "The **LORD** has not chosen these." ¹¹ And Samuel said to Jesse, "Are all your sons here?"

And he said, "There remains yet the youngest, but behold, he is keeping the sheep." And Samuel said to Jesse, "Send and fetch him; for we will not sit down till he comes here." ¹² And he sent, and brought him in. Now he was ruddy, and had beautiful eyes, and was handsome. And the LORD said, "Arise, anoint him; for this is he." ¹³ Then Samuel took the horn of oil, and anointed him in the midst of his brothers; and the Spirit of the LORD came mightily upon David from that day forward. And Samuel rose up, and went to Ramah.

The Lord's rejection of Saul (Ch. 15) is logically followed by the designation of his successor. This takes place when an obscure Bethlehem lad is anointed by the aged prophet Samuel, because, as the Lord puts it, "This is he!" Samuel does not undertake the anointing of a replacement for Saul with any enthusiasm. Just as he had hesitated in proclaiming Saul's rejection, so now he hesitates to anoint a successor. But the Lord insists that he go forth to Bethlehem on this mission, even suggesting that he remove any chance of reprisal from a suspicious Saul by making the actual anointing a secret part of a sacrificial ceremony at Bethlehem. For though the city elders are told by Samuel to prepare themselves ritually for participation in the holy ceremony in which they will meet the Lord, Samuel himself undertakes the consecration of the male members of Jesse's family, seemingly in such a way that Jesse's sons pass before him individually while outsiders remain unaware of what is transpiring. In fact, even when the actual anointing of the chosen son is carried out and the holy oil drips through the pierced narrow end of a horn and falls on the head of David, the word "king"

137

is never spoken aloud, though it is clear to the hearer
throughout that the Lord is thereby designating David
as the future king.

David does not become king by virtue of later military and political successes! He becomes king by virtue
of the Lord's choice, a choice made when he was yet
a lad. This is what is highlighted in the story: the Lord
even overrides the prophet's inclination to be impressed
by the kinglike appearance of the older brothers, and
He chooses the son who had apparently been considered
even too young for participation in the religious ceremony but on whom the Lord had nevertheless long
since had His eye. Only after the Lord explains that He
looks on the heart rather than on the superficial exter-
nals and says of David, "Anoint him; for this is he," do
we see more than a simple, wind-burned, unspoiled
shepherd lad; for thereupon the Spirit of the Lord leaps
upon him, descending with the force of lightning that
rends the very air. Moreover, we are told that this Spirit
will remain "upon David from that day forward." By
this anointing with the Holy Ghost David is not only
chosen to be God's future instrument for saving Israel
as its future king, but he is also placed in the continuing
line of charismatic leaders of God's people, like the
judges of old — a line that will extend to the King of the
end time (Is. 11:2), who in the fullness of time was baptized by the same Spirit, upon whom the Spirit was to
remain (John 1:33), and who, after His glorification,
would give His Spirit to His people in the Messianic
age without measure.

David Brought to the Court of Saul   *14-23*

**14 Now the Spirit of the LORD departed from
Saul, and an evil spirit from the LORD tormented**

138

him. ¹⁵ And Saul's servants said to him, "Behold
now, an evil spirit from God is tormenting you. ¹⁶ Let
our lord now command your servants, who are before
you, to seek out a man who is skilful in playing the
lyre; and when the evil spirit from God is upon you,
he will play it, and you will be well." ¹⁷ So Saul said
to his servants, "Provide for me a man who can play
well, and bring him to me." ¹⁸ One of the young men
answered, "Behold, I have seen a son of Jesse the
Bethlehemite, who is skilful in playing, a man of
valor, a man of war, prudent in speech, and a man
of good presence; and the LORD is with him." ¹⁹ Therefore Saul sent messengers to Jesse, and said, "Send
me David your son, who is with the sheep." ²⁰ And
Jesse took an ass laden with bread, and a skin of wine
and a kid, and sent them by David his son to Saul.
²¹ And David came to Saul, and entered his service.
And Saul loved him greatly, and he became his armor-
bearer. ²² And Saul sent to Jesse, saying, "Let David
remain in my service, for he has found favor in my
sight." ²³ And whenever the evil spirit from God was
upon Saul, David took the lyre and played it with his
hand; so Saul was refreshed, and was well, and the
evil spirit departed from him.

Though David received the Spirit of the Lord at
his anointing, it departed from Saul. Hence even though
Saul remains king for a number of years, he rules without this special divine endowment. In its place the Lord
sends an evil spirit to torment the disobedient king.
This spiritual affliction seems to manifest itself in sudden and unreasoning fits of terror. In seeking relief
for their king, Saul's concerned courtiers decide to
obtain a skillful lyre player. David of Bethlehem is rec-

ommended as possessing the ideal qualities of the perfect youth of his age: he is skillful in playing the lyre, a member of that sturdy, property-owning class of freeborn farmers that always furnished citizen-soldiers for Israel's army, a capable warrior, a man judicious in speech (a master of the new art of pleasant speech!), of good appearance. David's final qualification, "the LORD is with him," says more than the courtiers perhaps realized, for God's special blessing did indeed now rest on him. No wonder the king immediately sends to Jesse to ask for his son. We may note that even though the Israelite king wishes to attach valiant persons to his court (14:52), he does not simply take David (as a pagan king would feel his prerogative), but he respectfully requests his father to send his son; and Jesse respectfully sends him his son as well as a modest present.

David quickly becomes a favorite of the king, even attaining the position of king's armor-bearer, that is, his page in peacetime, and in wartime the one who supplied him with the weapons required in the varying phases of combat: the bow for long-range fighting, the javelin for medium range; the spear and sword for hand-to-hand combat. (An excellent color representation of Saul's fortress-palace appeared in the December 1957 *National Geographic Magazine*, p. 853.) David alone is able to banish Saul's evil spirit by his skillful lyre playing and by his singing of what must have been more than mere secular folk songs. The person whom the Lord has rejected appears side by side with the one whom He has chosen; the contrast between the two helps us see what kingship by God's grace really is. Thus David is already now beginning to rise to the throne.

140

DAVID AND GOLIATH 17

Goliath Challenges the Host of the Lord 17:1-11

¹ Now the Philistines gathered their armies for battle; and they were gathered at Socoh, which belongs to Judah, and encamped between Socoh and Azekah, in Ephesdammim. ² And Saul and the men of Israel were gathered, and encamped in the valley of Elah, and drew up in line of battle against the Philistines. ³ And the Philistines stood on the mountain on the one side, and Israel stood on the mountain on the other side, with a valley between them. ⁴ And there came out from the camp of the Philistines a champion named Goliath, of Gath, whose height was six cubits and a span. ⁵ He had a helmet of bronze on his head, and he was armed with a coat of mail, and the weight of the coat was five thousand shekels of bronze. ⁶ And he had greaves of bronze upon his legs, and a javelin of bronze slung between his shoulders. ⁷ And the shaft of his spear was like a weaver's beam, and his spear's head weighed six hundred shekels of iron; and his shield-bearer went before him. ⁸ He stood and shouted to the ranks of Israel, "Why have you come out to draw up for battle? Am I not a Philistine, and are you not servants of Saul? Choose a man for yourselves, and let him come down to me. ⁹ If he is able to fight with me and kill me, then we will be your servants; but if I prevail against him and kill him, then you shall be our servants and serve us." ¹⁰ And the Philistine said, "I defy the ranks of Israel this day; give me a man, that we may fight together." ¹¹ When Saul and all Israel heard these words of the Philistine, they were dismayed and greatly afraid.

Saul's first campaign against the Philistines had ended in the liberation of the mountains of Ephraim. Now the Philistines muster their hosts to invade the mountains of Judah, advancing to the Valley of Elah, a place of strategic importance, from which access could be gained to Hebron, Bethlehem, and the entire hilly region of Judah. Saul and Israel counter this move by marching out to occupy the other side of the valley. Thus the two armies are drawn up for battle facing each other, the dry river bottom forming the no-man's-land between them. At first there is no battle action; each morning the troops merely go forth with a war cry from their camps to their battle positions on the upper slopes of the valley. But after that neither army makes a move to begin a pitched battle.

The main reason for the stalemate is that from the Philistine ranks there daily steps forth a champion who not only challenges any Israelite champion but who strikes terror into the hearts of the poorly equipped Israelites. He is a giant of a man: over nine feet tall (were he to try to enter most of our rooms, he would break down the lintel!); he is fully armed with the latest and best equipment, including a coat of mail weighing at least 126 pounds, a mighty spear, the iron point of which weighs at least 16 pounds. The story puts just enough emphasis on the grotesque superiority of the giant's equipment to make hearers snicker a bit (the storyteller wants his audience to realize that "the bigger they come, the harder they fall!"). But despite this touch of grim humor — and why should the Bible not employ also humor to get its message across? — Goliath with his breastplate of bronze scales, greaves of bronze, and a special shield-bearer to go before him is no joke, for what he is proposing is no elegant duel like those

142

which meticulous Frenchmen fought in the 19th century, nor is it to be a Western movie mock fight, where all but the youngest children know that the combatants are really not hurting one another; Goliath is proposing a life-and-death duel the result of which will be that one of them will remain lying on the field dead. No wonder the Israelites' courage fails them at his challenge; even though the dueling of champions was a widespread custom of those ancient days (cf. Homer, early Rome), no one in Saul's army accepts the challenge to fight this man.

David at the Battlefield   12-30

¹² Now David was the son of an Ephrathite of Bethlehem in Judah, named Jesse, who had eight sons. In the days of Saul the man was already old and advanced in years.ˣ ¹³ The three eldest sons of Jesse had followed Saul to the battle; and the names of his three sons who went to the battle were Eliab the first-born, and next to him Abinadab, and the third Shammah. ¹⁴ David was the youngest; the three eldest followed Saul, ¹⁵ but David went back and forth from Saul to feed his father's sheep at Bethlehem. ¹⁶ For forty days the Philistine came forward and took his stand, morning and evening.

¹⁷ And Jesse said to David his son, "Take for your brothers an ephah of this parched grain, and these ten loaves, and carry them quickly to the camp to your brothers; ¹⁸ also take these ten cheeses to the commander of their thousand. See how your brothers fare, and bring some token from them."

¹⁹ Now Saul, and they, and all the men of Israel, were in the valley of Elah, fighting with the Philis-

ˣ Gk Syr: Heb *among men*

tines. ²⁰ And David rose early in the morning, and left the sheep with a keeper, and took the provisions, and went, as Jesse had commanded him; and he came to the encampment as the host was going forth to the battle line, shouting the war cry. ²¹ And Israel and the Philistines drew up for battle, army against army. ²² And David left the things in charge of the keeper of the baggage, and ran to the ranks, and went and greeted his brothers. ²³ As he talked with them, behold, the champion, the Philistine of Gath, Goliath by name, came up out of the ranks of the Philistines, and spoke the same words as before. And David heard him.

²⁴ All the men of Israel, when they saw the man, fled from him, and were much afraid. ²⁵ And the men of Israel said, "Have you seen this man who has come up? Surely he has come up to defy Israel; and the man who kills him, the king will enrich with great riches, and will give him his daughter, and make his father's house free in Israel." ²⁶ And David said to the men who stood by him, "What shall be done for the man who kills this Philistine, and takes away the reproach from Israel? For who is this uncircumcised Philistine, that he should defy the armies of the living God?" ²⁷ And the people answered him in the same way, "So shall it be done to the man who kills him."

²⁸ Now Eliab his eldest brother heard when he spoke to the men; and Eliab's anger was kindled against David, and he said, "Why have you come down? And with whom have you left those few sheep in the wilderness? I know your presumption, and the evil of your heart; for you have come down to see the battle." ²⁹ And David said, "What have I done

now? Was it not but a word?" [30] And he turned away from him toward another, and spoke in the same way; and the people answered him again as before.

At this crucial point a youth considered too young for military service, a mere lad, comes to the front — not with any intention of engaging in the fighting, however. His father Jesse has sent him with supplies for his enlisted brothers. He brings a bushel of parched grain, 10 round loaves of bread (as well as 10 cuts of soft cheese for the officer!). He is to bring back news to his father about the welfare of his sons (an ancient substitute for postal service). At the front this young teen-ager becomes aware both of the terror that is paralyzing the army and of the reason for that terror. He also hears the soldiers talking among themselves about the prizes King Saul has set up for the courageous man who would dare to accept the Philistine's challenge: great riches, a princess to wife, and exemption from taxes and labor service for himself and his entire family. This lad cannot understand why no one dares to respond, and it is not primarily interest in the prizes that causes David to repeat his question. His simple, unspoiled faith in the Lord cannot understand why the Philistine is allowed to reproach the armies of the living God. Thus it becomes clear that he is willing to accept the challenge. Eliab, David's eldest brother, can see only evil presumption in his "kid brother's" willingness to intervene (neglecting his duties at home to come to the front and be a "sidewalk superintendent" at a bloody slaughter!). David does not respond to his brother's nasty insinuations; rather, he continues unshaken on the path of faith, asking his brother only whether it is really wrong to even suggest

145

a word of hope in the midst of such hopelessness and then proceeding to interrogate the bystanders about what concerns him so very much. Thus it becomes clear not merely that David is willing to undertake being Israel's champion but that the Lord will show His might through this believing civilian who trusts Him while strong men of war are trembling before the enemy.

David Accepts the Challenge   *31-40*

[31] When the words which David spoke were heard, they repeated them before Saul; and he sent for him. [32] And David said to Saul, "Let no man's heart fail because of him; your servant will go and fight with this Philistine." [33] And Saul said to David, "You are not able to go against this Philistine to fight with him; for you are but a youth, and he has been a man of war from his youth." [34] But David said to Saul, "Your servant used to keep sheep for his father; and when there came a lion, or a bear, and took a lamb from the flock, [35] I went after him and smote him and delivered it out of his mouth; and if he arose against me, I caught him by his beard, and smote him and killed him. [36] Your servant has killed both lions and bears; and this uncircumcised Philistine shall be like one of them, seeing he has defied the armies of the living God." [37] And David said, "The LORD who delivered me from the paw of the lion and from the paw of the bear, will deliver me from the hand of this Philistine." And Saul said to David, "Go, and the LORD be with you!" [38] Then Saul clothed David with his armor; he put a helmet of bronze on his head, and clothed him with a coat of mail. [39] And David girded his sword over his armor, and he tried in vain to go, for he was not used to them.

Then David said to Saul, "I cannot go with these; for I am not used to them." And David put them off. **40** Then he took his staff in his hand, and chose five smooth stones from the brook, and put them in his shepherd's bag or wallet; his sling was in his hand, and he drew near to the Philistine.

Hearing of someone's willingness to accept the challenge, King Saul summons the shepherd boy from Bethlehem into his royal presence. But after one look at the lad, the seasoned warrior-king judges him utterly unqualified for such a battle; he is too young and too weak. The lad from Bethlehem does not, however, permit himself to be shaken in his resolve. He has, he reports, already experienced the Lord's aid a number of times before. As a shepherd stationed on the edge of the wilderness, he has pitted his courage against rapacious beasts that attacked his flock and him himself; his success there has convinced him that the Lord who delivered him then will deliver him now. This uncommon trust in the Lord convinces the king, and he sends him forth with the significant blessing "The LORD be with you!" Again a touch of humor is added to the story when we see how Saul wants to lend David his own armor. It does not fit David; it is in fact a hindrance to him, not merely militarily but religiously, since the Lord's champion does not need the royal helmet and coat of mail. He goes forth with a shepherd's club, sling, and five smooth stones from the brook.

The Combat 41-49

41 And the Philistine came on and drew near to David, with his shield-bearer in front of him. **42** And when the Philistine looked, and saw David, he disdained him; for he was but a youth, ruddy and comely in appearance. ⁴³ And the Philistine said to David, "Am I a dog, that you come to me with sticks?" And the Philistine cursed David by his gods. ⁴⁴ The Philistine said to David, "Come to me, and I will give your flesh to the birds of the air and to the beasts of the field." ⁴⁵ Then David said to the Philistine, "You come to me with a sword and with a spear and with a javelin; but I come to you in the name of the LORD of hosts, the God of the armies of Israel, whom you have defied. ⁴⁶ This day the LORD will deliver you into my hand, and I will strike you down, and cut off your head; and I will give the dead bodies of the host of the Philistines this day to the birds of the air and to the wild beasts of the earth; that all the earth may know that there is a God in Israel, ⁴⁷ and that all this assembly may know that the LORD saves not with sword and spear; for the battle is the LORD'S and he will give you into our hand."

⁴⁸ When the Philistine arose and came and drew near to meet David, David ran quickly toward the battle line to meet the Philistine. ⁴⁹ And David put his hand in his bag and took out a stone, and slung it, and struck the Philistine on his forehead; the stone sank into his forehead, and he fell on his face to the ground.

Armed with shepherd's equipment, David confronts the Philistine who is armed to the teeth. In fact, the giant feels insulted by the appearance of such a lad as his opponent. Asking, "Am I a dog, that you come to me with sticks?" the Philistine curses David by his gods and taunts him with the prospect of an ignominious death without benefit of proper burial. When David responds with the famous words (and this is certainly the theological point of the story!) "You come to me with a sword and with a spear and with a javelin; but I come to you in the name of the LORD of hosts, . . . The LORD will deliver you into my hand," he is employing the phraseology and imagery of the holy war (cf. p. 105, item 5), and it is clear that he is fighting the Lord's battle and that the Lord is fighting David's battle. David tops his opponent's boast with a boast that, when it is all over, the heathen will know that there is a God in Israel.

As for the brief description of the combat itself, it is important to note that even though David proves to be remarkably skillful with the sling, the enormous giant falls at David's feet not because of David's superior military prowess ("There was no sword in the hand of David" . . . "The LORD saves not with sword and spear"). Rather, David wins because "the battle is the LORD'S," because the Lord has given the giant into the hand of the boy who fights in His name. This is the central point of the story.

The Victory!   *50-54*

⁵⁰ So David prevailed over the Philistine with a sling and with a stone, and struck the Philistine, and killed him; there was no sword in the hand of David. ⁵¹ Then David ran and stood over the Philistine, and took his sword and drew it out of its sheath, and killed him, and cut off his head with it. When the Philistines saw that their champion was dead, they fled. ⁵² And the men of Israel and Judah rose with a shout and pursued the Philistines as far as Gath ʸ and the gates of Ekron, so that the wounded Philistines fell on the way from Shaaraim as far as Gath and Ekron. ⁵³ And the

ʸ Gk: Heb *Gai*

Israelites came back from chasing the Philistines, and they plundered their camp. 54 And David took the head of the Philistine and brought it to Jerusalem; but he put his armor in his tent.

The decapitation of the giant, performed by means of the giant's own sword (a great humiliation!), the headlong flight of the Philistines back to the very gates of Ekron, the way strewn with Philistine corpses, the enemy camp plundered — all these features of the story are told not with sadistic joy in others' misfortune but with heartfelt rejoicing and exultation in the Lord; the Israelites who heard the story undoubtedly laughed most heartily at this point. This is the Lord's victory over His enemy, a victory in which we hearers of it are also called upon to rejoice! David takes the head of the Philistine to Jerusalem, ostensibly as a trophy to be dedicated to the Lord. Despite a seeming lack of correlation of this information with what we know from 2 Sam. 5 and elsewhere (to the effect that at this time Jerusalem was still a Jebusite city not controlled by David; cf. Introduction, pp. 14 ff.), the meaning of this information in its present context is entirely clear: David considers this head of the enemy a trophy to be dedicated to the Lord, who has given the victory (cf. 1 Sam. 31:10), and he puts the armor into the tent in which it was presumably later displayed when this episode was recounted. (Cf. 1 Sam. 21:9)

David Joins Saul's Professional Army   *17:55 – 18:5*

55 When Saul saw David go forth against the Philistine, he said to Abner, the commander of the army, "Abner, whose son is this youth?" And Abner

said, "As your soul lives, O king, I cannot tell." [56] And the king said, "Inquire whose son the stripling is." [57] And as David returned from the slaughter of the Philistine, Abner took him, and brought him before Saul with the head of the Philistine in his hand. [58] And Saul said to him, "Whose son are you, young man?" And David answered, "I am the son of your servant Jesse the Bethlehemite."

[1] When he had finished speaking to Saul, the soul of Jonathan was knit to the soul of David, and Jonathan loved him as his own soul. [2] And Saul took him that day, and would not let him return to his father's house. [3] Then Jonathan made a covenant with David, because he loved him as his own soul. [4] And Jonathan stripped himself of the robe that was upon him, and gave it to David, and his armor, and even his sword and his bow and his girdle. [5] And David went out and was successful wherever Saul sent him; so that Saul set him over the men of war. And this was good in the sight of all the people and also in the sight of Saul's servants.

The ensuing section (omitted by a major Septuagint manuscript, as well as by some of the Dead Sea manuscripts; cf. Introduction, pp. 21 f.) is often regarded as another version of the story of how David came to Saul's attention. Again it is impossible for us to fit this into its exact chronological sequence; nevertheless, even a scientifically exact historian cannot simply exclude it as irrelevant, and we should follow God's Word in recognizing all these various versions (cf. Introduction, pp. 14 ff.). In its present position our account shows most clearly that David now is most graciously welcomed into the court and family of Saul. He is not an illegitimate usurper about to take the throne from a slipping man by violence, but he is introduced to the king by the commander, Abner, and received by the king and especially by the crown prince, Jonathan, with great love and respect. The crown prince not only enters the presence of the Lord with him but also makes a formal covenant with him, generously giving his own personal robe and armor to the shepherd lad who apparently has neither court nor military attire. But not only the crown prince honors David; the king also promotes him to a position of trust and respect.

The long chapter ends on the main motif of the entire section about David's rise (1 Sam. 16 – 2 Sam. 5): David is successful in every mission on which Saul sends him and is recognized both in the army and at court.

SAUL BECOMES JEALOUS
OF DAVID'S SUCCESS   18:6-30

The account of David's ascendancy continues in this chapter as we begin to hear of the surprising results of his entrance into the court of King Saul. Despite a number of attempts by Saul to check the rise of his young page, David emerges from each test stronger and more successful, whereas Saul becomes progressively more fearful and terrified. His own son, Crown Prince Jonathan, and his daughter Michal end up being firmly allied to this rival.

Saul's Jealousy Is Aroused   *6-16*

⁶ As they were coming home, when David returned from slaying the Philistine, the women came

152

out of all the cities of Israel, singing and dancing, to meet King Saul, with timbrels, with songs of joy, and with instruments ^{z} of music. ^{7} And the women sang to one another as they made merry,

> "Saul has slain his thousands,
> and David his ten thousands."

^{8} And Saul was very angry, and this saying displeased him; he said, "They have ascribed to David ten thousands, and to me they have ascribed thousands; and what more can he have but the kingdom?" ^{9} And Saul eyed David from that day on.

^{10} And on the morrow an evil spirit from God rushed upon Saul, and he raved within his house, while David was playing the lyre, as he did day by day. Saul had his spear in his hand; ^{11} and Saul cast the spear, for he thought, "I will pin David to the wall." But David evaded him twice.

^{12} Saul was afraid of David, because the LORD was with him but had departed from Saul. ^{13} So Saul removed him from his presence, and made him a commander of a thousand; and he went out and came in before the people. ^{14} And David had success in all his undertakings; for the LORD was with him. ^{15} And when Saul saw that he had great success, he stood in awe of him. ^{16} But all Israel and Judah loved David; for he went out and came in before them.

^{z} Or *triangle*, or *three-stringed instruments*

Saul's jealousy of David is aroused by the women who greet the returning army and ascribe greater credit for the victory to David than to the king. The result of the unpleasant incident is that Saul feels David has

everything but the kingdom itself. Ever after he eyes
David with suspicion and dislike. We moderns must
also realize that in that culture kingship had a monopoly
on success; hence any successful person was easily
considered a treasonable rival of the king. The phrase
"cast the spear" (v. 11) may be interpreted "lifted the
spear," implying merely an initial interrupted attempt
and not an actual deed. Saul raises the spear without,
however, casting it; he becomes more and more subject
to "raving" (v. 10), behaving with the wild excitement
characteristic of an ecstatic prophet. David, however,
evades the danger, and as a result Saul's suspicions
grow into actual fear of this man who is being so carefully protected by the Lord. Saul no longer trusts David
in personal attendance upon himself as armor-bearer.
Not wishing to insult the people's favorite, however,
Saul gives him a post of honor in the dangerous campaigns against the Philistines. The result is that David's
virtues are emphasized all the more highly. David
showed wisdom in all his ways, and the Lord was with
him. Hence Saul's fear of David is now heightened to a
dread of him—a dread all the more frightening as it
stands in contrast to the affection David enjoys among
the people whom he serves so faithfully.

David's Marriage into the Royal Family   *17-30*

**17 Then Saul said to David, "Here is my elder
daughter Merab; I will give her to you for a wife; only
be valiant for me and fight the LORD'S battles."
For Saul thought, "Let not my hand be upon him, but
let the hand of the Philistines be upon him." 18 And
David said to Saul, "Who am I, and who are my
kinsfolk, my father's family in Israel, that I should**

be son-in-law to the king?" ¹⁹ But at the time when Merab, Saul's daughter, should have been given to David, she was given to Adriel the Meholathite for a wife.

²⁰ Now Saul's daughter Michal loved David; and they told Saul, and the thing pleased him. ²¹ Saul thought, "Let me give her to him, that she may be a snare for him, and that the hand of the Philistines may be against him." Therefore Saul said to David a second time,*ᵃ* "You shall now be my son-in-law." ²² And Saul commanded his servants, "Speak to David in private and say, 'Behold, the king has delight in you, and all his servants love you; now then become the king's son-in-law.'" ²³ And Saul's servants spoke those words in the ears of David. And David said, "Does it seem to you a little thing to become the king's son-in-law, seeing that I am a poor man and of no repute?" ²⁴ And the servants of Saul told him, "Thus and so did David speak." ²⁵ Then Saul said, "Thus shall you say to David, 'The king desires no marriage present except a hundred foreskins of the Philistines, that he may be avenged of the king's enemies.'" Now Saul thought to make David fall by the hand of the Philistines. ²⁶ And when his servants told David these words, it pleased David well to be the king's son-in-law. Before the time had expired, ²⁷ David arose and went, along with his men, and killed two hundred of the Philistines; and David brought their foreskins, which were given in full number to the king, that he might become the king's son-in-law. And Saul gave him his daughter Michal for a wife. ²⁸ But when Saul saw and knew that the LORD was with David, and that all Israel *ᵇ* loved him, ²⁹ Saul was

ᵃ Heb *by two* *ᵇ* Gk: Heb *Michal, Saul's daughter*

still more afraid of David. So Saul was David's enemy continually.

[30] Then the princes of the Philistines came out to battle, and as often as they came out David had more success than all the servants of Saul; so that his name was highly esteemed.

The brief section about David and Merab (missing in an important family of Greek manuscripts) seems to be connected with Saul's previous promise of his daughter to the man who would smite the Philistine champion, for Saul here proposes that David marry his older daughter but mentions no evident occasion for such a proposal. It is perhaps connected with that previous claim on this daughter that David already has by right of his victory over Goliath. Saul evidently hopes that if David tries to win Merab by being valiant and fighting the Lord's battles, he will fall in combat. But when this does not happen, the jealous king unscrupulously breaks his word and gives his daughter to another man. If we consider this offering of the crown princess a separate incident (not a continuation of the offer first made in connection with the Philistine giant's challenge), we get the added impression that Saul is making repeated attempts at getting rid of David. We may in that case even imagine that the king's conscience bothers him when he has not given the promised daughter, but that he is happy when events permit him to deal "more magnanimously" with the second daughter.

Another major success of David is his winning of the princess Michal. Though the account does not explicitly emphasize the point, his marriage into the royal family also lays the foundation for David's future claims to be the legitimate successor to the first king. The report of Michal's affection for David comes to the king as a welcome occasion for luring David to danger and, he hopes, to death. Since it is unbecoming for the king himself to make direct advances to David in this delicate matter, Saul bids his servants speak to David privately. The servants, after having given a favorable account of David's status with king and people, advise him to marry into the king's family. David's objection to the effect that he does not have the qualifications nor sufficient money for the marriage present is not mere modesty. The fact is that David is unable to pay the customarily large marriage price required for a king's daughter. The king's countersuggestion of a different bride price, 100 foreskins of the Philistines, puts the bride within reach of a mighty warrior such as David was. There is grim humor in the idea of David's not merely "scalping the enemy" but circumcising these uncircumcised pagans! Publicly the king's purpose in sending David on such dangerous raids is to be avenged of his enemies; his real purpose, however, is to "cause David to fall by the hand of the Philistines." The king's proposition proves acceptable to David. In a shorter time than had been stipulated, David returns unscathed with 200 foreskins (double the amount required!) and counts them out in full to the king in order to win his bride and become the king's son-in-law. No wonder that Saul, on seeing David's continued and growing success with the people and with the Lord, fears David yet more. Saul is being forced to legitimatize the future king by making him his son-in-law, forever removing from David any stigma of having usurped his position. This dominant theme of growing success is repeated at the end of the chapter (v. 30); nothing succeeds like success!

Saul Seeks to Kill David 19

Two types of action predominate in the chain of episodes reported in this chapter. On the one hand, there are Saul's repeated attempts at killing David; on the other, there are David's successful escapes. In evaluating Saul's attempts at killing David we should not forget that in the ancient Near East a king was considered the supreme person in his realm and that it was therefore simply impermissible that he have a rival. Hence in his attempt to stop David, King Saul is not only acting out of personal jealousy and rivalry; he is doing what was expected of every king in that ancient world. The four attempts at murdering David recorded in this chapter are loosely coordinated with one another and with the preceding and following sections, reflecting, it seems, their origin in once separate traditions that the final compiler has not "steamrollered" into one seamless harmonization (cf. vv. 9 f. with 18:10 f.; v. 3 with 20:5; vv. 1-3 with 20:2 ff.; also cf Introduction, pp. 14 ff.). But instead of seeing our chapter as a patchwork of poorly coordinated duplicate traditions (and perhaps undertaking intricate harmonizations or practicing literary surgery to "reconstruct the original"), we must learn to see in these various episodes of our chapter the retarding action in what is a masterful drama, a drama in which Saul loses out most tragically but David goes on from success to success by the blessing of God.

Jonathan the Mediator Between Saul and David   19:1-7

¹ And Saul spoke to Jonathan his son and to all his servants, that they should kill David. But Jonathan, Saul's son, delighted much in David. ² And Jonathan told David, "Saul my father seeks to kill

you; therefore take heed to yourself in the morning, stay in a secret place and hide yourself; ³ and I will go out and stand beside my father in the field where you are, and I will speak to my father about you; and if I learn anything I will tell you." ⁴ And Jonathan spoke well of David to Saul his father, and said to him, "Let not the king sin against his servant David; because he has not sinned against you, and because his deeds have been of good service to you; ⁵ for he took his life in his hand and he slew the Philistine, and the LORD wrought a great victory for all Israel. You saw it, and rejoiced; why then will you sin against innocent blood by killing David without cause?" ⁶ And Saul hearkened to the voice of Jonathan; Saul swore, "As the LORD lives, he shall not be put to death." ⁷ And Jonathan called David, and Jonathan showed him all these things. And Jonathan brought David to Saul, and he was in his presence as before.

In the first episode it is, ironically, a member of Saul's own house, the heir apparent to the throne himself, who protects David from Saul's murderous plans by pointing out to his royal father not only David's innocence over against the king but, more important, the fact that through him "the LORD wrought a great victory for all Israel." Warning his father against shedding the innocent blood of the very person who took his life into his hand for the sake of the king, Jonathan obtains a promise, guaranteed by a sacred oath, that David will not be put to death. Hence David, instead of being obliged to hide, returns to favor at the court. Seen in relation to the broad context of the entire "drama" of David's rise, this episode serves masterfully to delay what must be the final outcome.

A Second Attempt on David's Life   *8-10*

⁸ And there was war again; and David went out and fought with the Philistines, and made a great slaughter among them, so that they fled before him. ⁹ Then an evil spirit from the LORD came upon Saul, as he sat in his house with his spear in his hand; and David was playing the lyre. ¹⁰ And Saul sought to pin David to the wall with the spear; but he eluded Saul, so that he struck the spear into the wall. And David fled, and escaped.

If we take this incident of Saul's attempt on David's life as a second attempt by Saul to kill David (cf. 18:10 f.), then we may imagine that the first time Saul had simply lifted the spear without throwing it, while David, prompted by the Lord, unconscious of the attempt, turned away at the right moment; the ill-will manifested in Saul's first attempt was temporarily checked by the reconciliation that Jonathan effected (19:1-7). Saul's second attempt is incited by David's renewed success in the continued war against the Philistines and by a second attack on Saul by the evil spirit sent by the Lord. Saul's old "fixation" on the idea that David is his enemy returns to the madman, even while David is trying to soothe him with music. But David again eludes him and escapes. What had once been an impetuous act prompted by jealousy now seems almost a plot.

Michal Saves David's Life   *11-17*

¹¹ That night Saul ˣ sent messengers to David's house to watch him, that he might kill him in the morning. But Michal, David's wife, told him, "If you

ˣ Gk Old Latin: Heb *escaped that night.* ¹¹ *And Saul*

do not save your life tonight, tomorrow you will be killed." ¹² So Michal let David down through the window; and he fled away and escaped. ¹³ Michal took an image *c* and laid it on the bed and put a pillow *d* of goats' hair at its head, and covered it with the clothes. ¹⁴ And when Saul sent messengers to take David, she said, "He is sick." ¹⁵ Then Saul sent the messengers to see David, saying, "Bring him up to me in the bed, that I may kill him." ¹⁶ And when the messengers came in, behold, the image *c* was in the bed, with the pillow *d* of goats' hair at it head. ¹⁷ Saul said to Michal, "Why have you deceived me thus, and let my enemy go, so that he has escaped?" And Michal answered Saul, "He said to me, 'Let me go; why should I kill you?'"

c Heb *teraphim*   *d* The meaning of the Hebrew word is uncertain

Again it is one of Saul's own family who saves the seemingly unsuspicious David, apparently on the wedding night when the king is again incensed against the hated upstart who now has taken his own daughter to his house as his bride. This time it is Michal who saves David from disaster. She lets him down through the window of a house situated, like Rahab's, on the city wall. David must flee without arms and attendants. To delay the pursuit, Michal then contrives to deceive the king's messengers. There is a real dash of intentional humor at this point in the story as we see Michal take an idolatrous object, an "image" (evidently the life-size anthropoid image representing the household god), place it on the bed with a pillow of goat's hair to give the illusion of David's hair, and then cover it all with a garment. The ruse is discovered only after considerable delay and in the king's own presence. ("Behold, the image was in the bed, with the pillow of goat's hair at its head"). Even Michal's response to her father's charge is contrived—that her life had been threatened! No doubt the intended result of the narration of this incident is again hearty laughter—laughter at those who dare interfere with the Lord's plans, like the laughter in which the Lord Himself indulges according to Psalm 2.

David Takes Refuge with Samuel   18-24

18 Now David fled and escaped, and he came to Samuel at Ramah, and told him all that Saul had done to him. And he and Samuel went and dwelt at Naioth. 19 And it was told Saul, "Behold, David is at Naioth in Ramah." 20 Then Saul sent messengers to take David; and when they saw the company of the prophets prophesying, and Samuel standing as head over them, the Spirit of God came upon the messengers of Saul, and they also prophesied. 21 When it was told Saul, he sent other messengers, and they also prophesied. And Saul sent messengers again the third time, and they also prophesied. 22 Then he himself went to Ramah, and came to the great well that is in Secu; and he asked, "Where are Samuel and David?" And one said, "Behold, they are at Naioth in Ramah." 23 And he went from *f* there to Naioth in Ramah; and the Spirit of God came upon him also, and as he went he prophesied, until he came to Naioth in Ramah. 24 And he too stripped off his clothes, and he too prophesied before Samuel, and lay naked all that day and all that night. Hence it is said, "Is Saul also among the prophets?"

f Gk: Heb lacks *from*

162

Saul's next attempt on David's life is made at Ramah, where David flees to the protection of the aged Samuel, at what seems to be a cloister for prophets in the vicinity of the sanctuary. The name Naioth can be translated "dwelling," or "school," and it seems to designate a well-known place where the prophets gathered, under the leadership of their "abbot" Samuel, for religious rites characterized by prophetic ecstasy. This ecstasy is stimulated, it seems, by circular dances that increase in intensity to such frenzy that even other people are infected by it, cast off all restraining outer garments (not necessarily becoming completely nude), and fall exhausted to the ground (cf. 10:5). This phenomenon, so strange and foreboding to modern men, is known elsewhere in the ancient world; it should therefore not be dismissed as fiction. Here in this account, however, the point is that not only are the successive groups of would-be captors seized by the Spirit of God, but King Saul himself is forced to travel on a road that is indistinguishable from that of the dervishlike prophets. He is consumed by a fever of ecstasy — with the result that, instead of people reporting, "Saul succeeded in capturing David," the old proverb is again repeated — with a great deal of humor! — "Is Saul also among the prophets?" Saul is out of place in the ranks of Samuel's men. Saul must realize that a superior force is being deployed against him. The Lord has found a new way to rescue David from harm: He has created a place of refuge for His anointed.

DAVID AND JONATHAN   20

In previous chapters Saul's daughter and the prophet Samuel have appeared to aid David in his escape from Saul. In this chapter Jonathan, the crown prince, Saul's son and heir, appears, not merely to help David escape (if that were all that is involved, our account would be told quite differently and much more briefly) but to aid David toward his future position as king. The present account of David's escape emphasizes especially the aspect that David the king is not a usurper but the legitimate successor of Saul. Jonathan himself guaranteed this to David. (Cf. Introduction, pp. 14 ff.)

David Confers with Jonathan 20:1-10

¹ Then David fled from Naioth in Ramah, and came and said before Jonathan, "What have I done? What is my guilt? And what is my sin before your father, that he seeks my life?" ² And he said to him, "Far from it! You shall not die. Behold, my father does nothing either great or small without disclosing it to me; and why should my father hide this from me? It is not so." ³ But David replied,*g* "Your father knows well that I have found favor in your eyes, and he thinks, 'Let not Jonathan know this, lest he be grieved.' But truly, as the LORD lives and as your soul lives, there is but a step between me and death." ⁴ Then said Jonathan to David, "Whatever you say, I will do for you." ⁵ David said to Jonathan, "Behold, tomorrow is the new moon, and I should not fail to sit at table with the king; but let me go, that I may hide myself in the field till the third day at evening. ⁶ If your father misses me at all, then say, 'David earnestly asked leave of me to run to Bethlehem his city; for there is a yearly sacrifice there for all the family.' ⁷ If he says, 'Good!' it will be well with your

g Gk: Heb *swore again*

servant; but if he is angry, then know that evil is determined by him. ⁸ Therefore deal kindly with your servant, for you have brought your servant into a sacred covenant ᴴ with you. But if there is guilt in me, slay me yourself; for why should you bring me to your father?" ⁹ And Jonathan said, "Far be it from you! If I knew that it was determined by my father that evil should come upon you, would I not tell you?" ¹⁰ Then said David to Jonathan, "Who will tell me if your father answers you roughly?"

ᴴ Heb a covenant of the LORD

The initial statement (about David's return from the prophets' settlement to the capital) serves to link the preceding episode about David's sojourn with Samuel to the present chapter. Though such a link presents us with the strange story that David reappears at Gibeah and the even more strange report that Jonathan is unconvinced of Saul's hostility to David, the implicit assumption of our account nevertheless seems to be that Saul's previous actions still seem to David to be so impossible and unbelievable that another inspection of the situation is called for. This implies, too, that Saul is here given another chance — one which he muffs, whereas David leaves the capital as an innocent refugee whose right to the throne is established even more clearly because the crown prince formally acknowledges him as the rightful successor to the throne.

The conversation between the two friends is told most vividly. It begins with David's complaint to the crown prince about the king's designs to kill him. Even Jonathan's well-meant attempt at reassuring David does not allay his misgivings; in fact, David suggests that the real reason for the king's concealing this from his son is his fear that Jonathan's great affection for David may upset the royal plan to kill him. Therefore, David suggests, Jonathan's assumption that he as crown prince enjoys his father's confidence in all matters and that he will therefore always be able to warn David is an assumption that must be tested. The next day's festival of the new moon, David suggests, offers an excellent opportunity for a test that will reveal Saul's real intentions. David can be said to be using the sacred day as an excuse for absenting himself from the king's fellowship in order to attend instead the annual sacrificial meal of his kinsmen at Bethlehem, thus allegedly putting duty to his family before that to his king. Jonathan agrees to the stratagem and assures David that he will under no circumstances betray the sacred covenant he had made with him but will most assuredly warn him of any possible danger.

Jonathan Entreats David for His Descendants   *11-17*

¹¹ And Jonathan said to David, "Come, let us go out into the field." So they both went out into the field.

¹² And Jonathan said to David, "The LORD, the God of Israel, be witness! *i* When I have sounded my father, about this time tomorrow, or the third day, behold, if he is well disposed toward David, shall I not then send and disclose it to you? ¹³ But should it please my father to do you harm, the LORD do so to Jonathan, and more also, if I do not disclose it to you, and send you away, that you may go in safety. May the LORD be with you, as he has been with my father. ¹⁴ If I am still alive, show me the loyal love of the LORD, that I may not die; *j* ¹⁵ and do not cut off your loyalty from my house for ever. When the LORD cuts

i Heb lacks *be witness*   *j* Heb uncertain

off every one of the enemies of David from the face
of the earth, [16] let not the name of Jonathan be cut
off from the house of David.[k] And may the LORD take
vengeance on David's enemies." [17] And Jonathan
made David swear again by his love for him; for he
loved him as he loved his own soul.

> [k] Gk: Heb *earth, and Jonathan made a covenant with the house
> of David*

This section about Jonathan's going out into the
field and there entreating David for his descendants
seemingly interrupts the main thread of the narrative.
Its tone is different from that of the preceding and
subsequent sections; also, instead of Jonathan being
the superior and David the suppliant, as in the first
part of this chapter, their positions are here reversed.
This may reflect a tradition that was originally separate
but has now been inserted into the more easily flowing
story (perhaps even damaging its text; cf. RSV notes
on vv. 12, 14, 16, and Introduction, pp. 14 ff.). Be that as
it may, this section nevertheless expresses one of the
major concerns of the chapter, that the noble Jonathan
could envision David as king of Israel without envy or
jealousy. Jonathan solemnly swears by the Lord that he
will most certainly inform David of his father's revealed
intentions, and, more important, he begs David, who will
be the future, God-appointed king, not to deal with him
and his descendants as ancient kings frequently dealt
with the previous royal family, that is, not to exterminate
them. Rather, Jonathan pleads that David show that
loyalty which their covenant made in the name of the
Lord demands. Jonathan insists that David renew that
covenant, or as the text puts it, "Jonathan made David
swear again by his love for him." Later 2 Samuel 9 tells

us how David kept this oath and spared Jonathan's house. The clear reference to David's future is important and therefore adds to the full picture at this point rather than detracting from it, because, as we hear the rest of the story of the escape, we are to know that this fugitive will one day be sovereign king. And then, "Let all of David's real enemies be cut off; but let not Jonathan's family be hurt." This tradition may well have been emphasized when the house of Jonathan later had to fear the superior house of David.

Jonathan Discovers Saul's Intentions 18-23

18 Then Jonathan said to him, "Tomorrow is the new moon; and you will be missed, because your seat will be empty. 19 And on the third day you will be greatly missed; *l* then go to the place where you hid yourself when the matter was in hand, and remain beside yonder stone heap.*m* 20 And I will shoot three arrows to the side of it, as though I shot at a mark. 21 And behold, I will send the lad, saying, 'Go, find the arrows.' If I say to the lad, 'Look, the arrows are on this side of you, take them,' then you are to come, for, as the LORD lives, it is safe for you and there is no danger. 22 But if I say to the youth, 'Look, the arrows are beyond you,' then go; for the LORD has sent you away. 23 And as for the matter of which you and I have spoken, behold, the LORD is between you and me for ever."

l Gk: Heb *go down quickly*   *m* Gk: Heb *the stone Ezel*

After having, so to say, rushed ahead into the future, the narrative now returns to tell about the "new-moon test" that David had suggested. Jonathan describes more distinctly his plan for revealing to David the intention of his father. It is difficult to identify "the place where you hid yourself when the matter was in hand." Is this a reference to David's hiding place after Saul's first attempt to kill David, or perhaps to another episode not presented here, or to all the details of the planned procedure? Nevertheless, the general sense is clear: Jonathan will choose some object by the side of David's hiding place at which to shoot, and he will communicate Saul's intentions to David by means of the instructions he gives to his servant, one set ("It is on this side of you," that is, "Come!") to indicate that all is well, and another ("It is beyond you," that is, "Go!") to indicate that he must flee. Jonathan's final statement again confirms the covenant between them, a covenant of which the Lord is the witness.

Saul's Intentions Revealed   *24-34*

24 So David hid himself in the field; and when the new moon came, the king sat down to eat food. 25 The king sat upon his seat, as at other times, upon the seat by the wall; Jonathan sat opposite,[n] and Abner sat by Saul's side, but David's place was empty.

26 Yet Saul did not say anything that day; for he thought, "Something has befallen him; he is not clean, surely he is not clean." 27 But on the second day, the morrow after the new moon, David's place was empty. And Saul said to Jonathan his son, "Why has not the son of Jesse come to the meal, either yesterday or today?" 28 Jonathan answered Saul, "David earnestly asked leave of me to go to Bethlehem; 29 he said, 'Let me go; for our family holds a sacrifice in the city, and my brother has commanded

[n] Cn See Gk: Heb *stood up*

me to be there. So now, if I have found favor in your eyes, let me get away, and see my brothers.' For this reason he has not come to the king's table."

³⁰ Then Saul's anger was kindled against Jonathan, and he said to him, "You son of a perverse, rebellious woman, do I not know that you have chosen the son of Jesse to your own shame, and to the shame of your mother's nakedness? ³¹ For as long as the son of Jesse lives upon the earth, neither you nor your kingdom shall be established. Therefore send and fetch him to me, for he shall surely die." ³² Then Jonathan answered Saul his father, "Why should he be put to death? What has he done?" ³³ But Saul cast his spear at him to smite him; so Jonathan knew that his father was determined to put David to death. ³⁴ And Jonathan rose from the table in fierce anger and ate no food the second day of the month, for he was grieved for David, because his father had disgraced him.

The next day the plan David had suggested for determining the king's real intentions begins to be put into effect. However, on that first day of the new-moon festival, David's absence is passed over. The king imagines that some accident (like contact with a dead body) has disqualified David from sharing in the royal meal, which had a religious significance and therefore required ritual preparation. It is only on the second day that Saul's intentions are clearly revealed. Since obligations to one's kin were among the most pressing and urgent duties of that day, the explanation that David had suggested and Jonathan now repeats is most skillful. More than that, David's obligation to his kin and their covenant with the Lord here supersedes that to Saul the king. Saul, however, does not acknowledge this. When Jonathan therefore excuses David on the ground that his duty to kinsmen takes precedence over that to the king, Saul breaks out in anger, practically disowning Jonathan as an illegitimate bastard who is unworthy of his high birth, claiming that it is rebellion for Jonathan to prefer any covenant bond with David over his undivided duty toward his family, the royal family.

Saul was chosen king on a personal basis; the principle of dynastic succession to Israel's throne has not yet been established. One could expect that Saul's successor would be a great warrior designated by God and acclaimed by the people; and that is just how David appears: as the probable successor to king Saul. Jonathan seems to share that common opinion about David. This does not mean a plot against Saul, even though Saul seems to be thinking of handing down kingship to his own family. So Jonathan now suffers affliction out of loyalty to his covenant of love with David. He remains loyal to it even when it brings him into conflict with his father, the king, and costs him the kingship. Had it not, in fact, been for selfless Jonathan's loyalty to the covenant, it seems doubtful that David would have succeeded in escaping from Saul. The fact that Jonathan could rise from the table and leave without being pinned to the wall is perhaps not due to the fact that he dodged Saul's spear (at least the text says nothing about this), but it is due perhaps to the fact that Saul only "took up," i. e. brandished, his spear at the crown prince without casting it (as in 18:11). In any case, Saul's intentions were now clearly revealed. Jonathan could acquaint David with his grave danger.

Jonathan Contacts David 35-42

³⁵ In the morning Jonathan went out into the field to the appointment with David, and with him a little lad. ³⁶ And he said to his lad, "Run and find the arrows which I shoot." As the lad ran, he shot an arrow beyond him. ³⁷ And when the lad came to the place of the arrow which Jonathan had shot, Jonathan called after the lad and said, "Is not the arrow beyond you?" ³⁸ And Jonathan called after the lad, "Hurry, make haste, stay not." So Jonathan's lad gathered up the arrows, and came to his master. ³⁹ But the lad knew nothing; only Jonathan and David knew the matter. ⁴⁰ And Jonathan gave his weapons to his lad, and said to him, "Go and carry them to the city." ⁴¹ And as soon as the lad had gone, David rose from beside the stone heap*^o* and fell on his face to the ground, and bowed three times; and they kissed one another, and wept with one another, until David recovered himself.*^p* ⁴² Then Jonathan said to David, "Go in peace, forasmuch as we have sworn both of us in the name of the LORD, saying, 'The LORD shall be between me and you, and between my descendants and your descendants, for ever.'" And he rose and departed; and Jonathan went into the city.*^q*

^o Gk: Heb *from beside the south*   *^p* Or *exceeded*
^q This sentence is 21. 1 in Heb

Though some aspects of the arrow-procedure are obscure (cf. 2 Kings 13:14-19), the main point is nevertheless clear. The instructions, ostensibly addressed to the lad, are really an instruction to David to "hurry, make haste." That David does not immediately flee but meets and takes leave of Jonathan is another surprising thing, perhaps incorporating another tradition, unless we are to imagine that at the last moment Jonathan could not let David go without a final farewell, no matter what the risk. In any case, the main point is emphasized: before they part, the Lord is called as witness between them and their descendants forever. This episode, at the beginning of the account of David's deepest humiliation, helps us see that the account is not merely a recital of events but the unfolding of the Lord's plans for David.

DAVID FLEES TO PHILISTINE TERRITORY   21

The tone of this chapter is in marked contrast to that of the previous one. It tells its story without expressing any pity for the priest Ahimelech, who gets involved in the deadly quarrel by unwittingly aiding David in his escape; it likewise expresses no charge against David for deceiving the priest; nor does it celebrate David's presence of mind in fabricating fictitious stories that get him out of tight spots. It merely mentions these things in passing, its main emphasis lying elsewhere, on the serious consequences David's flight had for all concerned. "The city of the priests" (22:19) does not seem to be a minor village cult place but the well-known central sanctuary of Israel, now on the border between Benjamin and Judah, just east of Jerusalem, called Nob. There the presiding high priest is Ahimelech, a grandson of Eli, the man who was Saul's own priest at the time of the war of liberation (14:3), where he appears under the variant name of Ahijah.

David and the Bread of the Presence   *21:1-6*

¹ ʳ Then came David to Nob to Ahimelech the priest; and Ahimelech came to meet David trembling,

ʳ Ch 21. 2 in Heb

173

and said to him, "Why are you alone, and no one with you?" [2] And David said to Ahimelech the priest, "The king has charged me with a matter, and said to me, 'Let no one know anything of the matter about which I send you, and with which I have charged you.' I have made an appointment with the young men for such and such a place. [3] Now then, what have you at hand? Give me five loaves of bread, or whatever is here." [4] And the priest answered David, "I have no common bread at hand, but there is holy bread; if only the young men have kept themselves from women." [5] And David answered the priest, "Of a truth women have been kept from us as always when I go on an expedition; the vessels of the young men are holy, even when it is a common journey; how much more today will their vessels be holy?" [6] So the priest gave him the holy bread; for there was no bread there but the bread of the Presence, which is removed from before the LORD, to be replaced by hot bread on the day it is taken away.

The high priest trembles as he greets David because only some extraordinary circumstance would make the king's captain and son-in-law travel alone. Perhaps Ahimelech was in a general way acquainted with the delicate situation existing between David and Saul. David's explanation is that he is on a secret mission for the king and that he has arranged to rendezvous with his men at a certain place. Meanwhile, because of his hasty departure, he needs rations, he says. The priest has scruples about giving consecrated bread to David and his men, lest they by their uncleanness contaminate the holy; but these scruples are allayed when David assures the priest that even when his men are not on a specific warlike mission they are in a state of holiness (cf. item 5 of the holy war imagery p. 105; also cf. 2 Sam. 11:11 ff.). Since on this occasion they have a military assignment, they and all their vessels are naturally in a state of holiness. Thereupon the priest gives David the bread of the Presence, that is, the sacrificial bread presented to the Lord, in accordance with Lev. 24:5-9, on the previous Sabbath, now replaced by fresh bread, and therefore available to be eaten by the priests. Strictly speaking, then, allowing David to partake of the holy bread broke the letter of the Law in much the same way that Jesus broke the letter of the Sabbath law (cf. Matt. 12:3-4), but in a similar way it is also a vague hint that something greater than the external regulation is involved here. David does partake of the holy food that brings him into communion with the Lord. (Cf. Ex. 24:9-11)

David and Goliath's Sword   7-9

⁷ Now a certain man of the servants of Saul was there that day, detained before the LORD; his name was Doeg the Edomite, the chief of Saul's herdsmen.

⁸ And David said to Ahimelech, "And have you not here a spear or a sword at hand? For I have brought neither my sword nor my weapons with me, because the king's business required haste." ⁹ And the priest said, "The sword of Goliath the Philistine, whom you killed in the valley of Elah, behold, it is here wrapped in a cloth behind the ephod; if you will take that, take it, for there is none but that here." And David said, "There is none like that; give it to me."

David also receives from the priest a holy weapon, the very one which had been consecrated to the Lord after David had won it from Goliath. Though he must flee for his life, this refugee remains under God's protection; this is not expressly said, of course, but it is implied, for Doeg later reports (22:9 f.) that the priest also inquired of the Lord for David, that is, obtained an oracle for him. Our account does not report that detail, though the oracle ephod is mentioned, and there seems to be no reason for denying Doeg's assertion. In any case, we must admit that this account touches only lightly on these matters because it wishes to hasten on to the subsequent story of David's flight. Even Doeg is mentioned only briefly at this point because of the part he will play in that subsequent story. He is an official of Saul, perhaps a courier entrusted with escorting the king. He was detained before the Lord because he had to undergo a rite of purification, fulfill a vow, or wait for an oracle. David later reported (22:22) that he was terrified on seeing Doeg there, grieving that he had not been more careful in the presence of that man.

David's Narrow Escape in Philistine Territory   *10-15*

¹⁰ **And David rose and fled that day from Saul, and went to Achish the king of Gath. ¹¹ And the servants of Achish said to him, "Is not this David the king of the land? Did they not sing to one another of him in dances,**

> **'Saul has slain his thousands,**
> **and David his ten thousands'?"**

¹² **And David took these words to heart, and was much afraid of Achish the king of Gath. ¹³ So he changed his behavior before them, and feigned him-**

self mad in their hands, and made marks on the doors of the gate, and let his spittle run down his beard. [14] Then said Achish to his servants, "Lo, you see the man is mad; why then have you brought him to me? [15] Do I lack madmen, that you have brought this fellow to play the madman in my presence? Shall this fellow come into my house?"

We now perhaps expect the conclusion of the story of David's flight, but our storyteller has some other important points to make first to help us understand David's rise to the throne. The present episode underlines David's quick thinking and resourcefulness so vividly that it evokes the hearers' hearty laughter at its climax. In a tight spot David succeeds in tricking the Philistines and escaping under a divine protection that cannot be thwarted by the enemy. David may be thinking that at the court of the Philistine king he can enter a service much the same as that which he rendered to Saul. But the attempt of the person who fought the Lord's battles to fight for the Philistines does not succeed; David's plans are countermanded by the Lord's superior strategy. The servants in Gath, recalling the acclaim David had won beyond that of Saul, recognize him as "the king of the land" (an inaccurate but significant statement of the Lord's ultimate purpose for David). Sensing a fate like that which befell captured Samson, David fears greatly when he suddenly realizes the danger. But proving equal to the occasion, he escapes by playing the part of a madman. In those days a madman, a person seized by a spirit, enjoyed divine protection and immunity from human punishment. What makes the final part of the incident so humorous is that the Philistine king, far from doubting the identification

177

his servants had made of David and the slayer of Goliath, upbraids them, asking: Don't we have enough madmen in Philistia already? "Shall this fellow come into my house?" The obvious answer of the Israelite hearer is: Of course not; David should not end up in the Philistine army or jail, but as "king of the land." They said it themselves.

DAVID ON THE BORDERS OF JUDAH   22

David at Adullam   *22:1-5*

¹ David departed from there and escaped to the cave of Adullam; and when his brothers and all his father's house heard it, they went down there to him. ² And every one who was in distress, and every one who was in debt, and every one who was discontented, gathered to him; and he became captain over them. And there were with him about four hundred men.

³ And David went from there to Mizpeh of Moab; and he said to the king of Moab, "Pray let my father and my mother stay *ˢ* with you, till I know what God will do for me." ⁴ And he left them with the king of Moab, and they stayed with him all the time that David was in the stronghold. ⁵ Then the prophet Gad said to David, "Do not remain in the stronghold; depart, and go into the land of Judah." So David departed, and went into the forest of Hereth.

ˢ Syr Vg: Heb *come out*

David's hideout at Adullam in the border country between Philistia and Judah had the advantages of a rugged region that provided "caves and strongholds" in the vicinity of rich crop-producing valleys and also

178

extensive pasture areas on the lower slopes of the hills. It is understandable that David is soon joined by others: by his family, who feared Saul's reprisals, and by a number of disorientated individuals, who for one reason or another found themselves cut off from the normal life of society, running away from insurmountable social pressures, debts, or failures. In turning to the Moabites for protection for his father and mother, David is turning to a people distantly related to his family through Ruth, his great-grandmother. He himself, however, is not permitted to remain living on foreign soil. In fact, the divine message of the prophet Gad calls on him to leave the border stronghold of Adullam and return to the hills of Judah proper. Despite the danger such a movement into Saul's sphere of influence entails, David obeys, moving southwestward up into the Judean hill country to the forest of Hereth.

Saul Massacres the Priest at Nob 6-23

⁶ Now Saul heard that David was discovered, and the men who were with him. Saul was sitting at Gibeah, under the tamarisk tree on the height, with his spear in his hand, and all his servants were standing about him. ⁷ And Saul said to his servants who stood about him, "Hear now, you Benjaminites; will the son of Jesse give every one of you fields and vineyards, will he make you all commanders of thousands and commanders of hundreds, ⁸ that all of you have conspired against me? No one discloses to me when my son makes a league with the son of Jesse, none of you is sorry for me or discloses to me that my son has stirred up my servant against me, to lie in wait, as at this day." ⁹ Then answered Doeg the Edomite, who stood by the servants of Saul, "I saw the son of

Jesse coming to Nob, to Ahimelech the son of Ahitub, [10] and he inquired of the LORD for him, and gave him provisions, and gave him the sword of Goliath the Philistine."

[11] Then the king sent to summon Ahimelech the priest, the son of Ahitub, and all his father's house, the priests who were at Nob; and all of them came to the king. [12] And Saul said, "Hear now, son of Ahitub." And he answered, "Here I am, my lord." [13] And Saul said to him, "Why have you conspired against me, you and the son of Jesse, in that you have given him bread and a sword, and have inquired of God for him, so that he has risen against me, to lie in wait, as at this day?" [14] Then Ahimelech answered the king, "And who among all your servants is so faithful as David, who is the king's son-in-law, and captain over[f] your bodyguard, and honored in your house? [15] Is today the first time that I have inquired of God for him? No! Let not the king impute anything to his servant or to all the house of my father; for your servant has known nothing of all this, much or little." [16] And the king said, "You shall surely die, Ahimelech, you and all your father's house." [17] And the king said to the guard who stood about him, "Turn and kill the priests of the LORD; because their hand also is with David, and they knew that he fled, and did not disclose it to me." But the servants of the king would not put forth their hand to fall upon the priests of the LORD. [18] Then the king said to Doeg, "You turn and fall upon the priests." And Doeg the Edomite turned and fell upon the priests, and he killed on that day eighty-five persons who wore the linen ephod. [19] And Nob, the city of the priests, he put to the sword; both men

[f] Gk Tg: Heb *and has turned aside to*

and women, children and sucklings, oxen, asses and sheep, he put to the sword.

²⁰ But one of the sons of Ahimelech the son of Ahitub, named Abiathar, escaped and fled after David. ²¹ And Abiathar told David that Saul had killed the priests of the LORD. ²² And David said to Abiathar, "I knew on that day, when Doeg the Edomite was there, that he would surely tell Saul. I have occasioned the death of all the persons of your father's house. ²³ Stay with me, fear not; for he that seeks my life seeks your life; with me you shall be in safekeeping."

In sharp contrast to this ascendant anointed of the Lord who trusts and obeys the Lord, stands the declining, discredited anointed of the Lord who has long since been rejected by the Lord because of His disobedience but who is still trying to establish his kingdom for himself and his family by his own devices. The news that David is no longer a solitary fugitive but has gathered about him a band of 400 tough and desperate men moves the king to break out in bitter indignation against his officials, whom he accuses of sympathizing with the insurgent and of withholding information. What really rankles with Saul is that Jonathan had actively cooperated with David in his escape. Saul even imagines — wrongly — that David is lying in wait to pounce on him and seize his throne. Utterly unsure of himself and insanely suspicious of everyone, Saul lashes out with accusations in all directions. He is therefore most easily sent off on quite a different track when the Edomite Doeg uses this opportunity to report "the subversive activity" he had observed on the part of the priesthood at Nob: there he saw the priest Ahimelech give

David not only provisions and a weapon but a divine oracle!

Saul's insane and ungovernable suspicions are now aroused to the fullest. He summons the priesthood to face the charges. Ahimelech's defense is masterfully cogent but in vain. Without bothering to refute his protestation of ignorance and innocence, Saul unreasonably and brutally pronounces the sentence of death. It is a sentence directed not merely at Ahimelech but, in keeping with the prevalent sense of the solidarity of the entire family, at the entire priestly house; and the execution is then described as the execution of the ban of a holy war—nothing is spared! What Saul had refused to do against the Lord's ancient enemies, the Amalekites (1 Sam. 15), he now does to the priests of the Lord! What a frightful divine judgment when a hardened sinner no longer can discern between right and wrong; what makes it even more terrifying is that the disaster on Eli's house is a fulfillment of the judgment proclaimed long ago on that degenerate priestly house (2:30 ff.; 3:14). When his own royal escort refuses to carry out such monstrous orders against holy men of God, Saul has to turn to a foreigner, an Edomite, to have the Lord's priests executed.

One of the priests, Abiathar, escapes the massacre, flees to David, and reports the atrocity. Though David reproaches himself as accessory to the disaster, the emphasis of the story is not to the effect that David must answer for his action; rather, Saul remains the guilty one. Abiathar is invited to remain with David, who vows he will protect Abiathar from Saul, who seeks both their lives. So the chapter ends with David accompanied not only by Gad, the representative of the prophets, but also by Abiathar, the legitimate representative of the priesthood. The events of the chapter mark another step in the rise of David and another step in Saul's decline. David must increase; Saul must decrease!

In the Lord's Hand   23

David Delivers Keilah from the Philistines   *23:1-5*

¹ Now they told David, "Behold, the Philistines are fighting against Keilah, and are robbing the threshing floors." ² Therefore David inquired of the LORD, "Shall I go and attack these Philistines?" And the LORD said to David, "Go and attack the Philistines and save Keilah." ³ But David's men said to him, "Behold, we are afraid here in Judah; how much more then if we go to Keilah against the armies of the Philistines?"⁴ Then David inquired of the LORD again. And the LORD answered him, "Arise, go down to Keilah; for I will give the Philistines into your hand." ⁵ And David and his men went to Keilah, and fought with the Philistines, and brought away their cattle, and made a great slaughter among them. So David delivered the inhabitants of Keilah.

When the Philistines attack the city of Keilah, south of Adullam, and begin to plunder the population's grain supplies, it is David who senses what his duty is. Confirmed by the word of God, like a heroic judge of old, he "delivers" his people. Though as yet uncrowned, he does for his people what the crowned king should have been doing. The fact that David is therewith fighting the Lord's battles is underlined by the concomitant fact that he consults the Lord about this matter twice, for his men question the wisdom of leaving the forest of Hereth, where their situation is already critical, for an even more dangerous engagement. David and his men are, however, not permitted to remain in "safety" and "ease" when the Lord's enemies attack; they must go forth into battle a second time, but with the added assurance in holy war terminology, "I will give the Philistines into your hand." Attacking first, it seems, the carts that were transporting Israelite grain to Philistia, David finally wins a great victory over the Philistines for the inhabitants of Keilah.

Saul Attempts to Seize David at Keilah　　　　　6-15

⁶ When Abiathar the son of Ahimelech fled to David to Keilah, he came down with an ephod in his hand. ⁷ Now it was told Saul that David had come to Keilah. And Saul said, "God has given him into my hand; for he has shut himself in by entering a town that has gates and bars." ⁸ And Saul summoned all the people to war, to go down to Keilah, to besiege David and his men. ⁹ David knew that Saul was plotting evil against him; and he said to Abiathar the priest, "Bring the ephod here." ¹⁰ Then said David, "O LORD, the God of Israel, thy servant has surely heard that Saul seeks to come to Keilah, to destroy the city on my account. ¹¹ Will the men of Keilah surrender me into his hand? Will Saul come down, as thy servant has heard? O LORD, the God of Israel, I beseech thee, tell thy servant." And the LORD said, "He will come down." ¹² Then said David, "Will the men of Keilah surrender me and my men into the hand of Saul?" And the LORD said, "They will surrender you." ¹³ Then David and his men, who were about six hundred, arose and departed from Keilah, and they went wherever they could go. When Saul

was told that David had escaped from Keilah, he gave up the expedition. ¹⁴ And David remained in the strongholds in the wilderness, in the hill country of the Wilderness of Ziph. And Saul sought him every day, but God did not give him into his hand.

¹⁵ And David was afraid because ^u Saul had come out to seek his life. David was in the Wilderness of Ziph at Horesh.

^u Or *saw that*

David is not allowed to enjoy the fruits of his victory, for when these Judeans become aware that Saul is moving against their city in the hope of trapping David there, they are minded to avoid opposing the superior might and at the same time to get rid of a band of bothersome freebooters who live off the land they protect. Even before the men of Keilah openly reveal the plans of their hearts, David learns of them from the Lord. In this connection the customary manner of consulting the Lord is vividly described: David's introductory petition, the posing of a yes-or-no question, the response obtained by the sacred Urim and Thummim lots (cf. p. 121), and the brief answer proclaimed to the inquirer by the priest Abiathar. On receiving the word of the Lord, David must leave. Saul's statement, "God has given David into my hand," seems true. David does find himself forsaken by God, abandoned to his mighty persecutor. He and his men go "wherever they could go." David is "afraid"; he abandons the hill country and withdraws to the desert of Judah, the age-old asylum of refugees and rebels on the eastern slope of the Judean mountains—a region traversed by a great number of valleys that form gorges with precipitous and craggy sides, virtually inaccessible to military units.

185

Jonathan Visits David at Horesh 16-18

¹⁶ And Jonathan, Saul's son, rose, and went to David at Horesh, and strengthened his hand in God. ¹⁷ And he said to him, "Fear not; for the hand of Saul my father shall not find you; you shall be king over Israel, and I shall be next to you; Saul my father also knows this." ¹⁸ And the two of them made a covenant before the LORD; David remained at Horesh, and Jonathan went home.

Just at this low point in his "passion," when the strain of unrelieved insecurity begins to weigh on David's spirits and he doubts his promised future, David is visited by Jonathan. His friend boosts David's morale with the assertion that not only will Saul's hand not find him but also that he will yet be king, a king who can count on Jonathan's support, so that for the joy that is set before him David may despise the present shame. What David in his loneliness had no longer been certain of is the unshakable conviction of his friend. Jonathan even adds, "Saul my father also knows this." And to guarantee this to David, he renews the covenant in the presence of the Lord, reestablishing a relationship that will take precedence over every other tie or claim.

A Close Call at the "Rock of Escape" 19-29

¹⁹ Then the Ziphites went up to Saul at Gibeah, saying, "Does not David hide among us in the strongholds at Horesh, on the hill of Hachilah, which is south of Jeshimon? ²⁰ Now come down, O king, according to all your heart's desire to come down; and our part shall be to surrender him into the king's

hand." ²¹ And Saul said, "May you be blessed by the LORD; for you have had compassion on me. ²² Go, make yet more sure; know and see the place where his haunt is, and who has seen him there; for it is told me that he is very cunning. ²³ See therefore, and take note of all the lurking places where he hides, and come back to me with sure information. Then I will go with you; and if he is in the land, I will search him out among all the thousands of Judah." ²⁴ And they arose, and went to Ziph ahead of Saul.

Now David and his men were in the wilderness of Maon, in the Arabah to the south of Jeshimon. ²⁵ And Saul and his men went to seek him. And David was told; therefore he went down to the rock which is ^v in the wilderness of Maon. And when Saul heard that, he pursued after David in the wilderness of Maon. ²⁶ Saul went on one side of the mountain, and David and his men on the other side of the mountain; and David was making haste to get away from Saul, as Saul and his men were closing in upon David and his men to capture them, ²⁷ when a messenger came to Saul, saying, "Make haste and come; for the Philistines have made a raid upon the land." ²⁸ So Saul returned from pursuing after David, and went against the Philistines; therefore that place was called the Rock of Escape. ²⁹ ^w And David went up from there, and dwelt in the strongholds of Engedi.

^v Gk: Heb *and dwelt*   ^w Ch 24. 1 in Heb

Upon the heels of Jonathan's encouragement follows David's hairbreadth escape from Saul's pursuit. Saul knows that the region will offer David's small band a great advantage unless the Ziphites cooperate with him by giving exact information about the lurking places. Saul's approach pays off when the actual pursuit begins. This pursuit takes place down a rocky gorge, one of the many canyons that cut through the wilderness of Judah and slope down toward the Dead Sea—David and his men making their way on one side of the gorge, Saul and his men on the other side of the same gorge. David is fleeing before Saul, and Saul and his men are in turn trying to cross to the side of David and his men, when the report of a Philistine attack on his home territory forces Saul to call off the pursuit.

DAVID SPARES SAUL'S LIFE 24

"The Golden Opportunity" at the Cave 24:1-7

¹ When Saul returned from following the Philistines, he was told, "Behold, David is in the wilderness of Engedi." ² Then Saul took three thousand chosen men out of all Israel, and went to seek David and his men in front of the Wildgoats' Rocks. ³ And he came to the sheepfolds by the way, where there was a cave; and Saul went in to relieve himself. Now David and his men were sitting in the innermost parts of the cave. ⁴ And the men of David said to him, "Here is the day of which the LORD said to you, 'Behold, I will give your enemy into your hand, and you shall do to him as it shall seem good to you.'" Then David arose and stealthily cut off the skirt of Saul's robe. ⁵ And afterward David's heart smote him, because he had cut off Saul's skirt. ⁶ He said to his men, "The LORD forbid that I should do this thing to my lord, the LORD'S anointed, to put forth my hand against him, seeing he is the LORD'S

anointed." ⁷ So David persuaded his men with these words, and did not permit them to attack Saul. And Saul rose up and left the cave, and went upon his way.

After the narrow escape from Saul in the gorge David and his men retreat still deeper into the desert and establish their next base in the fortresslike cliff that towers over the Dead Sea beside the important oasis on the western shore, Engedi. When Saul takes up the pursuit again, he comes first to that cliff which dominates the road from Hebron to Engedi, most descriptively called "The Wildgoats' Rocks." This region is honeycombed with caves, many with sheepfolds at their entrances. In such a cave David and his men take refuge and remain unseen by Saul as he comes in from the daylight. As the king now covers his feet, David has his tormenter in his power! This is not just an accident, his men insist; it is the Lord who has so arranged it! Without replying or indicating whether he agrees or not, David stealthily approaches the king, sword in hand—yet he does nothing but cut off the fringe of the royal mantle. Even at that, the feeling that by this act of his he has violated the holy person of the anointed of the Lord arouses David's sensitive conscience. His men, by contrast, are by no means satisfied with such a "half measure" against their enemy. Had David permitted, they would have executed "justice" on Saul themselves, using the "God-given" golden opportunity to the fullest.

David's Magnanimous Speech to His Foe   *8-15*

⁸ Afterward David also arose, and went out of the cave, and called after Saul, "My lord the king!" And when Saul looked behind him, David bowed with his

face to the earth, and did obeisance. [9] And David said to Saul, "Why do you listen to the words of men who say, 'Behold, David seeks your hurt'? [10] Lo, this day your eyes have seen how the LORD gave you today into my hand in the cave; and some bade me kill you, but I[x] spared you. I said, 'I will not put forth my hand against my lord; for he is the LORD'S anointed.' [11] See, my father, see the skirt of your robe in my hand; for by the fact that I cut off the skirt of your robe, and did not kill you, you may know and see that there is no wrong or treason in my hands. I have not sinned against you, though you hunt my life to take it. [12] May the LORD judge between me and you, may the LORD avenge me upon you; but my hand shall not be against you. [13] As the proverb of the ancients says, 'Out of the wicked comes forth wickedness'; but my hand shall not be against you. [14] After whom has the king of Israel come out? After whom do you pursue? After a dead dog! After a flea! [15] May the LORD therefore be judge, and give sentence between me and you, and see to it, and plead my cause, and deliver me from your hand."

[x] Gk Syr Tg: Heb *you*

Why did David refuse to take justice into his own hands, when, as he himself states, the Lord had given his enemy into his hand? The answer becomes clear in David's speech to Saul after the king has gone forth from the cave and David has disclosed himself to him. The reason is that David has come to realize that this accidental confrontation is not a golden opportunity for one human being to square accounts with another human being who has wronged him. Rather, he realizes that the Lord has sanctified the person of his enemy;

he is the inviolable anointed of the Lord. And even though this person has misused his office and powers to persecute him, the Lord is the judge between him and his opponent; He will plead David's case, establish justice, and vindicate him. This belief that God has taken his case into His hands is what gives David such freedom from self-service that he is able to act contrary to human expectations. He is able to refrain from attempting to play the role of God and is content to recognize his enemy as another human being standing alongside of him under God.

Saul Is Overcome by David's Magnanimity   *16-22*

16 When David had finished speaking these words to Saul, Saul said, "Is this your voice, my son David?" And Saul lifted up his voice and wept. 17 He said to David, "You are more righteous than I; for you have repaid me good, whereas I have repaid you evil. 18 And you have declared this day how you have dealt well with me, in that you did not kill me when the LORD put me into your hands. 19 For if a man finds his enemy, will he let him go away safe? So may the LORD reward you with good for what you have done to me this day. 20 And now, behold, I know that you shall surely be king, and that the kingdom of Israel shall be established in your hand. 21 Swear to me therefore by the LORD that you will not cut off my descendants after me, and that you will not destroy my name out of my father's house." 22 And David swore this to Saul. Then Saul went home; but David and his men went up to the stronghold.

David's unheard-of goodwill penetrates to the very depths of Saul's being, and recognizing David's innocence and genuine love for him, the king breaks out into weeping. His opponent's case has proved beyond all question to be the more righteous one. But more important, Saul now realizes, as Jonathan did before, that he himself has been truly rejected by the Lord and that David will be the next king of Israel. Therefore he begs David to swear a solemn oath that even as king he will deal kindly with his descendants. After David complies, we might expect some sort of statement as this, "Thus there was a reconciliation between David and Saul, and they both returned to the palace at Gibeah." Instead of that we hear that Saul indeed goes back to the palace but David and his men return to their hideout. We are not to draw the unwarranted conclusion that David's magnanimous deed ushers in a sort of millenium for everyone concerned. No, things remain much as they were before. Saul's professed change of heart cannot, it seems, be relied on. David's story will have to end with the triumph of him who is made perfect by suffering, for David is, even in his exaltation, merely a type of the Anointed One who could enter into His glory only by His self-sacrifice.

THE LORD KEEPS DAVID FROM POLLUTING HIMSELF WITH BLOOD AND REVEALS HIS LIFE'S SECRET — THROUGH A WOMAN   25

Though the temptation that comes to David in this chapter might seem at first glance less enticing for David than the preceding ones, which came when David was fleeing Saul's hot pursuit, nevertheless in some ways it is much more dangerous because here David is tempted to put forth his hand, not against the anointed of the Lord, but against an avaricious and stubborn fool whose shameless behavior toward his benefactor David cried aloud for punishment. It is the Lord, however, who prevents David from taking vengeance with his own hand. The Lord employs as the instrument of His guidance the foolish man's own beautiful and intelligent wife, Abigail.

Nabal Refuses to Pay for David's Protection   *25:1-13*

[1] **Now Samuel died; and all Israel assembled and mourned for him, and they buried him in his house at Ramah.**

Then David rose and went down to the wilderness of Paran. [2] **And there was a man in Maon, whose business was in Carmel. The man was very rich; he had three thousand sheep and a thousand goats. He was shearing his sheep in Carmel.** [3] **Now the name of the man was Nabal, and the name of his wife Abigail. The woman was of good understanding and beautiful, but the man was churlish and ill-behaved; he was a Calebite.** [4] **David heard in the wilderness that Nabal was shearing his sheep.** [5] **So David sent ten young men; and David said to the young men, "Go up to Carmel, and go to Nabal, and greet him in my name.** [6] **And thus you shall salute him: 'Peace be to you, and peace be to your house, and peace be to all that you have.** [7] **I hear that you have shearers; now your shepherds have been with us, and we did them no harm, and they missed nothing, all the time they were in Carmel.** [8] **Ask your young men, and they will tell you. Therefore let my young men find favor in your eyes; for we come on a feast day. Pray, give whatever you have at hand to your servants and to your son David.'"**

⁹ When David's young men came, they said all
this to Nabal in the name of David; and then they
waited. ¹⁰ And Nabal answered David's servants,
"Who is David? Who is the son of Jesse? There are
many servants nowadays who are breaking away
from their masters. ¹¹ Shall I take my bread and my
water and my meat that I have killed for my shearers,
and give it to men who come from I do not know
where?" ¹² So David's young men turned away, and
came back and told him all this. ¹³ And David said
to his men, "Every man gird on his sword!" And
every man of them girded on his sword; David also
girded on his sword; and about four hundred men
went up after David, while two hundred remained
with the baggage.

The brief note concerning the death of Samuel
should not be considered a mere misplaced gloss; in
its present context it also serves to indicate that, with
Samuel the kingmaker dead, the time is approaching
when the uncrowned David is to replace the rejected,
though still crowned Saul.

The wealth of Nabal, the Calebite sheikh, was
measured by the size of his flocks: 3,000 sheep, 1,000
goats. No wonder that the high point of the year for
him and his shepherds, the shearing-festival, was celebrated with a public feast comparable to the great
harvest and grape-gathering festivals in the agricultural regions of Palestine. It is also not surprising that
David, who had been protecting Nabal and his people
from desert marauders, takes advantage of this opportunity to ask for the customary "present" in return
for the protection of the sheikh's property, sending ten
men to respectfully pick up sorely needed rations.

Nabal's response is marked not only by base ingratitude and brutal insults, but more important, by a complete lack of understanding for David's position and destiny. He calls him a runaway slave. The result is that, after David's men have relayed this response back to their master, David gives the command, "Every man gird on his sword!" He is determined to settle scores with this fool immediately.

The Intervention of Abigail   *14-31*

¹⁴ But one of the young men told Abigail, Nabal's wife, "Behold, David sent messengers out of the wilderness to salute our master; and he railed at them. ¹⁵ Yet the men were very good to us, and we suffered no harm, and we did not miss anything when we were in the fields, as long as we went with them; ¹⁶ they were a wall to us both by night and by day, all the while we were with them keeping the sheep. ¹⁷ Now therefore know this and consider what you should do; for evil is determined against our master and against all his house, and he is so ill-natured that one cannot speak to him."

¹⁸ Then Abigail made haste, and took two hundred loaves, and two skins of wine, and five sheep ready dressed, and five measures of parched grain, and a hundred clusters of raisins, and two hundred cakes of figs, and laid them on asses. ¹⁹ And she said to her young men, "Go on before me; behold, I come after you." But she did not tell her husband Nabal. ²⁰ And as she rode on the ass, and came down under cover of the mountain, behold, David and his men came down toward her; and she met them. ²¹ Now David had said, "Surely in vain have I guarded all that this fellow has in the wilderness, so that nothing

was missed of all that belonged to him; and he has returned me evil for good. [22] God do so to David [y] and more also, if by morning I leave so much as one male of all who belong to him.''

[23] When Abigail saw David, she made haste, and alighted from the ass, and fell before David on her face, and bowed to the ground. [24] She fell at his feet and said, "Upon me alone, my lord, be the guilt; pray let your handmaid speak in your ears, and hear the words of your handmaid. [25] Let not my lord regard this ill-natured fellow, Nabal; for as his name is, so is he; Nabal [z] is his name, and folly is with him; but I your handmaid did not see the young men of my lord, whom you sent. [26] Now then, my lord, as the LORD lives, and as your soul lives, seeing the LORD has restrained you from bloodguilt, and from taking vengeance with your own hand, now then let your enemies and those who seek to do evil to my lord be as Nabal. [27] And now let this present which your servant has brought to my lord be given to the young men who follow my lord. [28] Pray forgive the trespass of your handmaid; for the LORD will certainly make my lord a sure house, because my lord is fighting the battles of the LORD; and evil shall not be found in you so long as you live. [29] If men rise up to pursue you and to seek your life, the life of my lord shall be bound in the bundle of the living in the care of the LORD your God; and the lives of your enemies he shall sling out as from the hollow of a sling. [30] And when the LORD has done to my lord according to all the good that he has spoken concerning you, and has appointed you prince over Israel, [31] my lord shall have no cause of grief, or pangs of conscience, for

[y] Gk Compare Syr: Heb *the enemies of David*   [z] That is *fool*

having shed blood without cause or for my lord taking vengeance himself. And when the LORD has dealt well with my lord, then remember your handmaid."

Meanwhile Nabal's intelligent wife, who had been utterly unaware of the crisis, learns of the attack that threatens their camp, a camp now rendered entirely defenseless by the festive carousing. Only swift action can avert disaster. She therefore quickly readies a ration of provisions, including, beside the staples of bread, wine, and mutton, such delicacies as parched grain, raisins, and figs, sending them on ahead of herself to hopefully placate the would-be attackers. We hear nothing of the effect of the gifts; we hear only David's angry soliloquy (spoken while Abigail is descending, under cover of a mountain, to what would be a rather sudden confrontation with him). David's words dramatize the seriousness of the situation: he will not leave any male alive; he is so convinced of the righteousness of his cause that there is no trace of any of the hesitancy that marked his approach to king Saul in the cave. Then suddenly they meet: David and Abigail, the wealthy sheikh's wife. Abigail most respectfully bows before David as if he were not an outlaw with a price on his head but a noble and royal personage, speaking a speech that is a masterpiece of oratorical pleading (just because of its agitated, breathless compilation of a dozen and one logical reasons why David should desist from his purpose!). Hers, she insists, is the guilt; she did not see David's messengers. As for Nabal (*nabal* in Hebrew means "fool"), he is so true to his name and so foolish in nature (a neat play on words!) that he should be disregarded! In fact, Abigail calls on David to look to the future when Nabal, as well as all of David's enemies,

197

will have been "slung out as from the hollow of a sling" (what rhetoric!) and David will be "the prince over Israel" and will have an enduring dynasty, a sure house (cf. 2 Sam. 7:13). That David is even now fighting the Lord's battles in holy wars is proof of what his real destiny is to be, that is, that his life "shall be bound in the bundle of the living in the care of the LORD." Does he then dare to ruin or at least mar this future by shedding blood in a policy of self-help, not permitting the Lord to be his avenger? In very fact, it is the Lord, Abigail claims, who is even now, this very moment — through Abigail — restraining him from staining his hands with blood and from attempting to save himself from his adversaries with his own hand. The artful speech ends with a telling punch line: P. S., "When the LORD has dealt well with my lord, then remember your handmaid."

David Marries Abigail   *32-43*

³² And David said to Abigail, "Blessed be the LORD, the God of Israel, who sent you this day to meet me! ³³ Blessed be your discretion, and blessed be you, who have kept me this day from bloodguilt and from avenging myself with my own hand! ³⁴ For as surely as the LORD the God of Israel lives, who has restrained me from hurting you, unless you had made haste and come to meet me, truly by morning there had not been left to Nabal so much as one male." ³⁵ Then David received from her hand what she had brought him; and he said to her, "Go up in peace to your house; see, I have hearkened to your voice, and I have granted your petition."

³⁶ And Abigail came to Nabal; and, lo, he was holding a feast in his house, like the feast of a king.

And Nabal's heart was merry within him, for he was very drunk; so she told him nothing at all until the morning light. [37] And in the morning, when the wine had gone out of Nabal, his wife told him these things, and his heart died within him, and he became as a stone. [38] And about ten days later the LORD smote Nabal; and he died.

[39] When David heard that Nabal was dead, he said, "Blessed be the LORD who has avenged the insult I received at the hand of Nabal, and has kept back his servant from evil; the LORD has returned the evil-doing of Nabal upon his own head." Then David sent and wooed Abigail, to make her his wife. [40] And when the servants of David came to Abigail at Carmel, they said to her, "David has sent us to you to take you to him as his wife." [41] And she rose and bowed with her face to the ground, and said, "Behold, your handmaid is a servant to wash the feet of the servants of my lord." [42] And Abigail made haste and rose and mounted on an ass, and her five maidens attended her; she went after the messengers of David, and became his wife.

[43] David also took Ahinoam of Jezreel; and both of them became his wives.

That Abigail's speech did make its point becomes clear when we hear David's response. He has been awakened to the frightful danger in which he had been standing; he had almost fallen into a terrible trap. Awakened to the danger, he now breaks out into blessing both the Lord and this prudent woman whom the Lord has sent to keep him from engaging in a punitive expedition to right his personal insults and neglecting the higher tasks to which he has been called.

The account is brought to a fitting conclusion with brief but bold strokes. The next morning the rich sheepherder has sobered up enough from his carousal to be able to hear a report of what has happened, a report that so shocks him that he, so to say, suffers a stroke ("his heart died within him"); after 10 days he falls by the hand of the Lord. David then blesses the Lord, who has fully accomplished for him what he had been tempted to do by his own hand. No time is lost as David quickly fetches the beautiful and intelligent widow, who comes to him as a lady of state, riding on an ass and accompanied by five maidens — a fitting bride for the future king. The final note (v. 43) about David's wives points out that although Saul's daughter Michal has been taken away from him, the persecuted David is building up a house by means of connections with wealthy and influential families of the land. Instead of judging these marriages by moral standards of a later age, we should follow the storyteller and realize that now the scales are beginning to tip in David's direction.

DAVID SPARES SAUL'S LIFE A SECOND TIME 26

No matter whether Chs. 24 and 26 are two versions of one original event (cf. Introduction, p. 14) or whether they tell of two similar events that were molded by early tradition into one similar pattern of reporting, the differences between them are clear. In Ch. 24 we were dealing with an accidental confrontation of David and Saul, one which put David in complete control of his enemy in the cave. In Ch. 26 we are, by contrast, dealing with a planned foray into the camp of the sleeping enemy and a confrontation that takes place at a distance — a deep gorge separating David and Saul.

200

David Raids Saul's Sleeping Camp   *26:1-12*

¹ Then the Ziphites came to Saul at Gibeah, saying, "Is not David hiding himself on the hill of Hachilah, which is on the east of Jeshimon?" ² So Saul arose and went down to the wilderness of Ziph, with three thousand chosen men of Israel, to seek David in the wilderness of Ziph. ³ And Saul encamped on the hill of Hachilah, which is beside the road on the east of Jeshimon. But David remained in the wilderness; and when he saw that Saul came after him into the wilderness, ⁴ David sent out spies, and learned of a certainty that Saul had come. ⁵ Then David rose and came to the place where Saul had encamped; and David saw the place where Saul lay, with Abner the son of Ner, the commander of his army; Saul was lying within the encampment, while the army was encamped around him.

⁶ Then David said to Ahimelech the Hittite, and to Joab's brother Abishai the son of Zeruiah, "Who will go down with me into the camp to Saul?" And Abishai said, "I will go down with you." ⁷ So David and Abishai went to the army by night; and there lay Saul sleeping within the encampment, with his spear stuck in the ground at his head; and Abner and the army lay around him. ⁸ Then said Abishai to David, "God has given your enemy into your hand this day; now therefore let me pin him to the earth with one stroke of the spear, and I will not strike him twice." ⁹ But David said to Abishai, "Do not destroy him; for who can put forth his hand against the LORD'S anointed, and be guiltless?" ¹⁰ And David said, "As the LORD lives, the LORD will smite him; or his day shall come to die; or he shall go down into battle and

perish. [11] The **LORD** forbid that I should put forth my hand against the **LORD'S** anointed; but take now the spear that is at his head, and the jar of water, and let us go." [12] So David took the spear and the jar of water from Saul's head; and they went away. No man saw it, or knew it, nor did any awake; for they were all asleep, because a deep sleep from the **LORD** had fallen upon them.

This confrontation of David and Saul is not an accident, as was the one in Ch. 24, though it is also occasioned by the Ziphites, who bring Saul news of David's whereabouts as they had done in the earlier instance (23:19 ff.). This time it is David who deliberately sends out spies to learn of Saul's camp and who then, under cover of darkness and accompanied only by his nephew Abishai, goes out to reconnoiter and even enter the camp where the king sleeps, surrounded by three companies of men. David's daring enterprise reminds us of Jonathan's daring exploit (1 Sam. 14:1); it was undoubtedly prompted by the same faith in the Lord, for the purpose of this dangerous foray into Saul's camp was not to harm Saul, but to remove the ill-feeling Saul still harbored against David. An especially deep sleep from the Lord (Gen. 2:21; 15:12) had rendered completely unconscious the royal task force that had come to capture David.

Again, as in Ch. 24, David is tempted by his companion to use the "God-given" opportunity to kill the sleeping king and thus end their miserable existence in exile. No, David replies, Saul is the Lord's Messiah (anointed one), and no one can put forth a hand against him with impunity. Only the Lord can deal with Saul—in His own good time. The royal spear, the well-known constant companion of Saul (see 22:6), together with his water flask, will be a new proof of how groundless Saul's suspicion has been and how righteous David has proved to be. Thus David, without having taken justice into his own hands, leaves the still undisturbed camp of the enemy, trophies in hand.

David's Message to Saul   *13-20*

13 Then David went over to the other side, and stood afar off on the top of the mountain, with a great space between them; 14 and David called to the army, and to Abner the son of Ner, saying, "Will you not answer, Abner?" Then Abner answered, "Who are you that calls to the king?" 15 And David said to Abner, "Are you not a man? Who is like you in Israel? Why then have you not kept watch over your lord the king? For one of the people came in to destroy the king your lord. 16 This thing that you have done is not good. As the LORD lives, you deserve to die, because you have not kept watch over your lord, the LORD'S anointed. And now see where the king's spear is, and the jar of water that was at his head."

17 Saul recognized David's voice, and said, "Is this your voice, my son David?" And David said, "It is my voice, my lord, O king." 18 And he said, "Why does my lord pursue after his servant? For what have I done? What guilt is on my hands? 19 Now therefore let my lord the king hear the words of his servant. If it is the LORD who has stirred you up against me, may he accept an offering; but if it is men, may they be cursed before the LORD, for they have driven me out this day that I should have no share in the heritage of the LORD, saying, 'Go, serve other gods.' 20 Now therefore, let not my blood fall to the earth

away from the presence of the LORD; for the king of Israel has come out to seek my life, [a] **like one who hunts a partridge in the mountains."**

[a] Gk: Heb *a flea* (as in 24. 14)

The second part of the episode, the actual confrontation of David and Saul, also takes place under cover of darkness. Separated from Saul and his sleeping men by a deep gorge, David calls out to them. By shouting Abner's name he succeeds in breaking through their leaden sleep. With humorous sarcasm David chides the sleepyhead commander for inefficiency in guarding the Lord's anointed. David even suggests that the sentence of death ought to be pronounced upon the entire group because of their dereliction of duty, and—as proof of all he said—he calls attention to the fact that the king's spear and water flask are missing. We hear nothing of Abner's consternation; but back in the darkness we hear King Saul call out in response as he recognizes David's voice and is again seized by his old affection for him.

Having gained a hearing in this way, David speaks freely of what was truly burdening his heart all these days of his exile. What, he asks, is the reason for this uninterrupted persecution? If it is (1) David himself who is responsible, let David learn of his guilt from the king. If it is (2) the Lord who has stirred Saul up against David, then let the Lord receive a sacrifice to placate Him. If, however, it is (3) men who are responsible, let curses be uttered against them for driving David from the Promised Land, to die far from the presence of the Lord in a place where he is tempted to serve "other gods." David describes himself as a "partridge in the mountains" hunted by Saul.

Saul Admits His Error   *21-25*

²¹ Then Saul said, "I have done wrong; return, my son David, for I will no more do you harm, because my life was precious in your eyes this day; behold, I have played the fool, and have erred exceedingly." ²² And David made answer, "Here is the spear, O king! Let one of the young men come over and fetch it. ²³ The LORD rewards every man for his righteousness and his faithfulness; for the LORD gave you into my hand today, and I would not put forth my hand against the LORD'S anointed. ²⁴ Behold, as your life was precious this day in my sight, so may my life be precious in the sight of the LORD, and may he deliver me out of all tribulation." ²⁵ Then Saul said to David, "Blessed be you, my son David! You will do many things and will succeed in them." So David went his way, and Saul returned to his place.

Though Saul confesses his folly and invites David to return to Gibeah with him, David takes no note of that invitation in his response, though he asks Saul to send a young man over to fetch the royal spear. Rather, David's concern is with the Lord, who must certainly see that David has justly refused to traffic with intrigue against the king. David's words are, however, not so much a pronouncement of personal moral stainlessness as a direct petition to the Lord for such mercy and undeserved love as David had shown to him who had trespassed against him. What is then significant is that the king thereupon does bless David, giving him an express promise of better days. Thus they part, David going on a path that will take him away from the beloved Promised Land and Saul going to Gibeah and the final crisis that will claim his life.

DAVID IN PHILISTIA

David Takes Refuge with Achish, King of Gath   27:1-4

¹ And David said in his heart, "I shall now perish one day by the hand of Saul; there is nothing better for me than that I should escape to the land of the Philistines; then Saul will despair of seeking me any longer within the borders of Israel, and I shall escape out of his hand." ² So David arose and went over, he and the six hundred men who were with him, to Achish the son of Maoch, king of Gath. ³ And David dwelt with Achish at Gath, he and his men, every man with his household, and David with his two wives, Ahinoam of Jezreel, and Abigail of Carmel, Nabal's widow. ⁴ And when it was told Saul that David had fled to Gath, he sought for him no more.

After David's attempts to remove Saul's ill will toward him have failed, he feels that at any time he may be destroyed by a surprise onslaught and decides that he must get out of Saul's reach. And where could a political refugee from Israel be more safe than in the territory of his native land's traditional enemies? Moreover, there he and his band of outlaws might take up service as mercenaries of King Achish of Gath. If we wonder about the relation of our present story concerning David's ready acceptance by Achish to the earlier incident when his life was endangered as he came to Gath, we must remember that at the earlier time David appeared in Gath as a solitary warrior coming from Saul's court, whereas he now comes as a well-known enemy of the king of Israel, accompanied also by a capable fighting force — all of which could prove to be a distinct asset to the Philistine king.

David Dupes the Philistine King 5-12

⁵ Then David said to Achish, "If I have found favor in your eyes, let a place be given me in one of the country towns, that I may dwell there; for why should your servant dwell in the royal city with you?" ⁶ So that day Achish gave him Ziklag; therefore Ziklag has belonged to the kings of Judah to this day. ⁷ And the number of the days that David dwelt in the country of the Philistines was a year and four months.

⁸ Now David and his men went up, and made raids upon the Geshurites, the Girzites, and the Amalekites; for these were the inhabitants of the land from of old, as far as Shur, to the land of Egypt. ⁹ And David smote the land, and left neither man nor woman alive, but took away the sheep, the oxen, the asses, the camels, and the garments, and came back to Achish. ¹⁰ When Achish asked, "Against whom *ᵇ* have you made a raid today?" David would say, "Against the Negeb of Judah," or "Against the Negeb of the Jerahmeelites," or, "Against the Negeb of the Kenites." ¹¹ And David saved neither man nor woman alive, to bring tidings to Gath, thinking, "Lest they should tell about us, and say, 'So David has done.'" Such was his custom all the while he dwelt in the country of the Philistines. ¹² And Achish trusted David, thinking, "He has made himself utterly abhorred by his people Israel; therefore he shall be my servant always."

ᵇ Gk Vg: Heb lacks *whom*

In a difficult situation that could easily prove disastrous for his future career, David succeeds not only in avoiding losses but in gaining considerable profits for himself and his people. After spending some time at the capital, David begs Achish to assign him and his men to one of the border towns, cleverly conveying the impression that it was too high an honor for him to dwell in the immediate vicinity of the king — prudently, however, not mentioning the crucial fact that only thus would he obtain the freedom of action necessary for playing the double role he had in mind. Achish gives David the border city of Ziklag.

While Achish imagines that David is making himself odious throughout Israel by attacking his former countrymen, David is in fact pursuing a shrewd policy designed to show that he is by no means a traitor to the Israelite cause. He is, in fact, accomplishing what Saul had failed to do; he is exterminating the enemies of the Lord. No prisoners are taken, so that the true state of affairs cannot be reported to Achish, who seems to have been well satisfied with the booty that is brought to him. Though we may be shocked by the brutality of David's raids, the ancient Israelites heard with great delight the story of how David duped the Philistine king and transformed a desperate situation to such an extent that, when the crucial hour would strike, he would be welcomed back to Israel.

SAUL VISITS THE WITCH AT ENDOR 28

David Mobilized for the Philistine Offensive
Against Israel 28:1-2

[1] **In those days the Philistines gathered their forces for war, to fight against Israel. And Achish said to David, "Understand that you and your men are to go out with me in the army."** [2] **David said to**

208

Achish, "Very well, you shall know what your servant can do." And Achish said to David, "Very well, I will make you my bodyguard for life."

As a Philistine vassal, David is summoned to take part in the new campaign of the combined Philistine forces against his own people, Israel. David's response to Achish's mobilization order is purposely ambiguous. Achish, however (unlike the readers and hearers who are already "in the know" and who realize where David's real loyalty lies), has no reason to suspect David. Therefore he understands David's ambiguous response as a promise of faithful service and even promotes him to be his personal bodyguard for life because of it!

An Act of Desperation 3-6

³ Now Samuel had died, and all Israel had mourned for him and buried him in Ramah, his own city. And Saul had put the mediums and the wizards out of the land. ⁴ The Philistines assembled, and came and encamped at Shunem; and Saul gathered all Israel, and they encamped at Gilboa. ⁵ When Saul saw the army of the Philistines, he was afraid, and his heart trembled greatly. ⁶ And when Saul inquired of the LORD, the LORD did not answer him, either by dreams, or by Urim, or by prophets.

While David is becoming deeply involved in the Philistine mobilization, Saul is pictured as caught in a somewhat similar crisis, one to which he, however, proves singularly unequal. Apparently to gain the favor of the Lord, Saul had cut off from the land those who sought to penetrate the secrets of the future by utilizing the supposedly superior knowledge possessed by the spirits of the dead. The narrative seems to share the ancient world's belief in the existence of such spirits (even though it also makes it clear that to invoke them is forbidden by God!), and this problem has occupied interpreters through the ages. In the main, three "explanations" have been advanced. Some say, "The divination described here is a case of divine intervention." Others say, "No, this is a case of demonic intervention." Still others say, "This is pure quackery attempted by the woman." Perhaps there is some truth to each "explanation." At any rate, any adequate explanation must realize that the divination begins, like similar stories, with Saul's superstitious belief in the power of this woman and with the woman's tricks of the trade to communicate with the dead. But then the Lord does intervene, permitting Samuel to appear in some way (it is at this point that the woman shrieks in utter terror). The Lord breaks through the necromantic ceremony (cf. Num. 23 f.) with His authentic message, proclaimed by His faithful prophet, who now again repeats to Saul what he had long since told him (cf. Luke 16:31). It is this message of God which is paramount here; we dare not lose ourselves in speculations about secondary matters concerning the next world, things that are not clearly taught here and, moreover, are beyond our ken.

In order to counter the Philistine strategy which aimed at cutting Israelite territory in two by occupying the Valley of Jezreel, King Saul moves up his lightly armed Israelites through the hill country to Mount Gilboa on the south side of that valley. Two neighboring mountains, Gilboa on the south and the hill of Moreh to the north, are to serve as strongholds and, if necessary, as places of refuge for the two armies. When Saul reconnoiters the enemy camp and thus becomes aware of

210

their vastly superior strength, he is seized by sudden terror and panic. His initial reflex is, it must be granted, a very good one; he wants to find out from God what he is to do. But the Lord does not respond to his search through any of the customary media. The Lord is silent.

*Saul Attempts to Communicate
with the Prophet Samuel*   *7-14*

⁷ Then Saul said to his servants, "Seek out for me a woman who is a medium, that I may go to her and inquire of her." And his servants said to him, "Behold, there is a medium at Endor."

⁸ So Saul disguised himself and put on other garments, and went, he and two men with him; and they came to the woman by night. And he said, "Divine for me by a spirit, and bring up for me whomever I shall name to you." ⁹ The woman said to him, "Surely you know what Saul has done, how he has cut off the mediums and the wizards from the land. Why then are you laying a snare for my life to bring about my death?" ¹⁰ But Saul swore to her by the LORD, "As the LORD lives, no punishment shall come upon you for this thing." ¹¹ Then the woman said, "Whom shall I bring up for you?" He said, "Bring up Samuel for me." ¹² When the woman saw Samuel, she cried out with a loud voice; and the woman said to Saul, "Why have you deceived me? You are Saul." ¹³ The king said to her, "Have no fear; what do you see?" And the woman said to Saul, "I see a god coming up out of the earth." ¹⁴ He said to her, "What is his appearance?" And she said, "An old man is coming up; and he is wrapped in a robe." And Saul knew that it was Samuel, and he bowed with his face to the ground, and did obeisance.

Despite the fact that he has received no response from the Lord, Saul realizes that he must act. In his desperation he resorts to necromancy, the very magic that he himself had only recently forbidden. He certainly does not resort to this pagan method because he has abandoned all relation to the Lord but simply to get a genuine message from the Lord through the faithful prophet of the Lord who in good and evil days had always told him the truth—Samuel. Despite the fact that he had been rejected by this very prophet, Saul now wants to force the Lord to respond to him through the spirit of the dead prophet. And wonder of wonders, the Lord does respond—in a manner unexpected by either the witch or the king!

Saul is disguised as he travels by night on his mysterious mission to Endor. The disguise enables him to pass through the dangerous no-man's-land between the two army camps and to hide his identity from the witch. The witch, in turn, fears that she will suffer ill for performing the forbidden rite of calling up the familiar spirit of the dead. Saul, however, reassures her by an oath sworn in the name of the Lord. He requests that she call up Samuel for him. And then—this is the climax—Samuel actually comes! When the woman sees what even she did not expect to see (the ancient prophet coming up out of the earth), she shrieks in utter terror. Recalling the relations between the prophet and King Saul, she rightly concludes that her disguised consultant is the king of Israel! To Saul's anxious questions about what she is seeing, she answers that she sees a supernatural being coming up out of the earth, an old man wrapped in a cloak such as Samuel wore (and Saul tore!) the very last time Samuel and Saul met (cf. 15:27). The king, who apparently does not see what the woman can see, nevertheless recognizes that he is now in the presence of the prophet and prostrates himself in worship before him.

The Prophet Samuel Speaks *15-19*

¹⁵ Then Samuel said to Saul, "Why have you disturbed me by bringing me up?" Saul answered, "I am in great distress; for the Philistines are warring against me, and God has turned away from me and answers me no more, either by prophets or by dreams; therefore I have summoned you to tell me what I shall do." ¹⁶ And Samuel said, "Why then do you ask me, since the LORD has turned from you and become your enemy? ¹⁷ The LORD has done to you as he spoke by me; for the LORD has torn the kingdom out of your hand, and given it to your neighbor, David. ¹⁸ Because you did not obey the voice of the LORD, and did not carry out his fierce wrath against Amalek, therefore the LORD has done this thing to you this day. ¹⁹ Moreover the LORD will give Israel also with you into the hand of the Philistines; and tomorrow you and your sons shall be with me; the LORD will give the army of Israel also into the hand of the Philistines."

Surprisingly enough, it is Samuel who begins a direct dialog with Saul, asking the king why he has disturbed him and brought him up from his abode of Sheol. His great distress, Saul answers, especially the fact that God had not responded to his urgent request in this crisis, has caused him to turn to the prophet. Samuel, however, refuses to help. The Lord, he says, has become the king's enemy; how does he expect the

213

prophet to change that? More than that, long ago the king sealed his own fate when he disobeyed the Lord's instructions given through His prophet concerning the holy war against Amalek. Therefore what the king does or wants to do in the present crisis will not change things a bit. His entire life's work of establishing Israelite independence will be ruined, for on the morrow the Lord will deliver him, his sons, and all Israel into the hands of the Philistines! The only ray of hope in Samuel's message is one that means little to Saul: the kingship will be given to David, his rival!

After the Proclamation of Doom 20-25

²⁰ Then Saul fell at once full length upon the ground, filled with fear because of the words of Samuel; and there was no strength in him, for he had eaten nothing all day and all night. ²¹ And the woman came to Saul, and when she saw that he was terrified, she said to him, "Behold, your handmaid has hearkened to you; I have taken my life in my hand, and have hearkened to what you have said to me. ²² Now therefore, you also hearken to your handmaid; let me set a morsel of bread before you; and eat, that you may have strength when you go on your way." ²³ He refused, and said, "I will not eat." But his servants, together with the woman, urged him; and he hearkened to their words. So he arose from the earth, and sat upon the bed. ²⁴ Now the woman had a fatted calf in the house, and she quickly killed it, and she took flour, and kneaded it and baked unleavened bread of it, ²⁵ and she put it before Saul and his servants; and they ate. Then they rose and went away that night.

The Lord has forsaken this stubborn man who has so persistently failed to trust and obey Him. The heartbreaking tragedy of it all becomes even clearer from the sequel. Already physically exhausted by a daylong fast and now overcome by the Lord's final verdict, Saul crashes to the ground, felled by Samuel's words of doom like some mighty oak in the forest. In stark contrast to the prophet's unrelenting proclamation of judgment is the sympathetic care the king receives from the witch, who, with the aid of Saul's two servants, restores him to consciousness and gives him the sustenance he will need to meet the demands of the new day. When Saul leaves the witch's house in Endor, still under cover of darkness, we have been prepared for the final act in a great tragedy. As Samuel had said, "The LORD has torn the kingdom out of your hand, and given it to your neighbor, David."

DAVID SENT BACK FROM THE FRONT 29

In order to set the rejected Saul in bold contrast to the ascendant David, our author had interrupted the chronological sequence of narration at 28:2 to tell the episode of the witch at Endor. Now at 29:1 he continues with the story of David's experiences during the mobilization of the Philistine army.

*Achish's Prize Regiment Dismissed
from the Campaign* *29:1-5*

¹ Now the Philistines gathered all their forces at Aphek; and the Israelites were encamped by the fountain which is in Jezreel. ² As the lords of the Philistines were passing on by hundreds and by thousands, and David and his men were passing on in

the rear with Achish, ³ the commanders of the Philistines said, "What are these Hebrews doing here?"
And Achish said to the commanders of the Philistines, "Is not this David, the servant of Saul, king of
Israel, who has been with me now for days and years,
and since he deserted to me I have found no fault
in him to this day." ⁴ But the commanders of the
Philistines were angry with him; and the commanders
of the Philistines said to him, "Send the man back,
that he may return to the place to which you have
assigned him; he shall not go down with us to battle,
lest in the battle he become an adversary to us. For
how could this fellow reconcile himself to his lord?
Would it not be with the heads of the men here? ⁵ Is
not this David, of whom they sing to one another in
dances,

> 'Saul has slain his thousands,
> and David his ten thousands'?"

Though a brief note tells of the gathering of Saul's
army at the spring of Harod at the foot of Mount Gilboa,
our chapter deals primarily with the incidents that ensue
at the Philistine mustering place on the coastal plain
at Aphek (cf. 4:1), where the lords of the Philistines
hold a review of their various contingents. In the parade
David and his men march in the rearguard with their
overlord Achish of Gath. What raises eyebrows among
the reviewing generals is not so much their characteristic dress or arms, but their very presence. After all,
the campaign is against Israel! Achish defends his
vassal against such suspicions by pointing out that
David is a deserter from Saul, a traitor to Israel's cause
who certainly cannot and will not return thither; moreover, he is a dependable soldier who has proved worthy

216

of every confidence Achish ever placed in him. The other generals, however, still consider him a bad security risk, a man possibly looking for an opportunity to sabotage this campaign against Israel and thus reconcile himself to his former master. Achish's protestations to the contrary notwithstanding, these lords of the Philistines angrily demand that Achish send the famous Hebrew back to his border station. These hardheaded generals are not as gullible as Achish. And their judgment of David was (as hearers and readers already know) truer than even they imagined. This entire account is therefore tinged with that typically ironical humor which Israelites relished in recounting episodes of their having deceived their archenemies.

King Achish Again a Comic Buffoon   *6-11*

⁶ Then Achish called David and said to him, "As the LORD lives, you have been honest, and to me it seems right that you should march out and in with me in the campaign; for I have found nothing wrong in you from the day of your coming to me to this day. Nevertheless the lords do not approve of you. ⁷ So go back now; and go peaceably, that you may not displease the lords of the Philistines." ⁸ And David said to Achish, "But what have I done? What have you found in your servant from the day I entered your service until now, that I may not go and fight against the enemies of my lord the king?" ⁹ And Achish made answer to David, "I know that you are as blameless in my sight as an angel of God; nevertheless the commanders of the Philistines have said, 'He shall not go up with us to the battle.' ¹⁰ Now then rise early in the morning with the servants of your lord who came with you; and start early in the morning, and

217

depart as soon as you have light." **11 So David set out
with his men early in the morning, to return to the
land of the Philistines. But the Philistines went up
to Jezreel.**

Achish considers the decision of the other generals
to dismiss one of his prize regiments a painful personal
rebuff, but he knows he dare not oppose the majority
and therefore summons David to delicately break the
"upsetting" news to him. He reports the decision in
words of fulsome praise, even calling on the Lord to
witness the truth of what he is saying, though every
reader and hearer very well knows that what he reports about David's "honesty and loyalty" is simply not
true—so completely has he been taken in by David's
double-dealing. Hence David can most easily—and in
a sense also most genuinely—express his disappointment and resentment at being barred from going to
"fight against the enemies of my lord, the king." Achish,
of course, does not understand that David's plan has
been to sabotage in some way the Philistine operation
against Israel and thus truly to fight against the enemies
of his lord, the king (Saul!). David, however, receives
Achish's renewed and exaggerated assurance that he
is as blameless as "an angel of God." The Greek version
of v. 10 (which includes an additional section, here ital-
icized) highlights Achish's concern lest the high-spirited
warrior feel insulted and be tempted to take revenge
for his dismissal: "Now then rise early in the morning
with the servants of your lord [This lord is really Saul!
Achish is again saying much more than he realizes.]
who came with you, and *go to the place where I have
stationed you and do not cherish resentment in your
heart, for I have a high opinion of you.* So start early

218

in the morning and depart as soon as you have light."
Thus the Philistines and David go their separate ways.
Israelite hearers undoubtedly enjoyed the comic aspect
of the story to the fullest and praised the Lord for
rescuing David from a potentially dangerous situation
in Philistine employ.

A CAMPAIGN AGAINST THE AMALEKITES 30

David's Border Town Sacked by Desert Raiders   30:1-6

¹ Now when David and his men came to Ziklag
on the third day, the Amalekites had made a raid
upon the Negeb and upon Ziklag. They had overcome
Ziklag, and burned it with fire, ² and taken captive
the women and all *c* who were in it, both small and
great; they killed no one, but carried them off, and
went their way. ³ And when David and his men came
to the city, they found it burned with fire, and their
wives and sons and daughters taken captive. ⁴ Then
David and the people who were with him raised their
voices and wept, until they had no more strength to
weep. ⁵ David's two wives also had been taken captive,
Ahinoam of Jezreel, and Abigail the widow of Nabal
of Carmel. ⁶ And David was greatly distressed; for
the people spoke of stoning him, because all the people were bitter in soul, each for his sons and daughters. But David strengthened himself in the LORD
his God.

   c Gk: Heb lacks *and all*

Unlike the preceding somewhat lighthearted episode (Ch. 29), the present chapter tells of the grim Amal-

ekite raid that, with one fell swoop, threatens with ir-
retrievable ruin all of David's past achievements as well
as his hopes for the future. Taking advantage of David's
absence from his border post, the Amalekites make so
successful a surprise attack that all persons can be
carried off, perhaps for eventual sale on the Egyptian
slave market. When David's men return to find only
smoking ruins, their utter hopelessness is expressed
not only in such copious weeping as dries up the very
fountains of their tears but, more seriously, in a bitter
feeling that David is really responsible for this disaster
by reason of an incompetence that left their city exposed to marauding bands while they were gone on
a wild-goose chase up north with "allies" who finally
dismissed them. David does not know what to do; all
of his brilliant planning and felicitous opportunism has
fallen round his ears. He, of course, does not know that
the people have not been killed and that the situation
can be mended. He can therefore expect nothing but
savage mutiny, which may well end with his being
stoned by his own bitter men. More than that, he does
not even know exactly who the enemies are, to say
nothing about where they might be.

David Pursues and Overtakes the Amalekites   *7-20*

**⁷ And David said to Abiathar the priest, the son
of Ahimelech, "Bring me the ephod." So Abiathar
brought the ephod to David. ⁸ And David inquired
of the LORD, "Shall I pursue after this band? Shall
I overtake them?" He answered him, "Pursue; for
you shall surely overtake and shall surely rescue."
⁹ So David set out, and the six hundred men who were
with him, and they came to the brook Besor, where**

those stayed who were left behind. ¹⁰ But David went on with the pursuit, he and four hundred men; two hundred stayed behind, who were too exhausted to cross the brook Besor.

¹¹ They found an Egyptian in the open country, and brought him to David; and they gave him bread and he ate; they gave him water to drink, ¹² and they gave him a piece of cake of figs and two clusters of raisins. And when he had eaten, his spirit revived; for he had not eaten bread or drunk water for three days and three nights. ¹³ And David said to him, "To whom do you belong? And where are you from?" He said, "I am a young man of Egypt, servant to an Amalekite; and my master left me behind because I fell sick three days ago. ¹⁴ We had made a raid upon the Negeb of the Cherethites and upon that which belongs to Judah and upon the Negeb of Caleb; and we burned Ziklag with fire." ¹⁵ And David said to him, "Will you take me down to this band?" And he said, "Swear to me by God, that you will not kill me, or deliver me into the hands of my master, and I will take you down to this band."

¹⁶ And when he had taken him down, behold, they were spread abroad over all the land, eating and drinking and dancing, because of all the great spoil they had taken from the land of the Philistines and from the land of Judah. ¹⁷ And David smote them from twilight until the evening of the next day; and not a man of them escaped, except four hundred young men, who mounted camels and fled. ¹⁸ David recovered all that the Amalekites had taken; and David rescued his two wives. ¹⁹ Nothing was missing, whether small or great, sons or daughters, spoil or anything that had been taken; David brought back

all. ²⁰ David also captured all the flocks and herds; and the people drove those cattle before him,ᵈ and said, "This is David's spoil."

ᵈ Cn: Heb *they drove before those cattle*

At the very time when he is utterly dejected, David strengthens himself "in the LORD his God." He lives by faith, not faith in himself and in his capabilities to deal with the situation but faith in God's word as he receives it through the Lord's priest, Abiathar, in the form of a gracious promise. The Lord promises David that he will most assuredly overtake the enemy and rescue the captives. One third of his men, however, are so exhausted by the three days' forced march from Aphek that they are unable to continue farther than the brook Besor, a watercourse that divides the sown area to the north from the truly desert region to the south. They are left as a kind of garrison on the banks of the watercourse while David continues his pursuit with those in the best physical condition.

The vivid incident involving the Egyptian slave who is found lying half-dead in the desert indicates that the Lord is removing every obstacle from David's path, for this slave is able to give exact information about the raiders and to guide David and his men to the Amalekite hideaway. There, by exploiting the element of surprise, David and his soldiers are able to recover all that the Amalekites had taken on their recent raids. The victory is complete; only a detachment of camel-riding cavalrymen is able to escape. What might well have proved to be a fatal failure of David's generalship turns out to be only a brief setback, from which David effects a complete recovery.

222

A Wise Division of the Spoils 21-31

²¹ Then David came to the two hundred men, who had been too exhausted to follow David, and who had been left at the brook Besor; and they went out to meet David and to meet the people who were with him; and when David drew near to the people he saluted them. ²² Then all the wicked and base fellows among the men who had gone with David said, "Because they did not go with us, we will not give them any of the spoil which we have recovered, except that each man may lead away his wife and children, and depart." ²³ But David said, "You shall not do so, my brothers, with what the LORD has given us; he has preserved us and given into our hand the band that came against us. ²⁴ Who would listen to you in this matter? For as his share is who goes down into the battle, so shall his share be who stays by the baggage; they shall share alike." ²⁵ And from that day forward he made it a statute and an ordinance for Israel to this day.

²⁶ When David came to Ziklag, he sent part of the spoil to his friends, the elders of Judah, saying, "Here is a present for you from the spoil of the enemies of the LORD"; ²⁷ it was for those in Bethel, in Ramoth of the Negeb, in Jattir, ²⁸ in Aroer, in Siphmoth, in Eshtemoa, ²⁹ in Racal, in the cities of the Jerahmeelites, in the cities of the Kenites, ³⁰ in Hormah, in Borashan, in Athach, ³¹ in Hebron, for all the places where David and his men had roamed.

David does not look upon either the victory or the spoils he won as belonging to himself or to his men. When therefore the baser men among those who had gone on the pursuit propose to keep the booty for themselves, David vetoes this proposal as being contrary to the will of the Lord, who had given them both the victory and the booty, which they must share as brothers. This decision dampens the greed of these sons of Belial, builds up the morale of the rank and file of his men, and becomes a precedent (cf. Num. 31:27) remembered in the couplet:

As the share of the one who goes down into battle,
So is the share of the one who stays with the baggage.

David's pursuit of the Amalekites is not considered an official holy war such as Saul the king had fought; there is therefore no ban on all booty. This is why David as leader of a raid receives the customary first portion of the booty when the people drive flocks and herds before him and designate them as "David's spoil" (v. 20). David is free to use this portion as he wishes, and he wisely uses it to repay the hospitality he had previously enjoyed in various Judean villages south of Hebron. This ought not be considered mere human politicking; David shows his religious attitude also at this point by accompanying the gifts with the message: "Here is a present for you from the spoil of the enemies of the LORD." Thus we see David fighting the Lord's battles and establishing already now the foundations of a kingdom that will extend even beyond his own empire to the kingdom of great David's greater son.

SAUL'S TRAGIC END 31

The previous episodes have prepared us for this final chapter in the life of Saul, his death in the battle

224

of Mount Gilboa. Instead of emphasizing Saul's guilt as the cause of the disaster (cf. 1 Chron. 10:13 f.), our account illustrates the heroism of Israel's first king in the midst of a hopeless tragedy: even the horrifying account of his body's shameful mutilation ends with an act of heroic bravery inspired by the memory of Saul's great days, performed in honor of Israel's first king.

The Tragic Battle of Mount Gilboa   31:1-6

[1] Now the Philistines fought against Israel; and the men of Israel fled before the Philistines, and fell slain on Mount Gilboa. [2] And the Philistines overtook Saul and his sons; and the Philistines slew Jonathan and Abinadab and Malchishua, the sons of Saul. [3] The battle pressed hard upon Saul, and the archers found him; and he was badly wounded by the archers. [4] Then Saul said to his armor-bearer, "Draw your sword, and thrust me through with it, lest these uncircumcised come and thrust me through and make sport of me." But his armor-bearer would not; for he feared greatly. Therefore Saul took his own sword, and fell upon it. [5] And when his armor-bearer saw that Saul was dead, he also fell upon his sword, and died with him. [6] Thus Saul died, and his three sons, and his armor-bearer, and all his men, on the same day together.

The description of the battle begins at the point where the Israelite battle line crumbles and a bloody pursuit begins. It seems, however, that Saul, his sons, and his professional army ("his men," in contrast to the people's army of conscripts, who had already fled) still fought on until they, too, were overwhelmed. Saul is finally unable to escape; he is forced to witness the

225

slaying of three of his sons, including Jonathan, before his own turn comes. One gets the impression from the description that the archers first "find him" and wound him severely. That is the reason why he asks his loyal armor-bearer to give him the *coup de grâce,* a blow which would put him out of his misery and prevent the uncircumcised Philistines from abusing their helpless but conscious royal captive. But the armor-bearer refuses to harm the sacrosanct person of the anointed of the Lord, with the result that Saul must dispatch himself, his example being then followed by his loyal armor-bearer. It seems that Saul's death did not mean, however, the immediate cessation of the resistance put up by his loyal professionals. They continued to fight round about the body of their fallen king until nightfall, for we hear that it was only the next morning that Saul's corpse was found by the Philistines.

The Results of the Defeat   7-10

7 And when the men of Israel who were on the other side of the valley and those beyond the Jordan saw that the men of Israel had fled and that Saul and his sons were dead, they forsook their cities and fled; and the Philistines came and dwelt in them.

8 On the morrow, when the Philistines came to strip the slain, they found Saul and his three sons fallen on Mount Gilboa. 9 And they cut off his head, and stripped off his armor, and sent messengers throughout the land of the Philistines, to carry the good news to their idols *e* and to the people. 10 They put his armor in the temple of Ashtaroth; and they fastened his body to the wall of Bethshan.

e Gk Compare 1 Chron. 10. 9: Heb *to the house of their idols*

The fall of the nation's great bulwark against the Philistines is a national catastrophe. Panic seizes the Israelite tribes north of the valley of Jezreel in Galilee as well as those east of the Jordan, and they flee their very homes. The next morning the customary stripping of the vanquished takes place, and Saul's body is shamefully mutilated. Messengers are sent with "the good news" to the temples and people of Philistia; Saul's armor and weapons are taken as trophies to the temple of Astarte (perhaps at Ashkelon or in nearby Bethshan, where excavators have found such a temple). The bodies of Saul and his sons are impaled on the walls of Bethshan, purposely exposed between heaven and earth to make the defilement as public and shameful as possible.

Saul's Body Heroically Rescued
from the Philistines   *11-13*

[11] But when the inhabitants of Jabesh-gilead heard what the Philistines had done to Saul, [12] all the valiant men arose, and went all night, and took the body of Saul and the bodies of his sons from the wall of Bethshan; and they came to Jabesh and burnt them there. [13] And they took their bones and buried them under the tamarisk tree in Jabesh, and fasted seven days.

The disgraceful mutilation scene is relieved at the end of our chapter by a scene of truly touching human sympathy. At a moment when most Israelites are paralyzed by panic, the inhabitants of the Jordan valley town of Jabesh-gilead recall that it was Saul who had once heroically rescued them from the Ammonites (Ch. 11), and they therefore, with genuine chivalry, risk their

227

lives in a night raid to rescue the corpses from the wall and bring them back to Jabesh for honorable burial under the sacred tamarisk of their city, having removed the defilement of the exposure by a rather uncustomary burning of the bodies. Thus our story ends with an account not of disgrace but of honor for the anointed of the Lord. The story of Saul had begun with his being honored by the prophet Samuel (Ch. 10), and now, even though the main part of the story is filled with the tragedy of his fall from God, it ends with his being honored, significantly, at the same place where he had won his first unsoiled victory. Truly a fitting end to the story of Israel's first king!

It is nevertheless true that Saul's end was a frightful one, for a suicide says "No" in the strongest way possible to men, to God, and to himself. To this dead end Saul had come. At the same time, however, we must realize that this tragic story is only part of a greater story of a greater Anointed of the Lord and that even David's story climaxes in Him who, in the fullness of times, was exposed on the accursed tree, buried—and rose again. That is the ultimate context of our chapter.

DAVID LAMENTS
HIS ENEMY'S FALL   2 SAMUEL 1

The Amalekite Messenger's Report of Saul's Death   1:1-16

¹ **After the death of Saul, when David had returned from the slaughter of the Amalekites, David remained two days in Ziklag; ² and on the third day, behold, a man came from Saul's camp, with his clothes rent and earth upon his head. And when he came to David, he fell to the ground and did obeisance. ³ David**

said to him, "Where do you come from?" And he said to him, "I have escaped from the camp of Israel." ⁴ And David said to him, "How did it go? Tell me." And he answered, "The people have fled from the battle, and many of the people also have fallen and are dead; and Saul and his son Jonathan are also dead." ⁵ Then David said to the young man who told him, "How do you know that Saul and his son Jonathan are dead?" ⁶ And the young man who told him said, "By chance I happened to be on Mount Gilboa; and there was Saul leaning upon his spear; and lo, the chariots and the horsemen were close upon him. ⁷ And when he looked behind him, he saw me, and called to me. And I answered, 'Here I am.' ⁸ And he said to me, 'Who are you?' I answered him, 'I am an Amalekite.' ⁹ And he said to me, 'Stand beside me and slay me; for anguish has seized me, and yet my life still lingers.' ¹⁰ So I stood beside him, and slew him, because I was sure that he could not live after he had fallen; and I took the crown which was on his head and the armlet which was on his arm, and I have brought them here to my lord."

¹¹ Then David took hold of his clothes, and rent them; and so did all the men who were with him; ¹² and they mourned and wept and fasted until evening for Saul and for Jonathan his son and for the people of the LORD and for the house of Israel, because they had fallen by the sword. ¹³ And David said to the young man who told him, "Where do you come from?" And he answered, "I am the son of a sojourner, an Amalekite." ¹⁴ David said to him, "How is it you were not afraid to put forth your hand to destroy the LORD'S anointed?" ¹⁵ Then David called one of the young men and said, "Go, fall upon him."

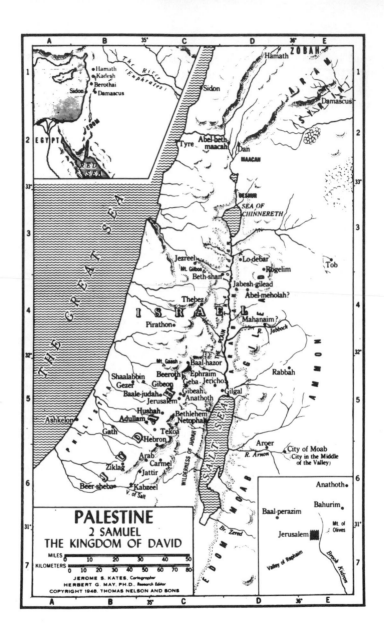

PALESTINE
2 SAMUEL
THE KINGDOM OF DAVID

MILES
0   10   20   30   40   50
KILOMETERS
0 10 20 30 40 50 60 70 80

JEROME S. KATES, *Cartographer*
HERBERT G. MAY, PH.D., *Research Editor*
COPYRIGHT 1948, THOMAS NELSON AND SONS

And he smote him so that he died. ¹⁶ And David said to him, "Your blood be upon your head; for your own mouth has testified against you, saying, 'I have slain the LORD'S anointed.'"

A messenger, his dress already foreboding bad tidings, arrives at David's camp, bows before the future king, without saying a word until David interrogates him. From him David hears not only the essential facts about the catastrophe of Mount Gilboa but also a number of details about Saul's end calculated — so the messenger thinks — to fetch a better-than-customary messenger gift from the long-term enemy of the dead king. The king who had fallen on the suicide weapon, the messenger reports, found the onset of death so unbearably slow that he requested him to terminate his agony. He complied, stripped the body of the royal insignia, and now offers them to David. We immediately recognize that many details of this Amalekite's report do not fit what we have heard in Ch. 31. We can conclude that he is fabricating and that in actual fact he perhaps merely stripped the corpse of the dead king. Others regard this as a varying account concerning the manner of Saul's death (cf. Introduction, pp. 14 ff.). Be that as it may, the main reason why the messenger's own testimony seals his doom is that he has not scrupled to put forth his hand to destroy the Lord's anointed. No Israelite, the report seems to imply, would have done this; this you could expect only of such a resident alien as this Amalekite, a traditional enemy of Israel who evidently was serving in Saul's professional army. Had David not executed this guilty man, the guilt would have rested on his own head; however, David says, the Amalekite's blood will not cry for venge-

231

ance, because he was justly executed. (Cf. 2 Sam. 3:28; Gen. 4:10)

A modern reader finds vv. 11 and 12 concerning the ritual lamentation for Saul an interruption in the rather smoothly flowing narrative about David's interrogation and punishment of the Amalekite. This modern obsession for a chronologically ordered narrative was apparently not shared by the ancient narrators who, for sound artistic and theological reasons, wished to emphasize that David and his men gave themselves to genuine lamentation for their persecutor Saul and for the Israelite dead, once they had been convinced by the insignia of the truth of the messenger's report.

David's Elegy on the Death of Saul and Jonathan   17-27

[17] And David lamented with this lamentation over Saul and Jonathan his son, [18] and he said it[a] should be taught to the people of Judah; behold, it is written in the Book of Jashar.[b] He said:

[19] "Thy glory, O Israel, is slain upon thy high places!
    How are the mighty fallen!
[20] Tell it not in Gath,
    publish it not in the streets of Ashkelon;
  lest the daughters of the Philistines rejoice,
    lest the daughters of the uncircumcised exult.

[21] "Ye mountains of Gilboa,
    let there be no dew or rain upon you,
    nor upsurging of the deep![c]
  For there the shield of the mighty was defiled,
    the shield of Saul, not anointed with oil.

[22] "From the blood of the slain,
    from the fat of the mighty,

---

[a] Gk: Heb *the Bow*   [b] Or *The upright*   [c] Cn: Heb *fields of offerings*

232

the bow of Jonathan turned not back,
    and the sword of Saul returned not empty.

23 "Saul and Jonathan, beloved and lovely!
    In life and in death they were not divided;
they were swifter than eagles,
    they were stronger than lions.

24 "Ye daughters of Israel, weep over Saul,
    who clothed you daintily in scarlet,
    who put ornaments of gold upon your apparel.

25 "How are the mighty fallen
    in the midst of the battle!

"Jonathan lies slain upon thy high places.
26   I am distressed for you, my brother Jonathan;
    very pleasant have you been to me;
    your love to me was wonderful,
    passing the love of women.

27 "How are the mighty fallen,
    and the weapons of war perished!"

David's elegy over Saul and Jonathan has rightly been considered one of the finest pieces of literature of all time. Its superscription shows that it was subsequently sung by the people (to accompany, some think, military training such as archery practice). It was also later collected into a poetry anthology called "The Book of Jashar" (cf. Joshua 10:13). This superscription gives us an insight into the literary path which this elegy, like much of the material in the books of Samuel, traveled: first, its original oral invention as a genuine lament; then, subsequent oral recital by others; collection of it in a written form into an anthology; finally, its incor-

233

poration into such a composite narrative as extends from Joshua through 2 Kings. (Cf. Introduction, pp. 14 ff.)

The plaintive lilt of the lament is clearest, of course, in the original Hebrew. But neither translation nor the fact that the lament conforms to a traditional pattern prevents it from speaking forcefully to us today. In the ancient world the dead were ritually lamented upon death according to a more or less fixed pattern that included the following traditional elements: cries of woe ("How are the mighty fallen!"), an expression of the lamenter's own bitter lot ("I am distressed for you, my brother Jonathan"), a recital of the deeds of the dead ("From the blood of the slain . . . the bow of Jonathan turned not back"), a contrast of the glorious past with present misery ("Thy glory, O Israel, is slain upon thy high places"), and, often, a curse upon the cause of the death ("Ye mountains of Gilboa, let there be no dew or rain upon you!").

If we understand that those are the typical elements of such a lament, we are equipped to let the poem itself, with its rich imagery, sink deep into our hearts. It may not be amiss, however, to point out the main sequence of lamentation and a few of the many excellencies in it. Israel's glory was her youth, but how different are things now that they have been slain! Let not the Philistine cities learn of it and rejoice; cursed be the place where Saul fell, his leather shield now lying there without needed care and oiling; let no crops grow there (even today its bare slopes are barren!). Therewith the poem begins to refer directly to Saul and Jonathan, who are celebrated for their prowess and loyalty to one another (despite their different attitudes toward David, they remained loyal to one another, Jonathan obeying his father in the Lord). An especially

234

interesting strophe is that in which the women of Israel are called on to remember how often Saul gave them war booty. But the climax of the elegy is certainly the touching strophe that expresses David's own tender friendship and love for Jonathan.

David received the news of Saul's death not as great good news for himself but as tragic news worthy of lament. Nevertheless, in this entire turn of events the Lord was with David, for Saul's death opens the way for him, as the immediately following episode shows.

David as King

2 Samuel 2 – 8

First Steps in Building the Future Empire 2:1-7

¹ After this David inquired of the LORD, "Shall I go up into any of the cities of Judah?" And the LORD said to him, "Go up." David said, "To which shall I go up?" And he said, "To Hebron." ² So David went up there, and his two wives also, Ahinoam of Jezreel, and Abigail the widow of Nabal of Carmel. ³ And David brought up his men who were with him, every one with his household; and they dwelt in the towns of Hebron. ⁴ And the men of Judah came, and there they anointed David king over the house of Judah.

When they told David, "It was the men of Jabesh-gilead who buried Saul," ⁵ David sent messengers to the men of Jabesh-gilead, and said to them, "May you be blessed by the LORD, because you showed this loyalty to Saul your lord, and buried him! ⁶ Now may the LORD show steadfast love and faithfulness to you! And I will do good to you because you have done this thing. ⁷ Now therefore let your hands be strong, and be valiant; for Saul your lord is dead, and the house of Judah has anointed me king over them."

It is in accordance with the expressly revealed will of the Lord that David and his men now move to Hebron. There at the central shrine of the Judean clans whom he had long since befriended he is elected and anointed king. Though later events would add to this initial office the lordship over many other regions and people, this is the first stone in the large empire structure he was to build. David seems to have remained, for the time being at least, a vassal of the Philistines; in fact, Achish may well have been pleased to see his vassal extending control over the Judean hill country.

David, however, has much more extensive ambitions. That is clear from the message he sends to the men of Jabesh-gilead, a message that not only congratulates them on their respectful burial of the late king but also most diplomatically adds a postscript about his own having been anointed king over Judah. This rather broad hint means: I'm available also for you, if you wish!

Ish-bosheth Made King of Israel by Abner   8-11

⁸ Now Abner the son of Ner, commander of Saul's army, had taken Ish-bosheth the son of Saul, and brought him over to Mahanaim; ⁹ and he made him king over Gilead and the Ashurites and Jezreel and Ephraim and Benjamin and all Israel. ¹⁰ Ish-bosheth, Saul's son, was forty years old when he began to reign over Israel, and he reigned two years. But the house of Judah followed David. ¹¹ And the time that

David was king in Hebron over the house of Judah was seven years and six months.

David's plans for the extension of his rulership to the North are made impossible by Abner, the real power in the North. He takes the initiative and enthrones Ish-bosheth at the relatively secure Transjordanian city of Mahanaim as king over the northern tribes. Since the principle of dynastic succession had not yet been established, Ish-bosheth was by no means recognized immediately at his father's death as the legitimate successor. He proves to be a mere puppet manipulated by Abner. The very form of the name here used (Ish-bosheth: "man of shame") seems to represent an effort to put him in a bad light. In its original form (Ish-baal: "the Lord's man"), the element *baal* did not refer to the Canaanite deity *(Baal)* but to the Lord (cf. 1 Chron. 8:33; 9:39). The obscure notes about Ish-bosheth's 2-year reign alongside David's 7½ years in Hebron can mean either (1) that Abner made his attempt at setting up Saul's dynasty after David had been king in Judah for 5 years or (2) that an original sentence such as "When Ishbaal had been king over Israel for two years, Abner went out from Mahanaim" has been interrupted by what were originally marginal notes about the age of Ish-bosheth and the length of David's rule in Hebron.

The Confrontation at Gibeon   *12-17*

¹² Abner the son of Ner, and the servants of Ish-bosheth the son of Saul, went out from Mahanaim to Gibeon. ¹³ And Joab the son of Zeruiah, and the servants of David, went out and met them at the pool of Gibeon; and they sat down, the one on the one side of the pool, and the other on the other side of the pool.

¹⁴ And Abner said to Joab, "Let the young men arise and play before us." And Joab said, "Let them arise." ¹⁵ Then they arose and passed over by number, twelve for Benjamin and Ish-bosheth the son of Saul, and twelve of the servants of David. ¹⁶ And each caught his opponent by the head, and thrust his sword in his opponent's side; so they fell down together. Therefore that place was called Helkath-hazzurim, *d* which is at Gibeon. ¹⁷ And the battle was very fierce that day; and Abner and the men of Israel were beaten before the servants of David.

d That is *the field of sword-edges*

It is Abner who undertakes a march into Benjaminite territory, approaching the border town of Gibeon at the edge of David's realm. Hence Joab moves up to checkmate him at the pool outside of Gibeon. The initial encounter of the two groups of professional soldiers (this confrontation does not involve the citizen-armies of the South and North!) is in the nature of a test of strength. Abner, in fact, suggests good naturedly to his friend and former colleague at Saul's court that 12 champions from each force come forth for some sort of "wrestling," possibly representative warfare or, more probably, amusement for the two forces. Whether in the ensuing contest the Benjaminites treacherously thrust hidden swords into their opponents' sides or not — one thing is clear: what began as either a friendly contest or representative warfare ends in a bloody battle, the effect of which will be far-reaching for all involved.

A Minor Incident with Great Future Significance   18-23

¹⁸ And the three sons of Zeruiah were there, Joab, Abishai, and Asahel. Now Asahel was as swift

of foot as a wild gazelle; [19] and Asahel pursued Abner, and as he went he turned neither to the right hand nor to the left from following Abner. [20] Then Abner looked behind him and said, "Is it you, Asahel?" And he answered, "It is I." [21] Abner said to him, "Turn aside to your right hand or to your left, and seize one of the young men, and take his spoil." But Asahel would not turn aside from following him. [22] And Abner said again to Asahel, "Turn aside from following me; why should I smite you to the ground? How then could I lift up my face to your brother Joab?" [23] But he refused to turn aside; therefore Abner smote him in the belly with the butt of his spear, so that the spear came out at his back; and he fell there, and died where he was. And all who came to the place where Asahel had fallen and died, stood still.

Joab and his men prove the stronger, and the Benjaminites must flee toward their Transjordanian base. The famous runner among the Judean mercenaries is Asahel, the youngest of David's nephews (the son of David's sister Zeruiah and the brother of Joab and Abishai). His ambition and overconfidence prove his undoing, for he imagines that he can overtake and kill the most important man in the fleeing enemy force, the commander Abner. Abner, overtaken by his fleet-footed pursuer but still conscious of his own superiority in combat, counsels him to be content with an antagonist of lesser rank (perhaps he means to suggest one of the young men whose treacherous action sparked the battle). Moreover, Abner fears that a blood feud will follow if he kills the brother of his old fellow soldier Joab.

The fact that it is the butt of Abner's spear that undoes the challenger can mean either that Asahel's swiftness was so great that when Abner suddenly halted, he caught him nicely on the butt of his spear; or Abner's use of the butt can indicate that he did not mean to kill but merely to put him out of action. But unfortunately it caught Asahel in the soft underpart of the body. In either case, it is clear that Abner wanted by all means to avoid further bloodshed.

The Aftermath of the Skirmish   *24-32*

²⁴ But Joab and Abishai pursued Abner; and as the sun was going down they came to the hill of Ammah, which lies before Giah on the way to the wilderness of Gibeon. ²⁵ And the Benjaminites gathered themselves together behind Abner, and became one band, and took their stand on the top of a hill. ²⁶ Then Abner called to Joab, "Shall the sword devour for ever? Do you not know that the end will be bitter? How long will it be before you bid your people turn from the pursuit of their brethren?" ²⁷ And Joab said, "As God lives, if you had not spoken, surely the men would have given up the pursuit of their brethren in the morning." ²⁸ So Joab blew the trumpet; and all the men stopped, and pursued Israel no more, nor did they fight any more.

²⁹ And Abner and his men went all that night through the Arabah; they crossed the Jordan, and marching the whole forenoon they came to Mahanaim. ³⁰ Joab returned from the pursuit of Abner; and when he had gathered all the people together, there were missing of David's servants nineteen men besides Asahel. ³¹ But the servants of David had slain of Benjamin three hundred and sixty of Abner's men.

³² And they took up Asahel, and buried him in the tomb of his father, which was at Bethlehem. And Joab and his men marched all night, and the day broke upon them at Hebron.

Even victorious Joab must recognize that the sword dare not devour forever; otherwise the sequel will be bitter. Hence when the Benjaminites are collected as a phalanx on one of the hills, Joab finally hearkens to Abner's reasonable arguments. Had Abner not spoken, Joab and his bloodthirsty men would have kept up the pursuit all night. Now, however, Joab relents—for the time being at least. At his signal the fighting is stopped, and both sides return homeward, Abner minus 360 men, Joab minus 20, one of whom, however, was his own brother Asahel, who must be buried on the way back at Bethlehem. The "war" is, however, prolonged, and David keeps getting stronger and stronger, while the house of Saul becomes weaker and weaker.

NEGOTIATIONS TOWARD MAKING DAVID KING ALSO OF THE NORTH   3

Abner Quarrels with His Stooge Ish-bosheth   *1-11*

¹ There was a long war between the house of Saul and the house of David; and David grew stronger and stronger, while the house of Saul became weaker and weaker.

² And sons were born to David at Hebron: his first-born was Amnon, of Ahinoam of Jezreel; ³ and his second, Chileab, of Abigail the widow of Nabal of Carmel; and the third, Absalom the son of Maacah the daughter of Talmai king of Geshur; ⁴ and the

fourth, Adonijah the son of Haggith; and the fifth, Shephatiah the son of Abital; [5] and the sixth, Ithream, of Eglah, David's wife. These were born to David in Hebron.

[6] While there was war between the house of Saul and the house of David, Abner was making himself strong in the house of Saul. [7] Now Saul had a concubine, whose name was Rizpah, the daughter of Aiah; and Ish-bosheth said to Abner, "Why have you gone in to my father's concubine?" [8] Then Abner was very angry over the words of Ish-bosheth, and said, "Am I a dog's head of Judah? This day I keep showing loyalty to the house of Saul your father, to his brothers, and to his friends, and have not given you into the hand of David; and yet you charge me today with a fault concerning a woman. [9] God do so to Abner, and more also, if I do not accomplish for David what the LORD has sworn to him, [10] to transfer the kingdom from the house of Saul, and set up the throne of David over Israel and over Judah, from Dan to Beersheba." [11] And Ish-bosheth could not answer Abner another word, because he feared him.

The list of David's Hebron-born sons (perhaps from an original royal archives document which continues with the Jerusalem-born sons in 5:13-16) is an offense to New Testament Christians whose view of marriage has been completely clarified by our Lord Jesus Christ. In Israel at this time, however, a large family, such as David's, was a concrete sign of divine blessing. In contrast to this large royal family in Hebron the continually deteriorating house of Saul can set only one genuinely superior person: not the king, weak Ish-bosheth, but his uncle, Abner, the real power among the northern tribes. He is accused of having designs on the throne; witness the report that he has gone in unto one of Saul's wives, and after all, the harem of a dead king always passed to his successor (cf. 12:8; 16:20-22; 1 Kings 2:22). In reply, Abner dismisses the serious charge as a trivial old wives' tale. Considering Ish-bosheth's attack on his person an irreparable insult to the loyal prop of the house of Saul, he vows he will be the very instrument by which the Lord's well-known promise to David will be accomplished: the kingdom will be transferred from the house of Saul to David, who will then rule one combined empire from Dan to Beersheba! Ish-bosheth's attempt at asserting independent authority ends with his being unable to reply to Abner's threat.

Abner Carries On Private Negotiations
with David   *12-16*

¹² And Abner sent messengers to David at Hebron,^e saying, "To whom does the land belong? Make your covenant with me, and behold, my hand shall be with you to bring over all Israel to you." ¹³ And he said, "Good; I will make a covenant with you; but one thing I require of you; that is, you shall not see my face, unless you first bring Michal, Saul's daughter, when you come to see my face." ¹⁴ Then David sent messengers to Ish-bosheth Saul's son, saying, "Give me my wife Michal, whom I betrothed at the price of a hundred foreskins of the Philistines." ¹⁵ And Ish-bosheth sent, and took her from her husband Paltiel the son of Laish. ¹⁶ But her husband went with her, weeping after her all the way to Bahurim. Then Abner said to him, "Go, return"; and he returned.

^e Gk: Heb *where he was*

David is surprisingly cool and formal toward Abner's welcome but nevertheless private and unofficial proposals. His counterstipulation is that first of all Michal, his rightful wife, Saul's daughter, be restored to him (thus clearly establishing the legitimacy of his own succession to King Saul). David emphasizes the same demand in an official communication to the official head of Saul's house, King Ish-bosheth himself. Surprisingly enough, Ish-bosheth readily complies. We wonder whether, with his usual shortsightedness, he is attempting to play David against his new enemy Abner, or whether — and this is more probable — Abner is still able to bend the weakling king to official action. In any case, the result is that despite the pathetic protests of Michal's devoted husband David receives Michal and therewith establishes the legitimacy of his succession to Saul. Abner seems to supervise the exchange at the border town of Bahurim.

Official Negotiations with the Elders of Israel   *17-21*

[17] And Abner conferred with the elders of Israel, saying, "For some time past you have been seeking David as king over you. [18] Now then bring it about; for the LORD has promised David, saying, 'By the hand of my servant David I will save my people Israel from the hand of the Philistines, and from the hand of all their enemies.'" [19] Abner also spoke to Benjamin; and then Abner went to tell David at Hebron all that Israel and the whole house of Benjamin thought good to do.

[20] When Abner came with twenty men to David at Hebron, David made a feast for Abner and the men who were with him. [21] And Abner said to David, "I will arise and go, and will gather all Israel to my

245

lord the king, that they may make a covenant with
you, and that you may reign over all that your heart
desires." So David sent Abner away; and he went in
peace.

While the negotiations concerning Michal are going
on, Abner also takes up negotiations with the elders
of the various tribes in Israel. Meeting with them, perhaps at some central point like Shechem, Abner first
draws their attention to their long-standing recognition
of David's qualifications and then to the Lord's oracle
("By the hand of my servant David I will save my people Israel from . . . their enemies"). Abner carries on
separate negotiations with the Benjaminites, who might
prove to be the most difficult to move because of their
ties with the house of Saul. Such successful preliminary
meetings enable Abner to begin the face-to-face negotiations with David in Hebron with substantial backing,
guaranteed by the presence of 20 elders from the North.
At a feast sealing their agreement, Abner, in a sort of
conference communique, announces that the final step
will be taken at a formal assembly of all Israel.

The Murder of Israel's Chief Negotiator   *22-39*

22 Just then the servants of David arrived with
Joab from a raid, bringing much spoil with them.
But Abner was not with David at Hebron, for he had
sent him away, and he had gone in peace. 23 When
Joab and all the army that was with him came, it
was told Joab, "Abner the son of Ner came to the king,
and he has let him go, and he has gone in peace."
24 Then Joab went to the king and said, "What have
you done? Behold, Abner came to you; why is it that

you have sent him away, so that he is gone? ²⁵ You know that Abner the son of Ner came to deceive you, and to know your going out and your coming in, and to know all that you are doing."

²⁶ When Joab came out from David's presence, he sent messengers after Abner, and they brought him back from the cistern of Sirah; but David did not know about it. ²⁷ And when Abner returned to Hebron, Joab took him aside into the midst of the gate to speak with him privately, and there he smote him in the belly, so that he died, for the blood of Asahel his brother. ²⁸ Afterward, when David heard of it, he said, "I and my kingdom are for ever guiltless before the LORD for the blood of Abner the son of Ner. ²⁹ May it fall upon the head of Joab, and upon all his father's house; and may the house of Joab never be without one who has a discharge, or who is leprous, or who holds a spindle, or who is slain by the sword, or who lacks bread!" ³⁰ So Joab and Abishai his brother slew Abner, because he had killed their brother Asahel in the battle at Gibeon.

³¹ Then David said to Joab and to all the people who were with him, "Rend your clothes, and gird on sackcloth, and mourn before Abner." And King David followed the bier. ³² They buried Abner at Hebron; and the king lifted up his voice and wept at the grave of Abner; and all the people wept. ³³ And the king lamented for Abner, saying,

"Should Abner die as a fool dies?

³⁴ Your hands were not bound,
    your feet were not fettered;
as one falls before the wicked
    you have fallen."

And all the people wept again over him. [35] Then all the people came to persuade David to eat bread while it was yet day; but David swore, saying, "God do so to me and more also, if I taste bread or anything else till the sun goes down!" [36] And all the people took notice of it, and it pleased them; as everything that the king did pleased all the people. [37] So all the people and all Israel understood that day that it had not been the king's will to slay Abner the son of Ner. [38] And the king said to his servants, "Do you not know that a prince and a great man has fallen this day in Israel? [39] And I am this day weak, though anointed king; these men the sons of Zeruiah are too hard for me. The LORD requite the evildoer according to his wickedness!"

Everything had been set for a peaceful and legal transfer of power to David when an upset occurs that threatens to ruin the entire undertaking. Hardly has Abner left the city when Joab, David's capable but sinister nephew and commander, returns from a raid and learns that in his absence his brother's slayer has successfully negotiated with the king. Joab does not shrink from directly upbraiding his royal kinsman and longtime army colleague for not having smitten "the enemy" while he had him in his power, ascribing treacherous motives to Abner's visit. Nor does Joab shrink from – unbeknown to David – enticing the unsuspecting Abner to return and to enter a corner of the gate with him, there to avenge his brother Asahel's blood by spilling that of his killer.

Modern states leave no room for blood-vengeance, and we expect the state (David in this case) to deal with homicide. In ancient Israel, however, this was not

248

expected. Moreover, even if David had personally wished to avenge Abner's blood on his nephews, he would have found the sons of Zeruiah "too hard" for him; they were the very props of his power, the leaders of his personal army. The gravest danger for David's plans at this point is the fact that Joab's deed might cause the Israelite tribes to recoil from the proposed alliance with him just at the moment their acceptance of him appeared to be secure. Therefore David must prove beyond the shadow of a doubt that he had no part in the deed. This David proves most effectively first by directing a withering curse against Joab's house, asking that the Lord be the avenger and waste their strength through disease (gonorrhea, leprosy, polio), suicide, and poverty. Such a devastating curse was not lightly spoken in the ancient world; but, once spoken, it was considered effective.

The second means David uses for disassociating himself from any suspicion of implication in Abner's death is the special public funeral he orders for the dead prince, in which David takes the position of chief mourner. Abner was, his lament points out, an experienced soldier, a seasoned statesman, a prince, and a great man. Had he been killed while handcuffed or clapped in the stocks, his lack of counterattack could be explained. As it is, he died like a simpleton — because treachery was afoot!

The result of such actions by David is that the people in Hebron as well as in all Israel understand that "it had not been the king's will to slay Abner." This episode represents a very "close call" for David, but by God's gracious guidance an irreparable breakdown between North and South is averted. David's progress toward the throne of all Israel can continue.

DAVID PUNISHES THE MURDERERS
OF ISH-BOSHETH

4

Two Malcontents Plot the Assassination   *4:1-4*

¹ When Ish-bosheth, Saul's son, heard that Abner had died at Hebron, his courage failed, and all Israel was dismayed. ² Now Saul's son had two men who were captains of raiding bands; the name of the one was Baanah, and the name of the other Rechab, sons of Rimmon a man of Benjamin from Beeroth (for Beeroth also is reckoned to Benjamin; ³ the Beerothites fled to Gittaim, and have been sojourners there to this day).

⁴ Jonathan, the son of Saul, had a son who was crippled in his feet. He was five years old when the news about Saul and Jonathan came from Jezreel; and his nurse took him up, and fled; and, as she fled in her haste, he fell, and became lame. And his name was Mephibosheth.

Now that mighty Abner no longer lives, weak Ish-bosheth stands alone, and all Israel is paralyzed by dismay and fear of revolution. Two disgruntled army men feel that this is the time to settle old scores with the house of Saul as well as to prepare for advancement in the future by removing the last obstacle that stands in the way of David's ascending to the throne over all Israel. These two men, Baanah and Rechab, are mercenary soldiers in Ish-bosheth's guard, having joined that "foreign legion" group while they lived in the Philistine city of Gittaim. Originally, however, they had lived in the Hivite town of Beeroth—until Saul had undertaken a purge of all non-Israelites from his Benjaminite territory. These men respond to the news of

250

Abner's death with anything but dismay; now is the time to murder Ish-bosheth! Jonathan's only son Mephibosheth is mentioned in the side-note of v. 4 presumably because Ish-bosheth and the house of Saul could expect no aid in the crisis from such a young and crippled person, who was also out of the question as a successor.

Bringing News of the Assassination to David   5-8

⁵ Now the sons of Rimmon the Beerothite, Rechab and Baanah, set out, and about the heat of the day they came to the house of Ish-bosheth, as he was taking his noonday rest. ⁶ And behold, the doorkeeper of the house had been cleaning wheat, but she grew drowsy and slept; so Rechab and Baanah his brother slipped in.*ᶠ* ⁷ When they came into the house as he lay on his bed in his bedchamber, they smote him, and slew him, and beheaded him. They took his head, and went by the way of the Arabah all night, ⁸ and brought the head of Ish-bosheth to David at Hebron. And they said to the king, "Here is the head of Ishbosheth, the son of Saul, your enemy, who sought your life; the LORD has avenged my lord the king this day on Saul and on his offspring."

ᶠ Gk: Heb ⁶ And hither they came into the midst of the house fetching wheat; and they smote him in the belly; and Rechab and Baanah his brother escaped

For their exploit Baanah and Rechab choose the drowsiest part of the day, when the king is taking his noonday siesta. Disguised, it seems, as household servants who have come to the palace to fetch wheat, they are able to slip past the drowsing doorkeeper, stab the sleeping king, cut off his head, and slip out again without hindrance. Traveling all night, they arrive in Hebron at David's residence to display the grisly trophy and say, "Here is the head of Ish-bosheth, son of Saul, your enemy, who sought your life." Moreover, they connect their foul deed with the divine promise given to David, claiming that their deed is God's own act of judgment upon Saul and his offspring. David had been tempted previously to play the part of God the Avenger and to kill those who stood in his path; such temptations had, however, been overcome partly because David saw King Saul as the Lord's anointed. Ish-bosheth, however, is never presented as the legitimately anointed and elected king but only as Abner's weak puppet. Therefore we should not underestimate the greatness of the temptation that now comes to David to at least rejoice in the fact that the evil deeds of Saul's house had now been avenged and that the last obstacle to his becoming king had been removed. Temptations to "smaller" sins at a time of success are often more difficult to withstand than temptation to "greater" sins at a time of defeat and humiliation.

David's Response to the Assassins' "Good News"   9-12

⁹ But David answered Rechab and Baanah his brother, the sons of Rimmon the Beerothite, "As the LORD lives, who has redeemed my life out of every adversity, ¹⁰ when one told me, 'Behold, Saul is dead,' and thought he was bringing good news, I seized him and slew him at Ziklag, which was the reward I gave him for his news. ¹¹ How much more, when wicked men have slain a righteous man in his own house upon his bed, shall I not now require his blood at your hand, and destroy you from the earth?" ¹² And David commanded his young men, and they killed them, and cut off their hands and

feet, and hanged them beside the pool at Hebron. But they took the head of Ish-bosheth, and buried it in the tomb of Abner at Hebron.

David does not rejoice in the murderers' deed. The message they brought in the hope that it would be received with joy and repaid with reward is not a message welcome to David. In fact, David's response to their report is a pronouncement of doom solemnly prefaced with an oath in the name of the living Lord, for He alone is the one who delivers David from every adversity. David had once killed the Amalekite who imagined he was bringing good news when he reported Saul's death; how much more, he asks, must he not prevent Ish-bosheth's innocent blood from crying in vain to heaven for vengeance. It is not enough for David to merely refrain from lifting his own hand against his rival or to avoid becoming implicated in this deed of theirs; no, to condone such evil, to be indifferent to wrong done to other people is also a sin that cries out to heaven. What David refrained from doing to his own strong kinsman Joab on behalf of the murdered Abner — and he felt a twinge of conscience because of it — he here does, straightforwardly and manfully, showing that also in the former instance he meant his lamentation and believed that one day Joab's wicked deed would be punished by the Lord!

We New Testament Christians are puzzled by the bloodshed and blood vengeance of these chapters. And we ask, "When will such a chain of bloodbaths come to an end?" We cannot avoid noticing that David, like many another ancient king, reached his throne only at the cost of shed blood. The answer to such questions we find, however, in the ultimate context of this chapter, in great David's greater Son, who came to the glory of His heavenly throne by the shedding of His own precious blood, blood which cries not for vengeance but for pardon.

A NEW CAPITAL
FOR AN INCIPIENT EMPIRE 5

With this chapter we arrive at the climax of the narrative about David's rise to kingship. What began when he was secretly anointed by Samuel (1 Sam. 16), what seemed at first to develop so naturally when he was a brilliant captain in Saul's professional army (1 Sam. 16:14 — 18:30), what was, however, delayed so long while he was forced to flee and live as a freebooter (Chs. 19 — 27), and what was postponed even after it had become clear that the Judean king in Hebron was the only possible king for all Israel (2 Sam. 1 — 4) — all this now comes to its climax with the establishment of a great united empire with Jerusalem as its capital. The teller of this colorful story of David's rise to kingship seems to have lived close to the events he describes, being a contemporary either of David or Solomon. He sees David's rise not as the merely political achievement of a crafty statesman but as the work of the Lord, who was with David (v. 10) and exalted David's kingdom "for the sake of his people Israel" (v. 12). It is God's own eternal kingship over the world that is here being foreshadowed and initiated.

David Anointed as King of Israel 5:1-5

[1] Then all the tribes of Israel came to David at Hebron, and said, "Behold, we are your bone and flesh. [2] In times past, when Saul was king over us,

it was you that led out and brought in Israel; and the LORD said to you, 'You shall be shepherd of my people Israel, and you shall be prince over Israel.'" ³ So all the elders of Israel came to the king at Hebron; and King David made a covenant with them at Hebron before the LORD, and they anointed David king over Israel. ⁴ David was thirty years old when he began to reign, and he reigned forty years. ⁵ At Hebron he reigned over Judah seven years and six months; and at Jerusalem he reigned over all Israel and Judah thirty-three years.

David's formal election and coronation as king of the northern tribes begins with two public acknowledgments by the Israelite representatives. First, they recognize David's excellent, long-term leadership of Israel, even while Saul was the crowned king. Secondly, they realize the Lord has designated David as His specially endowed leader to shepherd His people. Thereupon David takes Israel into a formal suzerain-vassal type of covenant with himself; and finally the elders anoint him king over Israel. This does not mean, however, that Israel is thereby fused into one political unit with Judah; rather, Judah and Israel continue as still separate realms, united only in the person of their common king, David—politically speaking, a rather shaky foundation for the subsequent imperial structure built upon it, one which indeed will not prove able to withstand the shocks of future history. The annalistic note (vv. 4-5) reminds us that David comes to the throne at the height of his natural strength and then reigns a full generation—a great blessing, especially if compared to weak Ish-bosheth's short-lived tenure.

Jerusalem Becomes David's Capital 6-16

⁶ And the king and his men went to Jerusalem against the Jebusites, the inhabitants of the land, who said to David, "You will not come in here, but the blind and the lame will ward you off" — thinking, "David cannot come in here." ⁷ Nevertheless David took the stronghold of Zion, that is, the city of David. ⁸ And David said on that day, "Whoever would smite the Jebusites, let him get up the water shaft to attack the lame and the blind, who are hated by David's soul." Therefore it is said, "The blind and the lame shall not come into the house." ⁹ And David dwelt in the stronghold, and called it the city of David. And David built the city round about from the Millo inward. ¹⁰ And David became greater and greater, for the LORD, the God of hosts, was with him.

¹¹ And Hiram king of Tyre sent messengers to David, and cedar trees, also carpenters and masons who built David a house. ¹² And David perceived that the LORD had established him king over Israel, and that he had exalted his kingdom for the sake of his people Israel.

¹³ And David took more concubines and wives from Jerusalem, after he came from Hebron; and more sons and daughters were born to David. ¹⁴ And these are the names of those who were born to him in Jerusalem: Shammua, Shobab, Nathan, Solomon, ¹⁵ Ibhar, Elishua, Nepheg, Japhia, ¹⁶ Elishama, Eliada, and Eliphelet.

The conquest of Jerusalem is the accomplishment of David's own private army of professionals. Hence this city is not tribal property but David's own personal property by right of conquest. The king does not set up his court at Shechem or Hebron or Gibeah but at a neutral place, situated, like Washington, D. C., on the border between the North and the South, where his freedom of action will not be influenced by regional pressures. The ancient Jebusite city had a long history and a rich culture. It provided David with a well-established personal city-state. By natural geographical endowment Jerusalem is not "the center of the land" (cf. Judg. 9:37); by God's gracious election, however, the Jebusite city becomes not only "David's city" but the Biblical prototype of the city of God. (Cf. Ezek. 16; Is. 2; Rev. 21)

The tactics by which David gained control of this ready-made capital are obscure. A probable explanation is that the Jebusites boasted that their strategically situated city was such an impregnable fortress that even the blind and the lame would be adequate to defend it against David. David, however, promised promotion to the first man to climb up the ancient tunnel that served as a protected descent to the Gihon spring and smite those enemies of his whom he sarcastically calls "the lame and the blind." According to 1 Chron. 11:6 Joab was the hero of the day. In any case, it is clear that David did not devastate the captured city but came to terms with its inhabitants and began to construct, it seems, a strong wall along its western and northern (Millo) sides to make it even more impregnable. The Bible's report of all this is theologically oriented: "David became greater and greater, for the LORD, the God of hosts, was with him" — so much so that Hiram of Tyre, taking a diplomatic step that was usual when there was a change in kingship (cf. 10:1), sent a delegation that included such skilled artisans as were not yet available in backward Israel to build a suitable palace for the great king. The writer's theological conclusion: It is the Lord who establishes David's kingdom "for the sake of his people Israel." The long list of Jerusalem-born royal sons (cf. 3:2-5) guarantees a lasting dynasty.

David's First Victory over the Philistines   17-21

[17] When the Philistines heard that David had been anointed king over Israel, all the Philistines went up in search of David; but David heard of it and went down to the stronghold. [18] Now the Philistines had come and spread out in the valley of Rephaim. [19] And David inquired of the LORD, "Shall I go up against the Philistines? Wilt thou give them into my hand?" And the LORD said to David, "Go up; for I will certainly give the Philistines into your hand." [20] And David came to Baal-perazim, and David defeated them there; and he said, "The LORD has broken through [g] my enemies before me, like a bursting flood." Therefore the name of that place is called Baal-perazim.[h] [21] And the Philistines left their idols there, and David and his men carried them away.

[g] Heb *paraz*   [h] That is *Lord of breaking through*

The Philistines had, it seems, viewed David's previous election as king over Judah without displeasure because he still remained their vassal. But now, disturbed by his growing power, they consider him a dangerous foe who must be stopped. Their first campaign against him is directed up the valleys southwest of Jerusalem, ostensibly in an attempt to cut communications between Judah and Israel. Moving only in accordance with the expressly revealed will of the Lord (cf. p. 121), David is told not to remain on the defensive

258

but to attack. In the battle David must have "broken through" the enemy ranks, since the place was called Baal-perazim ("Lord of breaking-through"). David, however, acknowledges that it was the Lord who decided the battle, bursting through His enemies like an erupting flood. The word *baal* in the name is a title referring to the Lord, not to the Canaanite fertility deity. The Lord's enemies in this case include not only the Philistine troops but also their gods, whose images had been brought to the battle to fight for them, much as the Israelites brought the ark (1 Sam. 4:1 ff.). In a reversal of the earlier capture of the Israelite ark by the Philistines, the Philistine images are now captured and taken away as booty by David.

The Decisive Victory over the Philistines 22-25

22 And the Philistines came up yet again, and spread out in the valley of Rephaim. 23 And when David inquired of the LORD, he said, "You shall not go up; go around to their rear, and come upon them opposite the balsam trees. 24 And when you hear the sound of marching in the tops of the balsam trees, then bestir yourself; for then the LORD has gone out before you to smite the army of the Philistines." 25 And David did as the LORD commanded him, and smote the Philistines from Geba to Gezer.

After an unspecified interval of time a second battle against the Philistines takes place, as a result of their second attempt at driving a wedge into Israelite territory at Rephaim. The action seems to have centered north of Jerusalem. Again it is the theological aspect of the battle that is paramount in the account. The Lord not only guides David into the battle (telling him to lead his men to the enemies' rear) but also engages in the battle Himself, the noise in the trees being the God-given sign to David that He has gone out in front to strike down the Philistines (on the holy war imagery cf. p. 105 f.). When David drives the Philistines back down the traditional invasion route to Gezer, he is putting an end to the Philistine menace. Their power is broken. But again David's deeds are the Lord's deeds, and the history of Israel is really the history of the Lord's mighty acts in behalf of Israel, for it is in their midst that He desires to set up His own eternal kingdom.

DAVID BRINGS THE ARK TO JERUSALEM 6

The ancient symbol of the Lord's kingship over the 12-tribe confederacy is now installed in the city that has recently become David's fortress-residence. With the advent of the ark it will henceforth be also Israel's central sanctuary, enjoying the prestige and traditions that have belonged to the sanctuaries where the ark has previously resided. Thus the ark serves to establish a continuity between the old and the new, between tenacious old religious loyalties and new developments in a united and expanding empire.

The transfer of the ark to Jerusalem takes the form of a religious procession. For this reason some scholars have concluded that our narrative was shaped by a later temple liturgy that celebrated either (1) David's being crowned "the divine king of Jerusalem" as signifying the Lord's enthronement in His sanctuary, or (2) the Lord's double choice of Mount Zion as His home and of David's dynasty to rule over His people (cf. Pss. 24, 89, 132). In any case, David's bringing of the ark to Mount Zion is itself a very significant religious act.

The Beginning of the Great Procession   *1-5*

¹ David again gathered all the chosen men of Israel, thirty thousand. ² And David arose and went with all the people who were with him from Baale-judah, to bring up from there the ark of God, which is called by the name of the LORD of hosts who sits enthroned on the cherubim. ³ And they carried the ark of God upon a new cart, and brought it out of the house of Abinadab which was on the hill; and Uzzah and Ahio,ⁱ the sons of Abinadab, were driving the new cartʲ ⁴ with the ark of God; and Ahioⁱ went before the ark. ⁵ And David and all the house of Israel were making merry before the LORD with all their might, with songsᵏ and lyres and harps and tambourines and castanets and cymbals.

ⁱ Or *and his brother*
ʲ Compare Gk: Heb *the new cart, and brought it out of the house of Abinadab which was on the hill*
ᵏ Gk 1 Chron. 13. 8: Heb *fir-trees*

As soon as the Philistines have been routed, David goes with a large military entourage to the border town of Kiriath-jearim (Baale-judah) to fetch the ark (cf. 1 Sam. 6). Using a cart unprofaned by common uses to convey the ark, its priestly protectors accompany its journey: Uzzah proceeding at its side, Ahio in front of it. Some scholars take the word *Ahio* to mean "his brother" and suggest that this anonymous priest was really the Jerusalemite priest Zadok, who appears in Jerusalem first alongside Abiathar (15:24 f.) and then in his place (1 Kings 2:35). David and the military escort now symbolize the ancient host of the Lord that fights His battles at His commands (mediated by His prophets and priests), as He proceeds with them on His triumphant course, invisibly enthroned above the ark. (On the holy war imagery cf. p. 105 f.)

Despite Interruptions and Obstacles
the Ark Is Brought to Jerusalem   6-16

⁶ And when they came to the threshing floor of Nacon, Uzzah put out his hand to the ark of God and took hold of it, for the oxen stumbled. ⁷ And the anger of the **LORD** was kindled against Uzzah; and God smote him there because he put forth his hand to the ark; *ᶦ* and he died there beside the ark of God. ⁸ And David was angry because the **LORD** had broken forth upon Uzzah; and that place is called Perez-uzzah,ᵐ to this day. ⁹ And David was afraid of the **LORD** that day; and he said, "How can the ark of the **LORD** come to me?" ¹⁰ So David was not willing to take the ark of the **LORD** into the city of David; but David took it aside to the house of Obed-edom the Gittite. ¹¹ And the ark of the **LORD** remained in the house of Obed-edom the Gittite three months; and the **LORD** blessed Obed-edom and all his household.

¹² And it was told King David, "The **LORD** has blessed the household of Obed-edom and all that belongs to him, because of the ark of God." So David went and brought up the ark of God from the house of Obed-edom to the city of David with rejoicing; ¹³ and when those who bore the ark of the **LORD** had gone six paces, he sacrificed an ox and a fatling. ¹⁴ And David danced before the **LORD** with all his might; and David was girded with a linen ephod.

ᶦ 1 Chron. 13. 10: Heb uncertain
ᵐ That is *The breaking forth upon Uzzah*

¹⁵ So David and all the house of Israel brought up the ark of the **LORD** with shouting, and with the sound of the horn.

¹⁶ As the ark of the **LORD** came into the city of David, Michal the daughter of Saul looked out of the window, and saw **King David leaping and dancing before the LORD**; and she despised him in her heart.

The joyous merrymaking of the triumphal procession is interrupted when, at the threshing floor later pointed out as Perez-uzzah, the stumbling oxen threaten to overturn the cart and Uzzah is smitten by the Lord as he disregards the lethal holiness of the Lord's throne and tries to steady it with his bare hand. It is characteristic of David's deep piety that, even though he is most angry with Uzzah's inept irreverence and disappointed with the failure of his plans ("How can the ark of the LORD come to me?" he asks in despair), nevertheless, he now interrupts the procession and cancels his own cherished plans. Only when he hears that the Lord has richly blessed the non-Israelite Obed-edom (in whose nearby house the ark had been kept) does David again undertake to fetch this highly desirable religious symbol to his city. Even then his first steps are taken with utmost delicacy; to avoid a new accident, porters take the place of the oxen and cart; the first hazardous steps taken to disturb the ark are breathlessly observed to see if the Lord now approves; and as soon as the initial process of disturbing the ark has been effected without calamity, a sacrifice is offered to the Lord. Only then does the procession begin with ritual cries, trumpetlike blasts on the ancient ram's horn, and, this time, king David's own ecstatic dancing. David dances "before

263

the LORD," clothed in a linen ephod—and, it seems, in little else—having taken off his long royal robe; it is not necessary, however, to conclude from Michal's subsequent charge (v. 20) that in dancing "with all his might" David exposed himself in utter nakedness, as Saul did at Ramah. (1 Sam. 19:23 f.)

The Great Celebration in Jerusalem   *17-19*

[17] And they brought in the ark of the LORD, and set it in its place, inside the tent which David had pitched for it; and David offered burnt offerings and peace offerings before the LORD. [18] And when David had finished offering the burnt offerings and the peace offerings, he blessed the people in the name of the LORD of hosts, [19] and distributed among all the people, the whole multitude of Israel, both men and women, to each a cake of bread, a portion of meat,[n] and a cake of raisins. Then all the people departed, each to his house.

[n] Vg: Heb uncertain

In Jerusalem the ark finds its resting place inside a tent—hardly the original wilderness-days tent of meeting but one that recalled those ancient traditions (cf. 1 Kings 1:39; 2:28 f.). On this occasion the offerings include both sacrifices burnt completely to the Lord and peace offerings in which the entire people partake as commensals with David and with the Lord before receiving the blessing from the king.

Michal and David Estranged   *20-23*

[20] And David returned to bless his household. But Michal the daughter of Saul came out to meet

David, and said, "How the king of Israel honored himself today before the eyes of his servants' maids, as one of the vulgar fellows shamelessly uncovers himself!" 21 And David said to Michal, "It was before the LORD, who chose me above your father, and above all his house, to appoint me as prince over Israel, the people of the LORD—and I will make merry before the LORD. 22 I will make myself yet more contemptible than this, and I will be abased in your *o* eyes; but by the maids of whom you have spoken, by them I shall be held in honor." 23 And Michal the daughter of Saul had no child to the day of her death.

o Gk: Heb *my*

David's wife Michal in no way shares her husband's spontaneous holy joy in the Lord's advent to Jerusalem. When therefore he returns to the palace to bless his own household, she greets him sarcastically, angrily attacking his ecstatic dancing as indecent exposure, unbecoming a king. She is a true daughter of proud Saul! David's answer is an honest confession of his faith and joy in the Lord. He does not think Israel's king too lofty a person to perform an ecstatic dance before the Lord. His "honor" comes from the Lord, who "opposes the proud, but gives grace to the humble." The common people will understand his religious zeal even if his royal wife despises him more than now. The final sentence of the chapter shows the sad result of this estrangement; Michal, David's first wife, who should have given him his first son and heir, bears no child. The house of Saul produces no offspring to be considered for the succession after David.

The Lord's Great Messianic Promise to David 7

The Lord's great promise to David about his dynasty is the very heart of the long Biblical narrative concerning David (1 Sam. 16 — 1 Kings 2). It provides the climactic conclusion to all the preceding stories of his rise to the throne and also a solid foundation that will stand firmly through the subsequent turbulences revolving about the succession to his throne.

A House of Flesh and Blood Instead of a House of Wood and Stone 7:1-17

[1] Now when the king dwelt in his house, and the LORD had given him rest from all his enemies round about, [2] the king said to Nathan the prophet, "See now, I dwell in a house of cedar, but the ark of God dwells in a tent." [3] And Nathan said to the king, "Go, do all that is in your heart; for the LORD is with you."

[4] But that same night the word of the LORD came to Nathan, [5] "Go and tell my servant David, 'Thus says the LORD: Would you build me a house to dwell in? [6] I have not dwelt in a house since the day I brought up the people of Israel from Egypt to this day, but I have been moving about in a tent for my dwelling. [7] In all places where I have moved with all the people of Israel, did I speak a word with any of the judges [p] of Israel, whom I commanded to shepherd my people Israel, saying, "Why have you not built me a house of cedar?"' [8] Now therefore thus you shall say to my servant David, 'Thus says the LORD of hosts, I took you from the pasture, from following

[p] 1 Chron. 17. 6: Heb *tribes*

266

the sheep, that you should be prince over my people Israel; [9] and I have been with you wherever you went, and have cut off all your enemies from before you; and I will make for you a great name, like the name of the great ones of the earth. [10] And I will appoint a place for my people Israel, and will plant them, that they may dwell in their own place, and be disturbed no more; and violent men shall afflict them no more, as formerly, [11] from the time that I appointed judges over my people Israel; and I will give you rest from all your enemies. Moreover the LORD declares to you that the LORD will make you a house. [12] When your days are fulfilled and you lie down with your fathers, I will raise up your offspring after you, who shall come forth from your body, and I will establish his kingdom. [13] He shall build a house for my name, and I will establish the throne of his kingdom for ever. [14] I will be his father, and he shall be my son. When he commits iniquity, I will chasten him with the rod of men, with the stripes of the sons of men; [15] but I will not take [q] my steadfast love from him, as I took it from Saul, whom I put away from before you. [16] And your house and your kingdom shall be made sure for ever before me; your throne shall be established for ever.'" [17] In accordance with all these words, and in accordance with all this vision, Nathan spoke to David.

[q] Gk Syr Vg 1 Chron. 17. 13: Heb *shall not depart*

The Lord has blessed David, giving him rest from his enemies and, besides, a magnificent Phoenician-built palace in a famous city, the proud capital of his great empire. Now that David's period of uncertain wandering from place to place has ended and Israel likewise has at long last gained firm possession of the Promised Land, David suggests to the Lord that He, too, ought really to settle down and enter an adequate permanent house. It was customary for pious kings in the ancient Near East to build such temples for their deities. The court prophet Nathan is delighted with the idea; in fact, he even thoughtlessly gives it what he considers the Lord's endorsement. But the Lord interrupts these plans, reverses His prophet's easy approval, and expressly forbids the royal project. The Lord asks the king, "Would you build me a house to dwell in?" He has been moving about, He says, staying only in temporary lodgings ever since the exodus from Egypt. Should He change His itinerant habits now and bind Himself to one place? He had never asked any of His people's previous leaders to build a permanent house for His throne, and He is not going to ask David to do it either. In fact, turning David's suggestion upside down, He says, "The LORD declares to you that the LORD will make you a house." The Lord will make David the founder of an enduring dynasty. That is, in fact, why He called him from a humble background, guided his checkered career to the present point where he has overcome the insecurity of the previous age when Israel was afflicted. The Lord does not wish to bind Himself to a house of cedar; but He does herewith bind Himself eternally to the living historical person of David and his family. David's own flesh, blood, and bones will be the starting point for an eternal development with worldwide goals, because the Lord wants to extend His rule over all nations and win back a rebellious creation to the "rest" of the beginning, when violence shall afflict them no longer. Therefore the Lord says not only of David or of his successor Solomon but of each succeeding king in David's line: I am your Father; you are My son. A Davidic king is not, to be sure, considered a physical incarnation of the Lord, as, for instance, the god-king in Egypt was idolatrously considered Horus incarnate; Israel's king is not deified. Nevertheless, he is an adopted son of the Lord, a prototype of the ideal King to come, in whom the Lord would truly become incarnate. Even though the individual Davidic king will reflect the image of that coming Messiah only imperfectly and must therefore be disciplined as a son is corrected by his father, nevertheless, the Lord's steadfast love will never annul this great promise. No wonder this promise became the source of much Old Testament liturgical and prophetic literature. (Cf. Pss. 2, 89, 110, 132; Is. 9:2 ff.; 11:1 ff.; Jer. 23:5 ff.)

Verse 13 refers to the puzzling fact that, despite the Lord's prohibition here, a temple for the Lord to dwell in was nevertheless actually to be built. This, however, only underscores the important fact about the temple Solomon did build: it was not Solomon's house of wood and stone to which the Lord bound Himself. In fact, whenever that house of wood and stone became an object of idolatry, a magic guarantee of national prosperity (cf. Jer. 7:11 f.), then that "box" was destroyed by the Lord's anger (Nebuchadnezzer, the Romans). The Davidic house of flesh and blood, however, was never destroyed, not even after it lost the kingship and was represented only by such a simple believer from the house and lineage of David as Mary of Nazareth. Then the eternal God in His ultimate Self-disclosure became flesh and tabernacled (John 1:14) among men. He told His enemies that even if they should destroy the temple of His body, He would raise it up in three

269

days (John 2:19 ff.). And that is just what He did on Easter morning. But when He in His own body rose from the dead, He also raised to life "His body," the church, into which we Christians are baptized and of which we are members. What Solomon could fulfill only in a very tentative and shadowy way has been fulfilled perfectly by the great Davidic King. In Him the royal house of David has grown to perfection; in the kingdom He has established, in the house He has built for the Lord's name, His throne is forever.

David's Response to the Promise: His Prayer 18-29

18 Then King David went in and sat before the LORD, and said, "Who am I, O LORD God, and what is my house, that thou hast brought me thus far? 19 And yet this was a small thing in thy eyes, O LORD God; thou hast spoken also of thy servant's house for a great while to come, and hast shown me future generations,^{r} O LORD God! 20 And what more can David say to thee? For thou knowest thy servant, O LORD God! 21 Because of thy promise, and according to thy own heart, thou hast wrought all this greatness, to make thy servant know it. 22 Therefore thou art great, O LORD God; for there is none like thee, and there is no God besides thee, according to all that we have heard with our ears. 23 What other^s nation on earth is like thy people Israel, whom God went to redeem to be his people, making himself a name, and doing for them ^{t} great and terrible things, by driving out ^{u} before his people a nation and its gods?^{v} 24 And thou didst establish for thyself thy

^{r} Cn: Heb *this is the law for man* ^{s} Gk: Heb *one* ^{t} Heb *you*
^{u} Gk 1 Chron 17. 21: Heb *for your land*
^{v} Heb *before thy people, whom thou didst redeem for thyself from Egypt, nations and its gods*

people Israel to be thy people for ever; and thou, O LORD, didst become their God. ²⁵ And now, O LORD God, confirm for ever the word which thou hast spoken concerning thy servant and concerning his house, and do as thou hast spoken; ²⁶ and thy name will be magnified for ever, saying, 'The LORD of hosts is God over Israel,' and the house of thy servant David will be established before thee. ²⁷ For thou, O LORD of hosts, the God of Israel, hast made this revelation to thy servant, saying, 'I will build you a house'; therefore thy servant has found courage to pray this prayer to thee. ²⁸ And now, O LORD God, thou art God, and thy words are true, and thou hast promised this good thing to thy servant: ²⁹ now therefore may it please thee to bless the house of thy servant, that it may continue for ever before thee; for thou, O LORD God, hast spoken, and with thy blessing shall the house of thy servant be blessed for ever."

Though David's royal proposal had been ruined, he is so overwhelmed by the magnificent counterproposal the Lord held out before him that he goes to the modest, now antique tent, and bowing low before the Lord, worships and adores Him. David's is a wonderful prayer, so full of the praise of God that he cannot find words enough to magnify Him adequately. He accepts the promise in genuine faith, knowing that the Lord's purposes stretch far beyond His dealings with himself personally. This promise is, the king says, indeed typical: the Lord always condescends to aid the poor; He graciously makes His saving presence known in the world of men (1 Sam. 2:4 ff.). The prayer also includes heartfelt petition, for David has not yet attained the goal. In the subsequent stories we shall witness violent upsets in his own household. David will then have to do repeatedly what he does already here: beg the Lord to confirm His promise and bless his unworthy house. This is truly a royal prayer, worthy to be prayed by all who live by faith in the same Lord who blessed and sustained David.

DAVID'S EMPIRE AND ITS ADMINISTRATION 8

In writing a history of Israel a modern historian describes the growth of David's empire in a manner that differs significantly from that of our chapter. After having assimilated all available information from Biblical and non-Biblical sources, a modern historian presents his readers with a consistent and compact account that is chronologically unified according to the various stages of growth, each carefully synchronized with simultaneous developments in the surrounding world where no great rival from Egypt or Mesopotamia challenged David's moves. A modern account is also adequately documented and readily verifiable. In fact, in order to be as objective as possible such a modern historian distinguishes sharply between what is clearly established fact, what is only probable, and what is merely possible. In describing David's empire such a modern historian deliberately refrains from employing religious language that would make divine intervention the cause of the events, even though he himself may be personally convinced that the prime and ultimate cause is divine. By contrast, in the present chapter our author presents us with what appear to be some excerpts from a very old document, perhaps from such royal archives as are referred to repeatedly in the

272

Books of Kings. The literary conventions of such chronicle-like report naturally differ from those in the highly developed subsequent narrative about the succession to the throne and from a modern historian's account. But the unique point of difference is that our Biblical account here views the growth of David's kingdom as the result of the Lord's activity, rather than of David's shrewd military and political maneuverings. Twice we hear the refrain: "The LORD gave victory to David wherever he went." David's empire points beyond itself to the future rule of the Lord. Significantly, our account follows the Lord's great promise about David's dynasty.

Military Successes Against the Philistines
and Moabites   *8:1-2*

¹ After this David defeated the Philistines and subdued them, and David took Methegammah out of the hand of the Philistines.
² And he defeated Moab, and measured them with a line, making them lie down on the ground; two lines he measured to be put to death, and one full line to be spared. And the Moabites became servants to David and brought tribute.

The first stage in the growth of David's empire, his victories over the Philistines, had been described in greater detail in 5:17-25; now we learn that, in addition, David took Methegammah ("the bridle of the mother city"; in 1 Chron. 18:1, "Gath and its dependencies"). In taking control of the Philistine mother city David does not seem to have done more than make the Philistines his tribute-paying vassals, thus becoming heir to the vast coastal heritage that the Philistine lords had themselves taken over from the previous Egyptian empire.

We moderns — despite our own age's atrocities — are shocked to learn of the punitive procedure whereby two out of every three defeated Moabites were put to death. If, however, David's action is evaluated in the light of the contemporary procedure of "devoting" or annihilating populations, then we may perhaps see an uncommon mildness in David's sparing at least one out of every three and, beyond that, measuring off a "full" measure for those who should live.

Further Military and Diplomatic Successes   *3-14*

³ David also defeated Hadadezer the son of Rehob, king of Zobah, as he went to restore his power at the river Euphrates. ⁴ And David took from him a thousand and seven hundred horsemen, and twenty thousand foot soldiers; and David hamstrung all the chariot horses, but left enough for a hundred chariots. ⁵ And when the Syrians of Damascus came to help Hadadezer king of Zobah, David slew twenty-two thousand men of the Syrians. ⁶ Then David put garrisons in Aram of Damascus; and the Syrians became servants to David and brought tribute. And the LORD gave victory to David wherever he went. ⁷ And David took the shields of gold which were carried by the servants of Hadadezer, and brought them to Jerusalem. ⁸ And from Betah and from Berothai, cities of Hadadezer, King David took very much bronze.

⁹ When Toi king of Hamath heard that David had defeated the whole army of Hadadezer, ¹⁰ Toi sent his son Joram to King David, to greet him, and to congratulate him because he had fought against Hadadezer and defeated him; for Hadadezer had

often been at war with **Toi**. And **Joram** brought with him articles of silver, of gold, and of bronze; [11] these also King **David** dedicated to the **LORD**, together with the silver and gold which he dedicated from all the nations he subdued, [12] from **Edom**, **Moab**, the **Ammonites**, the **Philistines**, **Amalek**, and from the spoil of **Hadadezer** the son of **Rehob**, king of **Zobah**.

[13] And David won a name for himself. When he returned, he slew eighteen thousand Edomites [w] in the Valley of Salt. [14] And he put garrisons in Edom; throughout all Edom he put garrisons, and all the Edomites became David's servants. And the **LORD** gave victory to David wherever he went.

[w] Gk: Heb *returned from smiting eighteen thousand Syrians*

David's procedure of hamstringing all but 100 of the valuable chariot horses of the defeated Aramaean king Hadadezer shows that his army was still, for the most part, infantry. In the second millenium B. C. the introduction of the chariot horse had represented a revolution in military procedure like the later introduction of gunpowder, tanks, and thermonuclear weapons. Is it not possible that what prevented David from employing the newest "weapons" of the great powers of his day was the same religious scruple that is voiced by the prophets (Is. 30:1 ff., especially v. 15; 31:1-3. Cf. Deut. 17:16)? The victory over the Aramaean king of Zobah and his Damascus allies gave David control of the interior of Syria all the way to the region of Hamath; it also sent a continuous stream of valuable tribute (especially bronze) flowing toward his capital. His sphere of influence, however, extended as far as the Euphrates, as we can see from the fact that a diplomatic mission from a North Syrian ally, Toi of Hamath, brings him gifts of great value, acknowledging his superiority. Significantly, David dedicates these "presents" to the Lord.

Some of the conquered territories are administered by governors with garrisons at their disposal (so, for instance, Damascus and Edom); other regions (like Moab and Philistia) seem to retain their previous kings and rulers, who as vassals are now pledged to send tribute to their new overlord. It seems that at this time David organized a new bodyguard made up of foreign mercenaries, consisting of Pelethites (perhaps meaning "Philistines") and Cherethites (perhaps "Cretans" who may well have accompanied the Philistines on their original folk-migration to Palestine after their stop-off in Crete).

The Administration of David's Realm   *15-18*

[15] So David reigned over all Israel; and David administered justice and equity to all his people. [16] And Joab the son of Zeruiah was over the army; and Jehoshaphat the son of Ahilud was recorder; [17] and Zadok the son of Ahitub and Ahimelech the son of Abiathar were priests; and Seraiah was secretary; [18] and Benaiah the son of Jehoiada was over *x* **the Cherethites and the Pelethites; and David's sons were priests.**

x Syr Tg Vg 20. 23; 1 Chron. 18. 17: Heb lacks *was over*

We gain an insight into the inner organization of the empire from the list that brings us the roster of David's officials (cf. 1 Sam. 14:49-52; 2 Sam. 3:2 f.; 5:13-16). Most important is the fact that the king not only functions personally as judge but is concerned that the Lord's will be done in Israel in accordance

276

with the stipulations of His covenant. Israel is not to be the nation in the history of the world which, like Assyria or Rome, is to teach the nations what imperial rule and administration mean but what the Lord's own righteous rule means for the welfare of communal life. The tendency to govern by means of a bureaucratic staff of officials is a new departure in Israel; as it grows out of hand, it comes into conflict with older Israelite conceptions.

The army, seemingly both the Israelite citizen army as well as the veteran mercenary army, was under David's capable nephew Joab. The special royal body-guard of Cherethites and Pelethites was under Benaiah. There is some evidence that David may have used the Egyptian government as a model for his administrative setup. Jehoshaphat was the recorder, a public-relations official like the Egyptian royal herald, responsible for regulating the ceremonies in the palace and for acting as the intermediary between king, officials, and people. The scribe, or royal secretary, had the functions of secretary of state.

Among the royal officials are the two priests Abi-athar and Zadok. Abiathar, a descendent of Eli and David's priest during his exile wanderings, was to be deposed by Solomon, whereupon the family of Zadok would gain a monopoly of the Jerusalemite priestly functions. Some scholars think the designation of Zadok here as "son of Ahitub" is meant to confer on this Jeb-usite newcomer to our story a priestly pedigree ac-ceptable to later Israelite priestly scruples (cf. 1 Chron. 6:8). Others hold that the text here has been disordered and should be emended to read: "And Zadok and Abi-athar, son of Ahimelech, son of Ahitub, were priests." It may have seemed natural for David to retain Zadok

277

as high priest of Jerusalem, and therefore we seem to have joint high priests serving the Lord in Jerusalem and aiding in the maintenance of justice in Israel.

Despite some progressive modernization, David remains the Lord's servant, building not for himself, nor for a day, but for the future which the Lord had already promised when in his dynasty He would establish His everlasting kingship over all the earth.

The Succession to
David's Throne

2 Samuel 9 – 20

The story of the succession to the throne of David
(2 Sam. 9 – 1 Kings 2) seems to have been an originally
independent account (written, it seems, by a person
intimately acquainted with the intricate details of
court events). It has now been incorporated, almost
without any editorial change, into the longer Biblical
narrative about the monarchy by the author-compiler
of the Books of Samuel. In a way, Nathan's prophecy
(Ch. 7) provides a preface to the famous story. The
story itself narrates how the succession to David finally
fell to Solomon, despite the survival of a descendant
of Saul (Ch. 9), the opposition of a Northerner, Sheba
(Ch. 20), and a series of tragic upsets in the royal family
(Chs. 10 – 19; 1 Kings 1 f.). It is one of the finest pieces
of historical writing from the ancient world, antedating
Herodotus, "the father of history," by about 500 years.

MEPHIBOSHETH, JONATHAN'S SON 9

*The Royal Pronouncement Concerning Survivors
of Saul's Family* 9:1

¹ And David said, "Is there still any one left of the house of Saul, that I may show him kindness for Jonathan's sake?"

This chapter begins abruptly, with no indication of its setting; a moment's reflection, however, makes it obvious that the king is speaking to his counselors when he expresses his desire to show kindness to possible survivors of Saul's house. Moreover, the reference to survivors from Saul's house presupposes that the house of Saul had suffered severe losses and was threatened with extinction. Many scholars suggest that our chapter presupposes the story now found in the Appendix (2 Sam. 21:1-14) about the king's execution of five of the sons of Saul at Gibeon (Shimei, a staunch supporter of the house of Saul, later during the revolution taunts David as a "man of blood" who had "shed the blood of the house of Saul" 16:7 f.).

In any case, Saul's house had suffered considerable bloodletting, and David's royal pronouncement that he wished to show kindness to that house could well have been understood by people to have been spoken with the same irony as King Herod's later statement that he wished to worship the newborn king of the Jews at Bethlehem (Matt. 2:8).

After all, people in the ancient Near East expected that the founder of a new royal dynasty would, and even should, exterminate all possible rivals. (Cf. also 16:1-4; 19:25-31.)

David Shows Shrewd Kindness to Jonathan's Son   *2-13*

² Now there was a servant of the house of Saul whose name was Ziba, and they called him to David; and the king said to him, "Are you Ziba?" And he said, "Your servant is he." ³ And the king said, "Is there not still some one of the house of Saul, that I may show the kindness of God to Him?" Ziba said to the king, "There is still a son of Jonathan; he is crippled in his feet." ⁴ The king said to him, "Where is he?" And Ziba said to the king, "He is in the house of Machir the son of Ammiel, at Lodebar." ⁵ Then King David sent and brought him from the house of Machir the son of Ammiel, at Lodebar. ⁶ And Mephibosheth the son of Jonathan, son of Saul, came to David, and fell on his face and did obeisance. And David said, "Mephibosheth!" And he answered, "Behold, your servant." ⁷ And David said to him, "Do not fear; for I will show you kindness for the sake of your father Jonathan, and I will restore to you all the land of Saul your father; and you shall eat at my table always." ⁸ And he did obeisance, and said, "What is your servant, that you should look upon a dead dog such as I?"

⁹ Then the king called Ziba, Saul's servant, and said to him, "All that belonged to Saul and to all his house I have given to your master's son. ¹⁰ And you and your sons and your servants shall till the land for him, and shall bring in the produce, that your master's son may have bread to eat; but Mephibosheth your master's son shall always eat at my table." Now Ziba had fifteen sons and twenty servants. ¹¹ Then Ziba said to the king, "According to all that my lord the king commands his servant, so will your servant do." So Mephibosheth ate at David's ᵞ table, like one

ᵞ Gk: Heb *my*

of the king's sons. [12] And Mephibosheth had a young son, whose name was Mica. And all who dwelt in Ziba's house became Mephibosheth's servants. [13] So Mephibosheth dwelt in Jerusalem; for he ate always at the king's table. Now he was lame in both his feet.

Saul's faithful servant Ziba also seems to expect the worst from the king's summons. That is apparently why his replies to the king's questions are so curt and why he emphasizes the lameness of the sole survivor of Saul's house, who could for that reason certainly not cause the king any harm. Through this man David contacts Mephibosheth (originally Merib-baal; cf. 2 Sam. 21:8; 1 Chron. 8:34), who is hiding out with a Transjordanian sheikh (in the very region where Ish-bosheth had once set up his rival kingdom).

We now understand why Mephibosheth comes to his command audience with the king, filled with great anxiety. David, however, bids him dismiss his fears, revealing to him his real reason for summoning him: the steadfast love or covenant-loyalty he is obligated to show to his friend Jonathan's house. As concrete proof of his good intentions David grants Mephibosheth all the crown land of his house, land which had fallen into David's royal possession. David's personal invitation that he live at the court is, however, more than a mere honor; it enables David to keep his eye on Saul's grandson and to counter any traitorous plans that might develop. Mephibosheth's response is so effusive that we are unable to judge whether he was truly happy with this arrangement or not. In any case, he obeys and comes to live in Jerusalem.

The cultivation of Saul's former royal estate is delegated by David to the servant Ziba, who has the necessary family and servants and who can therefore bring his master's household sufficient revenue to support it at the capital. A final note brings not only another description of Mephibosheth's privileged status at court ("like one of the king's sons") but also mention of his son Mica. We see that there still are rivals for the succession to David's throne from the house of Saul!

TRANSJORDANIAN CAMPAIGNS   10

The scene of our narrative shifts from the Jerusalem court to the realm of international events, and the reader is confronted with what seems to be an official campaign report from the royal archives, a document interrupted at 11:2 to present the David-Bathsheba story (11:2 – 12:25) but continued to its conclusion in 12:26-31.

The First Campaign Against Ammon   *10:1-14*

¹ **After this the king of the Ammonites died, and Hanun his son reigned in his stead. ² And David said, "I will deal loyally with Hanun the son of Nahash, as his father dealt loyally with me." So David sent by his servants to console him concerning his father. And David's servants came into the land of the Ammonites. ³ But the princes of the Ammonites said to Hanun their lord, "Do you think, because David has sent comforters to you, that he is honoring your father? Has not David sent his servants to you to search the city, and to spy it out, and to overthrow it?" ⁴ So Hanun took David's servants, and shaved off half the beard of each, and cut off their garments in the middle, at their hips, and sent them away. ⁵ When it was told David, he sent to meet them, for the men were greatly ashamed. And the king said,**

"Remain at Jericho until your beards have grown, and then return."

6 When the Ammonites saw that they had become odious to David, the Ammonites sent and hired the Syrians of Beth-rehob, and the Syrians of Zobah, twenty thousand foot soldiers, and the king of Maacah with a thousand men, and the men of Tob, twelve thousand men. 7 And when David heard of it, he sent Joab and all the host of the mighty men. 8 And the Ammonites came out and drew up in battle array at the entrance of the gate; and the Syrians of Zobah and of Rehob, and the men of Tob and Maacah, were by themselves in the open country.

9 When Joab saw that the battle was set against him both in front and in the rear, he chose some of the picked men of Israel, and arrayed them against the Syrians; 10 the rest of his men he put in the charge of Abishai his brother, and he arrayed them against the Ammonites. 11 And he said, "If the Syrians are too strong for me, then you shall help me; but if the Ammonites are too strong for you, then I will come and help you. 12 Be of good courage, and let us play the man for our people, and for the cities of our God; and may the LORD do what seems good to him." 13 So Joab and the people who were with him drew near to battle against the Syrians; and they fled before him. 14 And when the Ammonites saw that the Syrians fled, they likewise fled before Abishai, and entered the city. Then Joab returned from fighting against the Ammonites, and came to Jerusalem.

Our chapter describes two campaigns in Transjordan, the one against the Ammonites (10:1-14), the other against the Syrians, or Aramaeans (10:15-19). Believing his advisers' claim that the Israelite "courtesy call" on the occasion of his father's death is merely an excuse for more dangerous subversive activity, the young Ammonite king publicly humiliates David's distinguished ambassadors by cutting off half their beards and reducing their flowing robes to indecent brevity — to the jubilation of the mocking Ammonites but to the outrage of Israel and its king. David protects the ambassadors from further public shame by not requiring their immediate return to the court. Then he sends forth Joab and the special task force made up of the professional soldiers who had long since distinguished themselves in skill and valor. The Syrians, who had often represented a real danger for the existence and expansion of David's young empire, now suddenly appear in superior numbers as allies of the Ammonites.

The result is that Joab is caught, seemingly unexpectedly, between the Ammonite force (stationed at the gate of their capital Rabbah) and the approaching Syrians. He is forced to fight on two fronts, to divide his smaller force into two sections, himself turning with picked battalions against the more dangerous Syrians, while Abishai with the rest is to hold the Ammonites at bay.

The situation is touch and go. Defeat would seal the fate of Israel and of its new empire. Joab calls for courage and believing trust in the Lord, the mighty Man of War, who can give victory. His trust is not disappointed. The Syrians are routed before the onslaught of Joab's determined men, and the Ammonites flee back within their city's walls. The immediate threat is obviated, and since his force is not large enough to undertake a siege, Joab returns to Jerusalem.

Victory over the Syrians *15-19*

¹⁵ But when the Syrians saw that they had been defeated by Israel, they gathered themselves together. ¹⁶ And Hadadezer sent, and brought out the Syrians who were beyond the Euphrates; ᶻ and they came to Helam, with Shobach the commander of the army of Hadadezer at their head. ¹⁷ And when it was told David, he gathered all Israel together, and crossed the Jordan, and came to Helam. And the Syrians arrayed themselves against David, and fought with him. ¹⁸ And the Syrians fled before Israel; and David slew of the Syrians the men of seven hundred chariots, and forty thousand horsemen, and wounded Shobach the commander of their army, so that he died there. ¹⁹ And when all the kings who were servants of Hadadezer saw that they had been defeated by Israel, they made peace with Israel, and became subject to them. So the Syrians feared to help the Ammonites any more.

ᶻ Heb *river*

Soon David has to meet a renewed attack by gigantic Syrian forces led by the disappointed Hadadezer of Zobah, who for this second expedition musters reserve forces from as far away as the Euphrates region. David's opposing force is now also much larger, including not only the specialist task force of professionals but also the people's army of Israel. The result is a complete victory for David. Perhaps David now launched his devastating expedition against Syria, making it a vassal state (cf. 8:5 f.). The following year he sends forth his entire military force to ravage the Ammonite countryside and besiege the city of Rabbah (11:1, 22-24; 12: 26 ff.). Meanwhile something of greater significance for the succession to his throne is happening in Jerusalem.

DAVID AND BATHSHEBA   11

David's Adultery   *11:1-5*

¹ In the spring of the year, the time when kings
go forth to battle, David sent Joab, and his servants
with him, and all Israel; and they ravaged the Ammonites, and besieged Rabbah. But David remained
at Jerusalem.

² It happened, late one afternoon, when David
arose from his couch and was walking upon the roof
of the king's house, that he saw from the roof a woman
bathing; and the woman was very beautiful. ³ And
David sent and inquired about the woman. And one
said, "Is not this Bathsheba, the daughter of Eliam,
the wife of Uriah the Hittite?" ⁴ So David sent messengers, and took her; and she came to him, and he
lay with her. (Now she was purifying herself from
her uncleanness.) Then she returned to her house.
⁵ And the woman conceived; and she sent and told
David, "I am with child."

The famous story of David and Bathsheba is inserted between the two parts of the report on the campaign against Ammon. While the siege of the Ammonite
capital is delegated to Joab, the king remains in Jerusalem, perhaps prevented by popular demand from any
further personal participation in military combat after
a recent close call (cf. 21:15 ff.), and therefore, it seems,
somewhat at loose ends. One day that summer, after
spending the hottest hours of the day in a siesta indoors,
the king goes forth to the flat roof of the palace to enjoy
the usual evening breeze. From the palace roof which
is higher than the neighboring houses, he sees Bathsheba bathing in a courtyard below. Our account con-

centrates so exclusively on David's actions that we hear nothing about why she bathed where she could be seen or why David had to inquire about the identity of the wife of a prominent officer, the daughter of a leading family (23:34). We often spend time speculating about such secondary matters; our dramatic account, however, is so famous precisely because it pauses only very rarely to explain such matters while it masterfully concentrates on David's actions. Bathsheba's beauty is sufficient to inflame the king's desire, and the rest follows quickly. The only note of explanation offered is that she was bathing to purify herself from her monthly uncleanness—a time known even in the ancient world as especially favorable for conception. And that is exactly what results.

Unsuccessful Attempts at Covering Up His Sin   6-13

⁶ So David sent word to Joab, "Send me Uriah the Hittite." And Joab sent Uriah to David. ⁷ When Uriah came to him, David asked how Joab was doing, and how the people fared, and how the war prospered. ⁸ Then David said to Uriah, "Go down to your house, and wash your feet." And Uriah went out of the king's house, and there followed him a present from the king. ⁹ But Uriah slept at the door of the king's house with all the servants of his lord, and did not go down to his house. ¹⁰ When they told David, "Uriah did not go down to his house," David said to Uriah, "Have you not come from a journey? Why did you not go down to your house?" ¹¹ Uriah said to David, "The ark and Israel and Judah dwell in booths; and my lord Joab and the servants of my lord are camping in the open field; shall I then go to my house, to eat and to drink, and to lie with my wife? As you live,

and as your soul lives, I will not do this thing." **¹²** **Then David said to Uriah, "Remain here today also, and tomorrow I will let you depart." So Uriah remained in Jerusalem that day, and the next.** **¹³** **And David invited him, and he ate in his presence and drank, so that he made him drunk; and in the evening he went out to lie on his couch with the servants of his lord, but he did not go down to his house.**

At first David is by no means minded to murder the husband; in fact, by making it possible for Uriah to be considered the father of the child that is on the way, David wishes to both hide his own sin and save the wife. He therefore recalls Uriah from the front on a pretext and then tries to persuade him to go home and live with his wife, employing all sorts of subterfuges: beside the special leave from the front, a royal gift, a court drinking bout (to befuddle his wits), a postponement of his return to the front. Uriah's refusal to enjoy the pleasures of domestic life is based not merely on a strong feeling of solidarity with the army still at war but primarily on a religious scruple. Though a non-Israelite, Uriah takes seriously the ancient Israelite sex taboo for soldiers consecrated for a holy war (cf. p. 106, item 7). Speculations which view Uriah's decision to sleep in the guardhouse as sullenness based on a knowledge of the scandal go beyond the Biblical account into the usually fruitless attempts to get behind the narrative to "the original historical situation," which, however, cannot be established to any further degree than our purposely brief account permits. In the case of none of the chief characters involved do we find out precisely what is going on within him. That can, of course, be guessed at as we read between the lines, adding immeasurably to the interest with which we follow the narrative. Our narrator knows how to tell about the most delicate matters without giving offense, also he touches on most complex affairs without our being fully aware of the complexity of the events that are taking place.

Captain Joab Contrives the Murder of Uriah
for His Royal Master 14-17

[14] In the morning David wrote a letter to Joab, and sent it by the hand of Uriah. [15] In the letter he wrote, "Set Uriah in the forefront of the hardest fighting, and then draw back from him, that he may be struck down, and die." [16] And as Joab was besieging the city, he assigned Uriah to the place where he knew there were valiant men. [17] And the men of the city came out and fought with Joab; and some of the servants of David among the people fell. Uriah the Hittite was slain also.

Uriah's repeated refusals finally leave David with only one alternative: he must get rid of Uriah! Most unsparingly the Biblical account reveals how David himself commands Uriah's murder — in a letter which Uriah himself must deliver to Joab. At the front Joab proves to be much more skillful at disguising this murder than the king's instructions had stipulated. The actual murder is made much less obvious when Joab's purposely unwise tactics hazard the lives of others beside Uriah. Such an "improvement" on David's wickedness is typical of this extremely capable but sinister general, who had not shrunk from treacherously stabbing Abner (3:26 ff.) and who will not, in the future, shrink from murders he considers necessary for the welfare of the state (beside Uriah, Absalom, 18:14, and

290

Amasa, 20:10). Joab now knows that when his royal master is in a tight spot, he, too, resorts to murder — the very thing for which David had once cursed him and his family (3:29). In the light of David's later statement (1 Kings 2:5-7) Joab seems to have delighted in "being in on David's secret" and thus "having his number." In any case, the result of Joab's revised plan is that Uriah appears to have died a hero's death and no suspicious circumstances are attached to it.

A Cover-Up That Eludes Everyone —
Except the Lord!   18-27

¹⁸ Then Joab sent and told David all the news about the fighting; ¹⁹ and he instructed the messenger, "When you have finished telling all the news about the fighting to the king, ²⁰ then, if the king's anger rises, and if he says to you, 'Why did you go so near the city to fight? Did you not know that they would shoot from the wall? ²¹ Who killed Abimelech the son of Jerubbesheth? Did not a woman cast an upper millstone upon him from the wall, so that he died at Thebez? Why did you go so near the wall?' then you shall say, 'Your servant Uriah the Hittite is dead also.'"

²² So the messenger went, and came and told David all that Joab had sent him to tell. ²³ The messenger said to David, "The men gained an advantage over us, and came out against us in the field; but we drove them back to the entrance of the gate. ²⁴ Then the archers shot at your servants from the wall; some of the king's servants are dead; and your servant Uriah the Hittite is dead also." ²⁵ David said to the messenger, "Thus shall you say to Joab, 'Do not let this matter trouble you, for the sword devours now

one and now another; strengthen your attack upon the city, and overthrow it.' And encourage him."

²⁶ When the wife of Uriah heard that Uriah her husband was dead, she made lamentation for her husband. ²⁷ And when the mourning was over, David sent and brought her to his house, and she became his wife, and bore him a son. But the thing that David had done displeased the LORD.

Joab's communique from the front had to include a report of the unwise tactics that flouted elementary military principles and cost the lives of some of the king's best men. Joab knew that the king ordinarily held the lives of his men dear and that an investigation could therefore be anticipated. Hence Joab shrewdly prepares the messenger with one "incidental" piece of information that will cause the king to see the action in another light: the note that Uriah was among those who fell. The Septuagint version preserves a fuller and more vivid account of the messenger's report at the Jerusalem court (here its expansion of v. 22 is bracketed):

> So the messenger went and came and told David all that Joab sent him to tell [all the news of the war. And David's anger burned against Joab and he said to the messenger, "Why did you go so near to the city to fight? Did you not know that they would shoot from the wall? Who killed Abimelech, son of Jerubbesheth? Did not a woman cast an upper millstone upon him from the wall, so that he died at Thebez? Why did you go so near to the wall?"] The messenger said to David, "Because the men gained an advantage over us and came out against us in the field; but we drove . . .

Such verbatim repetition is the mark of superior storytelling, enabling the audience to feel more deeply the

292

impact of already familiar statements now repeated in a new context. Here such a repetition heightens the highly dramatic contrast between the king's initial anger at the casualties among his men (Joab's improved plan had disguised the murder so successfully that even David did not connect the news with the letter he had written!) and the sudden calm with which he greets the crucial point about Uriah's death. The king, to be sure, frivolously falls back on an old proverb to the effect that, after all, people do get killed in war; and then he encourages Joab to take heart and complete the siege! Therewith David has achieved his goal. Bathsheba, after the customary seven days of ritual mourning for her husband, is brought to the palace, where she subsequently bears David a son.

But now at the very end the narrator makes his important point, bringing in a short "punch line" — the Lord's evaluation of all of this. Up to this point there had been no such reference to the Lord. And it had almost seemed that the man whom the Lord had singled out to be the founder of the enduring dynasty would get by with his unbridled lust and his murder of a loyal officer. But now we hear the divine verdict: "But the thing that David had done displeased the LORD." What the Lord's displeasure will mean becomes clear in the continuation of the story in the next chapter.

DAVID'S REPENTANCE   12:1-25

David's Sin Exposed by the Lord's Messenger   *1-12*

¹ **And the LORD sent Nathan to David. He came to him, and said to him, "There were two men in a certain city, the one rich and the other poor. ² The**

293

rich man had very many flocks and herds; ³ but the poor man had nothing but one little ewe lamb, which he had bought. And he brought it up, and it grew up with him and with his children; it used to eat of his morsel, and drink from his cup, and lie in his bosom, and it was like a daughter to him. ⁴ Now there came a traveler to the rich man, and he was unwilling to take one of his own flock or herd to prepare for the wayfarer who had come to him, but he took the poor man's lamb, and prepared it for the man who had come to him." ⁵ Then David's anger was greatly kindled against the man; and he said to Nathan, "As the LORD lives, the man who has done this deserves to die; ⁶ and he shall restore the lamb fourfold, because he did this thing, and because he had no pity."

⁷ Nathan said to David, "You are the man. Thus says the LORD, the God of Israel, 'I anointed you king over Israel, and I delivered you out of the hand of Saul; ⁸ and I gave you your master's house, and your master's wives into your bosom, and gave you the house of Israel and of Judah; and if this were too little, I would add to you as much more. ⁹ Why have you despised the word of the LORD, to do what is evil in his sight? You have smitten Uriah the Hittite with the sword, and have taken his wife to be your wife, and have slain him with the sword of the Ammonites. ¹⁰ Now therefore the sword shall never depart from your house, because you have despised me, and have taken the wife of Uriah the Hittite to be your wife.' ¹¹ Thus says the LORD, 'Behold, I will raise up evil against you out of your own house; and I will take your wives before your eyes, and give them to your neighbor, and he shall lie with your wives in the sight of this sun. ¹² For you did it se-

cretly; but I will do this thing before all Israel, and before the sun.'"

It is the Lord who sends His messenger, the prophet Nathan, to the impenitent king, ostensibly to present a case for the king's judgment, a case of flagrant oppression of the poor by the rich. In order to avoid the social stigma of having refused traditional hospitality, a wealthy farmer had been forced to furnish a meal to a traveler. But instead of taking from his own numerous flocks, he brutally seized a poor family's pet lamb, so that his "hospitality" cost him nothing. David's sense of justice decrees nothing less than death for that culprit, besides a fourfold restitution for the poor man. The irony of the situation, however, is that David has unwittingly sentenced himself to death. For by means of the clear-cut hypothetical case it is easy for the prophet to persuade the king to see his own real situation and to condemn his own enormous wickedness. Nathan's interview with David is, however, much more than a private counseling session for the improvement of the king's moral health. The prophet had been sent as the Lord's messenger (hence the messenger formula: "Thus says the LORD"). First of all, therefore, Nathan recalls the riches of divine grace David had received. Thereupon the prophet demands, "Why have you despised the word of the LORD, to do what is evil in his sight?" And, finally, he pronounces a twofold divine verdict that links the recent crimes to future punishments: his bloody murder of a trusted officer will result in the sword's continuing to make a bloody path through David's own house (his sons Amnon, Absalom, Adonijah), and the punishment for his adultery will be as public as the original crime had been secret. (Cf. 16:22)

The Lord's Absolution to the Penitent David   *13-15a*

¹³ **David said to Nathan, "I have sinned against the LORD." And Nathan said to David, "The LORD also has put away your sin; you shall not die. ¹⁴ Nevertheless, because by this deed you have utterly scorned the LORD,^a the child that is born to you shall die." ¹⁵ Then Nathan went to his house.**

^a Heb *the enemies of the* LORD

The Lord responds to David's unqualified confession of sin (cf. 1 Sam. 15:20 f.; Ps. 51:4) with prompt and unqualified absolution, "The LORD also has put away your sin; you shall not die." We may ask: Why not? By what right is the royal culprit spared? The answer of our narrative is simple: The sinner is spared because the Lord is gracious. As He had long since been showering the riches of His grace on David in the past, so now in the present; though David strays from the Lord, He responds by graciously sending His prophet to bring David to a realization of the enormity of his failure and of his worthiness to die. And once this has been achieved, the Lord commutes the sentence into the gracious declaration, "You shall not die." This is, however, by no means "cheap grace," for in the very same pronouncement we hear also the other part of the verdict, introduced by the crucial connective "nevertheless," "the child that is born to you shall die." That is, of course, no selfish demand by a vindictive deity for a Shylock-like pound of flesh. The child must die in order that the sinner who has utterly scorned the Lord may experience in the death of his own innocent son what it means to be condemned and forgiven by God. It will not mean that David will now settle down to enjoy the fruits of divine mercy in complacent piety.

The Agony of Experiencing God's Forgiveness   *15b-23*

And the **LORD** struck the child that Uriah's wife bore to David, and it became sick. [16] David therefore besought God for the child; and David fasted, and went in and lay all night upon the ground. [17] And the elders of his house stood beside him, to raise him from the ground; but he would not, nor did he eat food with them. [18] On the seventh day the child died. And the servants of David feared to tell him that the child was dead; for they said, "Behold, while the child was yet alive, we spoke to him, and he did not listen to us; how then can we say to him the child is dead? He may do himself some harm." [19] But when David saw that his servants were whispering together, David perceived that the child was dead; and David said to his servants, "Is the child dead?" They said, "He is dead." [20] Then David arose from the earth, and washed, and anointed himself, and changed his clothes; and he went into the house of the **LORD**, and worshiped; he then went to his own house; and when he asked, they set food before him, and he ate. [21] Then his servants said to him, "What is this thing that you have done? You fasted and wept for the child while it was alive; but when the child died, you arose and ate food." [22] He said, "While the child was still alive, I fasted and wept; for I said, 'Who knows whether the **LORD** will be gracious to me, that the child may live?' [23] But now he is dead; why should I fast? Can I bring him back again? I shall go to him, but he will not return to me."

When the child is smitten by the Lord with fatal illness, David begins an excruciating daily experience

of the enormity of his wicked deeds and of the inflex-
ibility of the Lord's own gracious and just judgment.
Grace is not cheap for David. He finds the believing
appropriation of such strange divine grace to be much
more difficult and bitter than his initial admission of
guilt. What goes on is therefore an amazing wrestling
with God for the life of his doomed son. Breaking the
usual routine of his royal court, the king spends his
days in the sanctuary on his knees, fasting and praying,
and his nights like a penitent, lying on the bare earth,
consumed with concern for the innocent victim of his
sin. The courtiers are offended at a king who strips
himself of all royal prerogatives and refuses to function
as king out of merely overexaggerated grief for the illness of one of his many sons. They do not realize that
what has brought the king to his knees in genuine repentance and crushing anguish is the high cost of the
Lord's gracious sparing of his own life. Vain therefore
are all their attempts to take David out from under the
crushing load of the Lord's judgment.

But the Lord does not hearken to the king's passionate pleadings. After seven days the child dies. The
courtiers are afraid to break the news to the king,
thinking that his fasting and praying involved only a
father's overfond affection for a dear child and fearing
an outbreak of violent emotion and unpredictable action,
once the bitter news of his death is broken. How much
they have misunderstood their king is clear when the
actual news has the very opposite effect on him. David
surmises what has happened when he sees them whispering to one another, and then abruptly ends his self-
humiliation and returns to normal living with a deter-
mination which surprises and shocks the courtiers, who
expected that he would now certainly raise a lamenta-

tion for the dead son that would be much greater than his pleading for the living child. They are offended at his disregard of the customary rites of mourning. The fact, however, is not that David has been, as the courtiers imagined, too quickly comforted; rather, David has experienced both the inexorability of God-sent death (nothing can change that!) and, at the same time, the forgiveness of his sins, a personal guarantee of which was the death of the child. Therefore David does acquiesce in the death of his son when it comes, knowing that the Lord spared his own life at the cost of his son's life. More is involved in David's response to the courtier's accusation "I shall go to him, but he will not return to me" than deep hopelessness over against the relentlessness of death. In these bitter days David experiences God's own justification of his sinful existence. Spared by God's mercy, he goes to the house of the Lord and worships Him there. Then he goes down to his house, justified!

The Birth of Solomon *24-25*

²⁴ Then David comforted his wife, Bathsheba, and went in to her, and lay with her; and she bore a son, and he called his name Solomon. And the LORD loved him, ²⁵ and sent a message by Nathan the prophet; so he called his name Jedidiah,ᵇ because of the LORD.

ᵇ That is *beloved of the* LORD

David not only returns to normal court life but also consoles the mother of the dead child. The final result is reconciliation: even though the evil cannot be undone and the judgment cannot be turned back, the Lord does bring good out of evil. In place of the lost son the king and his favorite wife receive a son whose name Solomon indicates that health and peace have been restored. Moreover, the brief sentence "And the LORD loved him" is a clear pointer toward future developments, indicating that among the large number of royal sons who will soon be involved in the tumultuous family struggle for the succession to David's throne this child will be the chosen one. This is not a child doomed to die because of the sin of his parents but one "Beloved of the LORD" as Jedidiah, the name the prophet Nathan gives him, indicates. The son of that wife who might be considered most unworthy of all is the one designated as the Lord's darling "because of the LORD," that means, by grace, not on the basis of merit.

David Finally Takes Ammon   *26-31*

[26] Now Joab fought against Rabbah of the Ammonites, and took the royal city. [27] And Joab sent messengers to David, and said, "I have fought against Rabbah; moreover, I have taken the city of waters. [28] Now, then, gather the rest of the people together, and encamp against the city, and take it; lest I take the city, and it be called by my name." [29] So David gathered all the people together and went to Rabbah, and fought against it and took it. [30] And he took the crown of their king [c] from his head; the weight of it was a talent of gold, and in it was a precious stone; and it was placed on David's head. And he brought forth the spoil of the city, a very great amount. [31] And he brought forth the people who were in it, and set them to labor with saws and iron picks and iron axes, and made them toil at [d] the brickkilns; and thus he

[c] Or *Milcom* See Zeph 1. 5
[d] Cn: Heb *pass through*

did to all the cities of the Ammonites. Then David and all the people returned to Jerusalem.

Now that the Bathsheba story has been completed, the report on the campaign against Ammon (begun at 10:1, but interrupted at 11:1) can be concluded. This campaign is crucial for the future of David's young empire. Hence shrewd General Joab summons David to a larger effort once the decisive point in the protracted siege has been reached (he has successfully assaulted the section of the city where the Ammonite king had certain crown properties — perhaps royal gardens — and a large cistern — supplying water to the city during the siege). Joab calls not merely for the king's own royal presence but, more important, for an entirely new levy of troops. The tribal armies of citizen soldiers had heretofore traditionally served only for brief periods of time in exclusively defensive campaigns. David's employment of them now for bringing foreign territories into the private possession of the Davidic monarchy seems to have taxed the old tribal system beyond endurance — certainly beyond their will to partake year after year in the king's personal empire building. Crises, like the subsequent revolutions of Absalom and Sheba (in which the northern tribes looked to other leaders in attempts to retrieve their old rights), show that David had gone too far. After such revolutions do not succeed, those tribes, who had originally chosen David voluntarily, are forced to serve him against their will. The subsequent defection of the northern tribes from the Davidic monarchy began not merely when Solomon's foolish son Rehoboam would not reduce labor conscriptions; it began already at this time, during David's own lifetime.

In this particular campaign, however, David is successful in mustering "all the people" and in taking the citadel of Rabbah as well as all the cities of the Ammonites. David receives personally both the vast booty and the crown that symbolizes sovereignty over the land of the Ammonites. Since a talent (more than 75 lbs!) seems heavy for an ordinary crown, some scholars hold that such a heavy crown was meant for Milcom, the god of the Ammonites, and that David either (1) took the crown off the head of the Ammonite national cult statue and set the jewel which it contained in his own crown, or (2) did not hesitate to put the crown of the conquered god-king on his own head. In any case, this crown is the fifth that David won (after those of Ziklag, Judah, Israel, and Jerusalem). It becomes David's not through the aid of only his own professional mercenaries or by special covenant but by aid of the united military power of his entire empire, including the people's armies of North and South.

The inhabitants of the conquered city-state are either enslaved—prisoners of war in the ancient Near East often became slaves—or merely subjected to periodic forced labor on specific projects (cf. Ex. 1:11-14). In any case, the subjugated peoples aided in the building up of David's empire.

THE BEGINNING
OF AN AVALANCHE OF EVIL   13:1 — 14:3

There appears to be little connection between this new story and the preceding one until we realize that what now begins as a private affair (Amnon is smitten with uncontrollable lust for Absalom's sister) sets off a chain reaction that will spread into public life and cause tremendous upheavals throughout the nation — in the process eliminating the most likely successors to the throne, first Amnon, and then Absalom — with the result that when the full story has been told in Chs. 13 — 20, only one prince, Adonijah, remains as Solomon's rival for the throne.

The Crown-Prince Rapes His Half-Sister   *1-19*

¹ Now Absalom, David's son, had a beautiful sister, whose name was Tamar; and after a time Amnon, David's son, loved her. ² And Amnon was so tormented that he made himself ill because of his sister Tamar; for she was a virgin, and it seemed impossible to Amnon to do anything to her. ³ But Amnon had a friend, whose name was Jonadab, the son of Shimeah, David's brother; and Jonadab was a very crafty man. ⁴ And he said to him, "O son of the king, why are you so haggard morning after morning? Will you not tell me?" Amnon said to him, "I love Tamar, my brother Absalom's sister." ⁵ Jonadab said to him, "Lie down on your bed, and pretend to be ill; and when your father comes to see you, say to him, 'Let my sister Tamar come and give me bread to eat, and prepare the food in my sight, that I may see it, and eat it from her hand.'" ⁶ So Amnon lay down, and pretended to be ill; and when the king came to see him, Amnon said to the king, "Pray let my sister Tamar come and make a couple of cakes in my sight, that I may eat from her hand."

⁷ Then David sent home to Tamar, saying, "Go to your brother Amnon's house, and prepare food for him." ⁸ So Tamar went to her brother Amnon's house,

where he was lying down. And she took dough, and kneaded it, and made cakes in his sight, and baked the cakes. ⁹ And she took the pan and emptied it out before him, but he refused to eat. And Amnon said, "Send out every one from me." So every one went out from him. ¹⁰ Then Amnon said to Tamar, "Bring the food into the chamber, that I may eat from your hand." And Tamar took the cakes she had made, and brought them into the chamber to Amnon her brother. ¹¹ But when she brought them near him to eat, he took hold of her, and said to her, "Come, lie with me, my sister." ¹² She answered him, "No, my brother, do not force me; for such a thing is not done in Israel; do not do this wanton folly. ¹³ As for me, where could I carry my shame? And as for you, you would be as one of the wanton fools in Israel. Now therefore, I pray you, speak to the king; for he will not withhold me from you." ¹⁴ But he would not listen to her; and being stronger than she, he forced her, and lay with her.

¹⁵ Then Amnon hated her with very great hatred; so that the hatred with which he hated her was greater than the love with which he had loved her. And Amnon said to her, "Arise, be gone." ¹⁶ But she said to him, "No, my brother; for this wrong in sending me away is greater than the other which you did to me." *e* But he would not listen to her. ¹⁷ He called the young man who served him and said, "Put this woman out of my presence, and bolt the door after her." ¹⁸ Now she was wearing a long robe with sleeves; for thus were the virgin daughters of the

---

e Cn Compare Gk Vg: Heb *No, for this great wrong in sending me away is (worse) than the other which you did to me*

king clad of old.*f* So his servant put her out, and
bolted the door after her. **19 And Tamar put ashes
on her head, and rent the long robe which she wore;
and she laid her hand on her head, and went away,
crying aloud as she went.**

f Cn: Heb *clad in robes*

David's firstborn, Amnon, is a sensual brute whose
vicious lust for Tamar had been frustrated only by the
impossibility of seducing a virgin princess who lives
in the seclusion of the palace and does not enjoy the
freedom of movement that the royal princes have, each
of whom lives in his own house. A crafty cousin, a court
ne'er-do-well, by the name of Jonadab, suggests to
the lustsick Amnon that he satisfy his desire by making
use of a prevailing custom that called for a sick man's
repast to be prepared by specially trained women. By
feigning illness and getting his indulgent royal father
to order the princess Tamar to prepare the heart-shaped
cakes that were presumably to melt the sick man's
heart with their succulence, he could get the object
of his passion into his bedroom and power. The carefully laid plan proves successful. Since both attendants
and princess obey the sick man's every whim, step by
step Amnon finally reaches the point where he has
Tamar alone and at his mercy in his bedroom. In vain
are her many cogent appeals — even her willingness to
enter honorable marriage with him.

Amnon Abandons Tamar
While Absalom Bides His Time   *20-22*

**20 And her brother Absalom said to her, "Has
Amnon your brother been with you? Now hold your**

305

peace, my sister; he is your brother; do not take this to heart." So Tamar dwelt, a desolate woman, in her brother Absalom's house. ²¹ When King David heard of all these things, he was very angry. ²² But Absalom spoke to Amnon neither good nor bad; for Absalom hated Amnon, because he had forced his sister Tamar.

Having raped Tamar, the brutal monster further outrages her distraught feelings by cruelly ordering her out of his presence. He even gives the servant who is to throw her out of the house the impression that she has been forcing her unwelcome attention on him. She finally leaves the barred door — her disheveled hair befouled by ashes, her long-sleeved robe torn, her hands beating her head, crying loudly and bitterly, as she enters a future of living death, a ravished and abandoned woman.

Angered though he is, her brother Absalom does not choose to make an immediate issue of the outrage but purposely plays it down, perhaps in order to hide the family's shame, but most certainly in order to wait for a more favorable opportunity. In the meantime, however, he gives no indication of his thoughts or feelings. On hearing of the atrocity, King David is very angry. Surprisingly enough, however, he does nothing, undoubtedly because Amnon, as his firstborn son, has a special place in his affections (so the Septuagint), but even more likely because he looks upon Amnon as the next king. David does not seem to realize what the narrator has already pointed out, that the successor will be not Amnon but Solomon, the "Beloved of the LORD." Though the narrator does not explicitly say so, we get the impression that David failed at this point when he neglected to punish Amnon, thus leaving Absalom with a reason for taking the law into his own hands and starting an avalanche of evil. But as usual, our narrator does not stop to explain such undercurrents. In any case, Absalom is determined to vindicate his sister's honor and perhaps also to become first candidate for the throne by virtue of Amnon's death, though again the narrator does not explicitly bring out the latter reason.

Absalom's Murder of Amnon
Unsettles the Kingdom's Stability   23-36

23 After two full years Absalom had sheepshearers at Baal-hazor, which is near Ephraim, and Absalom invited all the king's sons. 24 And Absalom came to the king, and said, "Behold, your servant has sheepshearers, pray let the king and his servants go with your servant." 25 But the king said to Absalom, "No, my son, let us not all go, lest we be burdensome to you." He pressed him, but he would not go but gave him his blessing. 26 Then Absalom said, "If not, pray let my brother Amnon go with us." And the king said to him, "Why should he go with you?" 27 But Absalom pressed him until he let Amnon and all the king's sons go with him. 28 Then Absalom commanded his servants, "Mark when Amnon's heart is merry with wine, and when I say to you, 'Strike Amnon,' then kill him. Fear not; have I not commanded you? Be courageous and be valiant." 29 So the servants of Absalom did to Amnon as Absalom had commanded. Then all the king's sons arose, and each mounted his mule and fled.

30 While they were on the way, tidings came to David, "Absalom has slain all the king's sons, and

not one of them is left." ³¹ Then the king arose, and rent his garments, and lay on the earth; and all his servants who were standing by rent their garments. ³² But Jonadab the son of Shimeah, David's brother, said, "Let not my lord suppose that they have killed all the young men the king's sons, for Amnon alone is dead, for by the command of Absalom this has been determined from the day he forced his sister Tamar. ³³ Now therefore let not my lord the king so take it to heart as to suppose that all the king's sons are dead; for Amnon alone is dead."

³⁴ But Absalom fled. And the young man who kept the watch lifted up his eyes, and looked, and behold, many people were coming from the Horonaim road ᵍ by the side of the mountain. ³⁵ And Jonadab said to the king, "Behold, the king's sons have come; as your servant said, so it has come about." ³⁶ And as soon as he had finished speaking, behold, the king's sons came, and lifted up their voice and wept; and the king also and all his servants wept very bitterly.

ᵍ Cn Compare Gk: Heb *the road behind him*

Two years go by. Absalom bides his time – typical of the cold calculation that is an outstanding characteristic of this proud son of a princess from Aramaean Geshur. His well-laid plans make use of the festival of sheep-shearing celebrated on his estate north of Jerusalem at Baal-hazor. First he invites all the royal princes except the heir apparent. Then he goes to the palace to invite the head of the family. He expects, it seems, that the king will not come himself, but that he will for that very reason all the more surely send the crown prince as his representative. Absalom is most persistent in pressing his royal father, wresting the key concession from a seemingly suspicious, but nevertheless indulgent father even after the king had actually broken off the audience with his impetuous son by means of a farewell blessing. The result therefore is that the crown prince Amnon must attend the celebration and thus go to certain death — at the command of the king, who, as usual, is unable to overcome his indulgence toward his children.

At the farm a truly royal banquet readies the unsuspecting victim for the slaughter. The murder, of course, brings the festivities to an abrupt end, and the guests hastily bestraddle their royal mules in headlong flight. At the court in Jerusalem, a false initial rumor proclaims that Absalom has killed all the royal sons, thus bringing the king to the brink of utter despair. Struck by the divine judgment Nathan had proclaimed, the king is rightly concerned about the continuance of the promise of an enduring dynasty that Nathan had also proclaimed.

The king's nephew Jonadab advises David to discount the rumor, correctly surmising that Absalom has been concerned only with killing Amnon. Jonadab rejoices when the watchman corroborates his guess and reports the approach of many royal sons from the north. Only Amnon is dead. Even at that the heir apparent has been assassinated in bloody vengeance; the prince next in line, Absalom, is now an exile; and everyone knows that there will be no real stability in the realm until the question about the succession is settled.

The King Relents and Joab Moves
to Settle an Unsettled Situation   *13:37 — 14:3*

37 But Absalom fled, and went to Talmai the son of Ammihud, king of Geshur. And David mourned

for his son day after day. [38] So Absalom fled, and went to Geshur, and was there three years. [39] And the spirit [h] of the king longed to go forth to Absalom; for he was comforted about Amnon, seeing he was dead.

[1] Now Joab the son of Zeruiah perceived that the king's heart went out to Absalom. [2] And Joab sent to Tekoa, and fetched from there a wise woman, and said to her, "Pretend to be a mourner, and put on mourning garments; do not anoint yourself with oil, but behave like a woman who has been mourning many days for the dead; [3] and go to the king, and speak thus to him." So Joab put the words in her mouth.

[h] Gk: Heb *David*

David's mourning for Amnon continues day after day for a long time. Actually the king has lost two sons, one fallen by the sword (Amnon), the other banished for murder (Absalom), as good as dead, living in exile at the court of his maternal grandfather in Geshur, east of the Sea of Galilee. But again David is not master of his own emotions. Though he makes no moves for three years, even though the future of the state is beset by uncertainty and intrigue as to the succession, gradually his attitude toward Absalom softens. And when the king begins to long for Absalom, shrewd General Joab thinks it time to move forward and settle the unsettled and unsettling question about the succession to the throne. It is perhaps also natural for Joab to work for the recall of that royal son who seems to him to be most qualified to succeed David, especially since Absalom is, like himself, energetic, gifted, capable. But since even the

310

suggestion that the king recall Amnon's murderer is
a delicate matter, Joab shrewdly approaches the king
about it only indirectly, through a wise woman from the
village of Tekoa, 10 miles south of Jerusalem, the
prophet Amos' native town.

JOAB NEGOTIATES THE RECALL
OF ABSALOM   14:4-33

The King Hears a Case Involving Blood Vengeance 4-11

**⁴ When the woman of Tekoa came to the king,
she fell on her face to the ground, and did obeisance,
and said, "Help, O king." ⁵ And the king said to her,
"What is your trouble?" She answered, "Alas, I am
a widow; my husband is dead. ⁶ And your handmaid
had two sons, and they quarreled with one another
in the field; there was no one to part them, and one
struck the other and killed him. ⁷ And now the whole
family has risen against your handmaid, and they
say, 'Give up the man who struck his brother, that
we may kill him for the life of his brother whom he
slew'; and so they would destroy the heir also. Thus
they would quench my coal which is left, and leave
to my husband neither name nor remnant upon the
face of the earth."**

**⁸ Then the king said to the woman, "Go to your
house, and I will give orders concerning you." ⁹ And
the woman of Tekoa said to the king, "On me be the
guilt, my lord the king, and on my father's house;
let the king and his throne be guiltless." ¹⁰ The king
said, "If any one says anything to you, bring him to
me, and he shall never touch you again." ¹¹ Then she
said, "Pray let the king invoke the LORD your God,**

that the avenger of blood slay no more, and my son be not destroyed." He said, "As the **LORD** lives, not one hair of your son shall fall to the ground."

The remarkable woman who acts as Joab's agent comes to the royal court, disguised in a widow's mourning garments, to present a case for his judgment. She is appealing from the judgment of her local clansmen to the highest legal authority in the land. She tells David that she had two sons. In a quarrel one killed the other, and now the clan demands the blood of the murderer. But, she pleads, if he is killed, her entire family will be snuffed out and her property will be taken over by the clan. This woman is not satisfied with David's vague promise to take the case under advisement (v. 8), nor even with his prohibiting the clan from taking blood revenge. She also wants her own life protected from possible reprisals by the clan (v. 9), and she even insists that the king bind himself with a solemn oath sworn by the name of the Lord, to the effect that the avenging kinsman will not be permitted to carry out his normal duty. (V. 11)

The Surprising Point of an Ambiguous Speech
Becomes Clear to the King!　　　　　　　　*12-17*

[12] Then the woman said, "Pray let your handmaid speak a word to my lord the king." He said, "Speak." [13] And the woman said, "Why then have you planned such a thing against the people of God? For in giving this decision the king convicts himself, inasmuch as the king does not bring his banished one home again. [14] We must all die, we are like water spilt on the ground, which cannot be gathered up

again; but God will not take away the life of him who devises [i] means not to keep his banished one an outcast. [15] Now I have come to say this to my lord the king because the people have made me afraid; and your handmaid thought, 'I will speak to the king; it may be that the king will perform the request of his servant. [16] For the king will hear, and deliver his servant from the hand of the man who would destroy me and my son together from the heritage of God.' [17] And your handmaid thought, 'The word of my lord the king will set me at rest'; for my lord the king is like the angel of God to discern good and evil. The LORD your God be with you!"

[i] Cn: Heb *and he devises*

After she has successfully obtained the king's guarantee for her son's life, she continues in her suit to plead for his recall from banishment and his restoration to normal status at home. At this point her disguise becomes very thin; it is even momentarily dropped in v. 13 where it is quite clear that she is really pleading for the banished Absalom. The disguise is soon put on again, however, ostensibly to win the final part of her appeal, but actually to make the king truly aware of all that is implied in his own keeping Absalom in banishment. Her entire speech with its delightful ambiguity is a psychological masterpiece, for, though she makes believe that she is really concerned for her own son and the future of her own family, at the same time she clearly reveals the situation of the "widowed" nation, which has been deprived of the sorely needed heir apparent by the action of the king, who is acting in behalf of his own aggrieved family rather than for the future well-being of the entire nation.

313

Joab Negotiates the Return of Absalom 18-27

¹⁸ Then the king answered the woman, "Do not hide from me anything I ask you." And the woman said, "Let my lord the king speak." ¹⁹ The king said, "Is the hand of Joab with you in all this?" The woman answered and said, "As surely as you live, my lord the king, one cannot turn to the right hand or to the left from anything that my lord the king has said. It was your servant Joab who bade me; it was he who put all these words in the mouth of your handmaid. ²⁰ In order to change the course of affairs your servant Joab did this. But my lord has wisdom like the wisdom of the angel of God to know all things that are on the earth."

²¹ Then the king said to Joab, "Behold now, I grant this; go, bring back the young man Absalom." ²² And Joab fell on his face to the ground, and did obeisance, and blessed the king; and Joab said, "Today your servant knows that I have found favor in your sight, my lord the king, in that the king has granted the request of his servant." ²³ So Joab arose and went to Geshur, and brought Absalom to Jerusalem. ²⁴ And the king said, "Let him dwell apart in his own house; he is not to come into my presence." So Absalom dwelt apart in his own house, and did not come into the king's presence.

²⁵ Now in all Israel there was no one so much to be praised for his beauty as Absalom; from the sole of his foot to the crown of his head there was no blemish in him. ²⁶ And when he cut the hair of his head (for at the end of every year he used to cut it; when it was heavy on him, he cut it), he weighed the hair of his head, two hundred shekels by the king's

weight. ²⁷ There were born to Absalom three sons, and one daughter whose name was Tamar; she was a beautiful woman.

The concluding scene of her audience with the king (vv. 18-20) is especially well constructed — calculated to make the hearers and readers chuckle at the outcome. For the king does, of course, finally see through the comedy that has been played before his eyes, but only after he is unable to endanger the success of the entire maneuver. Not even her being unmasked as Joab's agent discomfits this "wise" and talkative woman. In fact, it gives her another opportunity to unabashedly flatter the king. By this time our narrator has his audience snickering not only at this precious bit of persistent feminine talkativeness but also at the enforced long-suffering of the king, who "finally gets the message." In playing a hunch that his royal master would be indulgent to his banished child, Joab had taken a risk, but he had now won. Hence the king speaks directly to him and grants his request: Absalom is to be brought back from banishment, a completely free man but not yet permitted to enter the royal presence. Joab is happy to go to Geshur to escort the prince back to the capital.

The subsequent description of Absalom's outstanding beauty and of his fine young family serves to present him at this point as a noble prince who is well suited to be the successor to David. The mention of his luxurious hair, weighing 3½ to 4 lbs. at each shearing, not only prepares us for the story of his end but also reflects the popular impression the young prince made on his contemporaries. V. 27 is seemingly contradicted by 18:18. Since vv. 25-27 interrupt the main narrative, some scholars consider them an insertion from another tradition (cf. Introduction, pp. 14 ff.). But it is equally possible that these sons died in the meantime, possibly in childhood. In fact, it may be that the daughter, Tamar, is specially noted here because she alone survived to carry on the family line.

Absalom Is Pardoned and Fully Restored
at the Court   *28-33*

²⁸ So Absalom dwelt two full years in Jerusalem, without coming into the king's presence. ²⁹ Then Absalom sent for Joab, to send him to the king; but Joab would not come to him. And he sent a second time, but Joab would not come. ³⁰ Then he said to his servants, "See, Joab's field is next to mine, and he has barley there; go and set it on fire." So Absalom's servants set the field on fire. ³¹ Then Joab arose and went to Absalom at his house, and said to him, "Why have your servants set my field on fire?" ³² Absalom answered Joab, "Behold, I sent word to you, 'Come here, that I may send you to the king, to ask, "Why have I come from Geshur? It would be better for me to be there still." Now therefore let me go into the presence of the king; and if there is guilt in me, let him kill me.'" ³³ Then Joab went to the king, and told him; and he summoned Absalom. So he came to the king, and bowed himself on his face to the ground before the king; and the king kissed Absalom.

Joab raises no finger to get the impetuous and ambitious prince fully restored to his former status until the brilliant young man forces the issue with violent action and an ultimatum that shows that he is not only tired of marking time but also dissatisfied with the half-measures Joab and his royal father have so far taken. He demands either complete restoration or execution. Then Joab undertakes Absalom's cause again — also this time successfully. For David finally grants Absalom the long-denied audience. Then Absalom on his part prostrates himself before his father, and David on his part falls upon his neck and kisses him. After seven long years the prodigal son has come home, and the entire evil affair seems to have worked itself out well. But this is just the moment when a new and more deadly conflict will break out in David's house and empire.

DAVID'S FLIGHT
FROM ABSALOM   15:1 — 16:14

Absalom's Intrigue   *15:1-6*

¹ After this Absalom got himself a chariot and horses, and fifty men to run before him. ² And Absalom used to rise early and stand beside the way of the gate; and when any man had a suit to come before the king for judgment, Absalom would call to him, and say, "From what city are you?" And when he said, "Your servant is of such and such a tribe in Israel," ³ Absalom would say to him, "See, your claims are good and right; but there is no man deputed by the king to hear you." ⁴ Absalom said moreover, "Oh that I were judge in the land! Then every man with a suit or cause might come to me, and I would give him justice." ⁵ And whenever a man came near to do obeisance to him, he would put out his hand, and take hold of him, and kiss him. ⁶ Thus Absalom did to all of Israel who came to the king for judgment; so Absalom stole the hearts of the men of Israel.

No matter what doubts David and Joab might have had about Absalom's claim to the throne, the prince himself wastes no time in advertising himself as the next king by introducing the non-Israelite prestige symbols associated with royal status in the world of that day (chariot, horses, a 50-man bodyguard). Beside such general public propaganda a more guarded but equally effective technique is the criticism which he directs against the king's seemingly inadequate provisions for the administration of justice. Absalom not only makes himself easily available to petitioners but also halts their attempts at bowing and treating him as more than a helpful friend — all in sharp contrast to the prevailing court ceremonial by means of which the king had made himself increasingly remote from his people. By such measures Absalom seduces the hearts of the people, skillfully exploiting the sectional grievances of the northern tribes, who feel that David has long since violated the covenant they had made with him by forcing them into costly expeditions for the advancement of his personal empire.

The Revolution Begins Most Successfully   7-12

[7] And at the end of four[j] years Absalom said to the king, "Pray let me go and pay my vow, which I have vowed to the LORD, in Hebron. [8] For your servant vowed a vow while I dwelt at Geshur in Aram, saying, 'If the LORD will indeed bring me back to Jerusalem, then I will offer worship to the LORD.'" [9] The king said to him, "Go in peace." So he arose, and went to Hebron. [10] But Absalom sent secret messengers throughout all the tribes of Israel, saying, "As soon as you hear the sound of the trumpet, then

[j] Gk Syr: Heb *forty*

say, 'Absalom is king at Hebron!'" [11] With Absalom went two hundred men from Jerusalem who were invited guests, and they went in their simplicity, and knew nothing. [12] And while Absalom was offering the sacrifices, he sent for [k] Ahithophel the Gilonite, David's counselor, from his city Giloh. And the conspiracy grew strong, and the people with Absalom kept increasing.

[k] Or *sent*

Absalom does not stop at merely courting general popularity with an eye to future advancement. He seems convinced that he must replace his father as soon as possible. For four years he patiently lays the foundation for his coup d'etat. Having won the allegiance of the North, he reckons that a revolt begun with his coronation at the South's ancient sanctuary in Hebron will paralyze the tribe of Judah and keep it from aiding David. The king, blinded as always by paternal affection, gives Absalom permission to fulfill a religious vow sworn to the Lord of his birthplace Hebron. Although the two hundred invited participants seem to have accompanied Absalom to Hebron without any awareness of the real purpose of his visit, in the North secret agents had prepared for the insurrection so well that only relayed trumpet signals are needed to declare Absalom's coronation an accomplished fact. When David's wisest counselor joins the revolutionaries, the conspiracy is assured of intelligent leadership. Every hour sees it grow stronger.

Our narrator's masterful description of the king's flight brilliantly illuminates both David's personality and his precarious situation by confronting the fleeing king with a number of people.

The Fleeing King Is Assured of a Loyal Following

¹³ And a messenger came to David, saying, "The hearts of the men of Israel have gone after Absalom." ¹⁴ Then David said to all his servants who were with him at Jerusalem, "Arise, and let us flee; or else there will be no escape for us from Absalom; go in haste, lest he overtake us quickly, and bring down evil upon us, and smite the city with the edge of the sword." ¹⁵ And the king's servants said to the king, "Behold, your servants are ready to do whatever my lord the king decides." ¹⁶ So the king went forth, and all his household after him. And the king left ten concubines to keep the house. ¹⁷ And the king went forth, and all the people after him; and they halted at the last house. ¹⁸ And all his servants passed by him; and all the Cherethites, and all the Pelethites, and all the six hundred Gittites who had followed him from Gath, passed on before the king.

¹⁹ Then the king said to Ittai the Gittite, "Why do you also go with us? Go back, and stay with the king; for you are a foreigner, and also an exile from *l* your home. ²⁰ You came only yesterday, and shall I today make you wander about with us, seeing I go I know not where? Go back, and take your brethren with you; and may the LORD show *m* steadfast love and faithfulness to you." ²¹ But Ittai answered the king, "As the LORD lives, and as my lord the king lives, wherever my lord the king shall be, whether for death or for life, there also will your servant be." ²² And David said to Ittai, "Go then, pass on." So Ittai the Gittite passed on, with all his men and all the little ones who

l Gk Syr Vg: Heb *to*   *m* Gk: Heb lacks *may the* LORD *show*

were with him. **23 And all the country wept aloud as all the people passed by, and the king crossed the brook Kidron, and all the people passed on toward the wilderness.**

Instead of attempting to hold the city where, it seems, he had no great following and where he might easily be cut off from escape, David wisely decides to evacuate Jerusalem and flee eastward toward Transjordan. As he comes to the last house, presumably at the bottom of the valley of the Kidron, he and his immediate officials halt to let the remainder of his following pass before them, as if for inspection. The ensuing episodes must have given David much encouragement, for not only does he find that his own immediate household, civil servants, and bodyguard are loyal, but even a newcomer to his court, Ittai from Gath, brings the welcome addition of 600 men as well as a redoubtable spirit.

David Is Encouraged by Loyal Priests   *24-29*

24 And Abiathar came up, and lo, Zadok came also, with all the Levites, bearing the ark of the covenant of God; and they set down the ark of God, until the people had all passed out of the city. 25 Then the king said to Zadok, "Carry the ark of God back into the city. If I find favor in the eyes of the LORD, he will bring me back and let me see both it and his habitation; 26 but if he says, 'I have no pleasure in you,' behold, here I am, let him do to me what seems good to him." 27 The king also said to Zadok the priest, "Look, *n* go back to the city in peace, you and Abiathar,*o* with your two sons, Ahimaaz your son, and

---

n Gk:ˉHeb *Are you a seer* or *Do you see?*
o Cn: Heb lacks *and Abiathar*

Jonathan the son of Abiathar. ²⁸ See, I will wait at the fords of the wilderness, until word comes from you to inform me." ²⁹ So Zadok and Abiathar carried the ark of God back to Jerusalem; and they remained there.

Another very bright spot in the midst of the dark catastrophe is the appearance of the priests Zadok and Abiathar, who also leave the city, bringing the ark, ostensibly so that the Lord of hosts may accompany David and his company. The loyalty of these priests inspires David with so much fresh confidence in his own ultimate return to the capital that even though he does also reckon with the possibility of his own rejection by the Lord, he nevertheless sends the priests and the ark back into the city to the place where they belong. A shrewd political reason is combined with this religious decision: Abiathar and Zadok with their respective sons can form part of an effective spy ring inside Absalom's court.

A Loyal Counselor Replaces
the Traitorous Ahithophel   *30-37*

³⁰ But David went up the ascent of the Mount of Olives, weeping as he went, barefoot and with his head covered; and all the people who were with him covered their heads, and they went up, weeping as they went. ³¹ And it was told David, "Ahithophel is among the conspirators with Absalom." And David said, "O LORD, I pray thee, turn the counsel of Ahithophel into foolishness."

³² When David came to the summit, where God was worshiped, behold, Hushai the Archite came to meet him with his coat rent and earth upon his head.

³³ David said to him, "If you go on with me, you will be a burden to me. ³⁴ But if you return to the city and say to Absalom, 'I will be your servant, O king; as I have been your father's servant in time past, so now I will be your servant,' then you will defeat for me the counsel of Ahithophel. ³⁵ Are not Zadok and Abiathar the priests with you there? So whatever you hear from the king's house tell it to Zadok and Abiathar the priests. ³⁶ Behold, their two sons are with them there, Ahimaaz, Zadok's son, and Jonathan, Abiathar's son; and by them you shall send to me everything you hear." ³⁷ So Hushai, David's friend, came into the city, just as Absalom was entering Jerusalem.

Once the review of the entire company has been completed, the group begins to climb the Mount of Olives, a procession of penitents in deep sorrow and lamentation, the king himself leading the way with feet bare, head covered, and robbed of all royal glory. Thus stripped of all proud claims, he dares to hope that the Lord will have mercy on him. David's thoughts become clear when he hears the unnerving report that his wisest statesman Ahithophel has gone over to Absalom's side, thus assuring Absalom of the very best advice and increasing the gravity of the situation. David responds to that news with an appeal to the Lord to turn the wisdom of the traitor into foolishness.

The Lord responds almost immediately to David's prayer by sending another helper, Hushai, an elderly court official with the title "The King's Friend" (1 Chron. 27:33). David urges him to return to thwart the sagacity of Ahithophel, thus planting a spy inside Absalom's council of war. Hushai returns to the city at the very

moment when Absalom (whom David had bitterly
called the new "king") enters the capital.

Ziba Provisions David — and Slanders
His Master!   *16:1-4*

¹ **When David had passed a little beyond the summit, Ziba the servant of Mephibosheth met him, with
a couple of asses saddled, bearing two hundred loaves
of bread, a hundred bunches of raisins, a hundred
of summer fruits, and a skin of wine.** ² **And the king
said to Ziba, "Why have you brought these?" Ziba
answered, "The asses are for the king's household
to ride on, the bread and summer fruit for the young
men to eat, and the wine for those who faint in the
wilderness to drink."** ³ **And the king said, "And where
is your master's son?" Ziba said to the king, "Behold,
he remains in Jerusalem; for he said, 'Today the house
of Israel will give me back the kingdom of my father.'"**
⁴ **Then the king said to Ziba, "Behold, all that belonged to Mephibosheth is now yours." And Ziba
said, "I do obeisance; let me ever find favor in your
sight, my lord the king."**

When David has proceeded a little beyond the summit, another helper appears with provisions for the
flight. Ziba, Mephibosheth's servant (cf. Ch. 9) thereby
strengthens the king's morale immeasurably, even
though it later becomes apparent (19:27-30) that he was
slandering his crippled master when he falsely reported
his defection. David, however, trusts this man who has
shown him such kindness in his hour of need and, without waiting to hear the other side of the story, gives
him all of Mephibosheth's property. We cannot blame
David for still harboring suspicions of possible treason-

ous action on the part of Saul's descendants. After all, this would be *the* moment for them to make a comeback.

A Hostile Descendant of Saul Curses
and Stones the Fleeing King   *5-14*

⁵ When King David came to Bahurim, there came out a man of the family of the house of Saul, whose name was Shimei, the son of Gera; and as he came he cursed continually. ⁶ And he threw stones at David, and at all the servants of King David; and all the people and all the mighty men were on his right hand and on his left. ⁷ And Shimei said as he cursed, "Begone, begone, you man of blood, you worthless fellow! ⁸ The LORD has avenged upon you all the blood of the house of Saul, in whose place you have reigned; and the LORD has given the kingdom into the hand of your son Absalom. See, your ruin is on you; for you are a man of blood."

⁹ Then Abishai the son of Zeruiah said to the king, "Why should this dead dog curse my lord the king? Let me go over and take off his head." ¹⁰ But the king said, "What have I to do with you, you sons of Zeruiah? If he is cursing because the LORD has said to him, 'Curse David,' who then shall say, 'Why have you done so?'" ¹¹ And David said to Abishai and to all his servants, "Behold, my own son seeks my life; how much more now may this Benjaminite! Let him alone, and let him curse; for the LORD has bidden him. ¹² It may be that the LORD will look upon my affliction,ᵖ and that the LORD will repay me with good for this cursing of me today." ¹³ So David and his men went on the road, while Shimei went along on the hillside opposite him and cursed as he went,

ᵖ Gk Vg: Heb *iniquity*

and threw stones at him and flung dust. 14 And the king, and all the people who were with him, arrived weary at the Jordan; [q] and there he refreshed himself.

[q] Gk: Heb lacks *at the Jordan*

The final episode of the flight is the most humiliating for David. It occurs when on his way toward Jericho he travels alongside the Benjaminite tribal boundary and a hostile descendant of Saul, Shimei, comes out to pelt the king and his company with flying stones and passionate curses. By traveling on a path that runs along the opposite side of the valley from the one on which David is traveling, Shimei is able to pursue a parallel course to that of the king and to hurl insults and stones across the deep ravine at the king and his retinue. Shimei looks upon the fleeing king as smitten by God with a just punishment for the blood-guilt he incurred when he allegedly executed seven of Saul's sons (cf. Ch. 9 and Ch. 21). David, surprisingly enough, does not permit his hotheaded nephew Abishai to cross over and avenge the insults. Rather, he accepts Shimei's claim (despite its partisan malice) that his humiliation is a punishment from God, the God who had long since exposed his iniquity. More than that, David sees this bitter experience as an experience that is most necessary if he is to be restored to Jerusalem and kingship. But restored or not, he is not going to take his fate into his own hands. Precisely at this point David appears as a prototype of Him who humbled Himself as He crossed the brook Kidron at the beginning of His Passion. David finally arrives at Jericho, exhausted but at least out of immediate danger. What will happen next is still undecided and therefore the narrative skillfully employs this pause to shift the scene back to Jerusalem, where Absalom is taking over.

THE GREAT DEBATE BETWEEN
AHITHOPHEL AND HUSHAI   16:15 — 17:23

David's Secret Agent Established
in Absalom's Court   *15-19*

¹⁵ **Now Absalom and all the people, the men of Israel, came to Jerusalem, and Ahithophel with him.** ¹⁶ **And when Hushai the Archite, David's friend, came to Absalom, Hushai said to Absalom, "Long live the king! Long live the king!" ¹⁷ And Absalom said to Hushai, "Is this your loyalty to your friend? Why did you not go with your friend?" ¹⁸ And Hushai said to Absalom, "No; for whom the LORD and this people and all the men of Israel have chosen, his I will be, and with him I will remain. ¹⁹ And again, whom should I serve? Should it not be his son? As I have served your father, so I will serve you."**

Among the men who enter Jerusalem with Absalom it is Ahithophel who receives special mention, since he is the heart and soul of the insurrection and David's real opponent. His rival Hushai's offer to serve Absalom is at first rudely rejected by the new king, who makes a sarcastic pun on Hushai's official court title, "The King's Friend," and accuses him of betraying his "friend" David. Hushai, however, claims that, since Absalom is now the legitimate king (chosen by both the people and the Lord at Hebron), nothing is more natural than that he should serve Absalom now that he is king, just as he once served his father when he was king.

327

*Ahithophel's Brilliant
but Godless Counsel to Absalom*   *20-23, 17:1-4*

[20] Then Absalom said to Ahithophel, "Give your counsel; what shall we do?" [21] Ahithophel said to Absalom, "Go in to your father's concubines, whom he has left to keep the house; and all Israel will hear that you have made yourself odious to your father, and the hands of all who are with you will be strengthened." [22] So they pitched a tent for Absalom upon the roof; and Absalom went in to his father's concubines in the sight of all Israel. [23] Now in those days the counsel which Ahithophel gave was as if one consulted the oracle [r] of God; so was all the counsel of Ahithophel esteemed, both by David and by Absalom.

[1] Moreover Ahithophel said to Absalom, "Let me choose twelve thousand men, and I will set out and pursue David tonight. [2] I will come upon him while he is weary and discouraged, and throw him into a panic; and all the people who are with him will flee. I will strike down the king only, [3] and I will bring all the people back to you as a bride comes home to her husband. You seek the life of only one man,[s] and all the people will be at peace." [4] And the advice pleased Absalom and all the elders of Israel.

[r] Heb *word*
[s] Gk: Heb *like the return of the whole (is) the man whom you seek*

Hushai's rival, the counselor Ahithophel, soon displays his impeccable sagacity by counseling that Absalom's first act of state show everyone that he has irrevocably broken with his father. He is to assume the full rights of kingship publicly by taking possession of

328

his father's harem — in keeping with widespread practice of usurpers in the ancient Near East. This act, Ahithophel knows, will force any of Absalom's partisans who still feared an eventual reconciliation of father and son to see that Absalom is irrevocably committed to the revolt, thus removing any sense of insecurity and raising their morale. The narrator's note in v. 23 (to the effect that Ahithophel's counsel had the same sort of authority as an inerrant divine oracle) serves to help the perceptive reader realize that this seemingly brilliant but nevertheless godless counsel leads to the ruin of both Ahithophel and Absalom.

For the moment, however, Ahithophel is confident of success. He suggests that he himself immediately set out with a force to overtake David's retinue that very night. Once David's slow-moving and weary company has been panicked and scattered by the surprise night attack, Ahithophel argues, it will be easy for him to kill "only one man," David. The danger of extended civil war will be over, and he will soon lead the people back to the new king, "like a bride to her husband." Neither Absalom nor the elders of the northern tribes who attend this war council have any scruples about laying hands on the anointed of the Lord. Without exception they all agree that Ahithophel's plan is excellent in all details. It does seem that if Absalom had actually carried out this plan, David's cause would have been lost. But God is guiding these plans and events, hearkening to David's passionate prayer that He turn wise Ahithophel's traitorous counsel into foolishness. (15:31)

Hushai Counteracts Ahithophel's Counsel   *5-14*

5 Then Absalom said, "Call Hushai the Archite also, and let us hear what he has to say." 6 And when

Hushai came to Absalom, Absalom said to him, "Thus has Ahithophel spoken; shall we do as he advises? If not, you speak." ⁷ Then Hushai said to Absalom, "This time the counsel which Ahithophel has given is not good." ⁸ Hushai said moreover, "You know that your father and his men are mighty men, and that they are enraged, like a bear robbed of her cubs in the field. Besides, your father is expert in war; he will not spend the night with the people. ⁹ Behold, even now he has hidden himself in one of the pits, or in some other place. And when some of the people fall *f* at the first attack, whoever hears it will say, 'There has been a slaughter among the people who follow Absalom.' ¹⁰ Then even the valiant man, whose heart is like the heart of a lion, will utterly melt with fear; for all Israel knows that your father is a mighty man, and that those who are with him are valiant men. ¹¹ But my counsel is that all Israel be gathered to you, from Dan to Beer-sheba, as the sand by the sea for multitude, and that you go to battle in person. ¹² So we shall come upon him in some place where he is to be found, and we shall light upon him as the dew falls on the ground; and of him and all the men with him not one will be left. ¹³ If he withdraws into a city, then all Israel will bring ropes to that city, and we shall drag it into the valley, until not even a pebble is to be found there." ¹⁴ And Absalom and all the men of Israel said, "The counsel of Hushai the Archite is better than the counsel of Ahithophel." For the LORD had ordained to defeat the good counsel of Ahithophel, so that the LORD might bring evil upon Absalom.

f Or *when he falls upon them*

Ironically enough, Absalom's own hankering after all possible advice and his dependence on the sagacity of professional political advisors now proves his undoing, for, before acting on Ahithophel's plan, he summons the other counselor who had not been present at the war council, David's secret friend Hushai. Hushai is faced with a situation much more difficult than the one he found at Absalom's initial entry into Jerusalem. Then Hushai had to somehow reestablish himself at the court; now he has to replace Ahithophel's perfect plan with one that will appear to lead to David's ruin but will actually rescue him and ruin Absalom. His speech is a masterpiece of persuasive oratory. Knowing that delay will work for David, Hushai at the outset warns against Ahithophel's scheme as being unwise; then with a series of colorful figures of speech, which are more brilliant than the bad argument they veil, he proceeds to "refute" Ahithophel's counsel. He compares David's entourage to "a bear robbed of her cubs" and predicts such a formidable defense by the seasoned veterans in a battle of desperation that even a slight mistake by Ahithophel's hastily levied troops will result in irreparable harm. In his own counterproposal Hushai calls for a muster of the combined forces of all Israel, so that Absalom may proceed against David with an army as numerous as "the sand by the sea." Not the least of Hushai's slyly flattering suggestions is that, instead of entrusting the expedition to Ahithophel, Absalom should "go to battle in person." Then, he predicts, his invincible host will overwhelm David's inferior forces like the dew which descends in such abundance that it covers the entire surface of the whole land. And even if David should in the meantime find refuge in some city—by this time Hushai's rhetoric has almost run away with

331

him and his audience—soon not even a pebble will be left of such an enemy city! Hushai's oratory carries the day; Absalom is blinded to his own best interests. This is, however, in accordance with the Lord's own ordering. In this third of the surprisingly few explicit references to divine guidance in the narrative of the succession (cf. 11:27; 12:24) we hear that this surprising turn of events is the Lord's doing. Our narrator here explicitly mentions the Lord's intervention, something that is otherwise implicit between the lines, so that we may realize that He is guiding the complicated human actions and events of this history in keeping with His promise to David's line (Ch. 7). Just as Amnon was not to be David's successor, so the usurper Absalom is also not the chosen one.

Forewarned, David Crosses the Jordan   *15-22*

15 Then Hushai said to Zadok and Abiathar the priests, "Thus and so did Ahithophel counsel Absalom and the elders of Israel; and thus and so have I counseled. 16 Now therefore send quickly and tell David, 'Do not lodge tonight at the fords of the wilderness, but by all means pass over; lest the king and all the people who are with him be swallowed up.'" 17 Now Jonathan and Ahimaaz were waiting at Enrogel; a maidservant used to go and tell them, and they would go and tell King David; for they must not be seen entering the city. 18 But a lad saw them, and told Absalom; so both of them went away quickly, and came to the house of a man at Bahurim, who had a well in his courtyard; and they went down into it. 19 And the woman took and spread a covering over the well's mouth, and scattered grain upon it; and nothing was known of it. 20 When Absalom's servants

came to the woman at the house, they said, "Where are Ahimaaz and Jonathan?" And the woman said to them, "They have gone over the brook [u] of water." And when they had sought and could not find them, they returned to Jerusalem.

21 After they had gone, the men came up out of the well, and went and told King David. They said to David, "Arise, and go quickly over the water; for thus and so has Ahithophel counseled against you." 22 Then David arose, and all the people who were with him, and they crossed the Jordan; by daybreak not one was left who had not crossed the Jordan.

[u] The meaning of the Hebrew word is uncertain

It is only by a hair's breadth that David actually receives the necessary intelligence from Jerusalem. According to vv. 15 f. either (1) Hushai himself is not present when Absalom and his elders make the final decision to take his advice, or (2) if Hushai knows of that decision, he is nevertheless afraid that Absalom may change his mind. In any case, the hearer and reader of the story is kept in suspense as to the relaying of the secret intelligence. In order to inform David of what has happened and to advise him to cross to Transjordan as quickly as possible, Hushai is to make use of the long line of communication that stretches from (1) the priests, Zadok and Abiathar, through (2) a servant girl who goes to get water at a spring and through (3) the priests' two sons who have to remain hidden outside the city near that spring to (4) David's company still descending toward Jericho. This complicated intelligence organization almost breaks down when a lad observes the servant girl talking to Ahimaaz and Jonathan at the well and reports this to the court. The messengers are saved only by the ruse of a farmer's wife at Bahurim who hides them in a cistern and tells the searchers, with a pun (which must have delighted the listeners), that they had left the courtyard to get closer to the water. Finally the young men are able to escape and to bring David the important message about Absalom's plans. By the next morning David has succeeded in bringing his entire company over the Jordan to the comparative safety of Transjordan.

The Loser in the Debate, Ahithophel,
Draws His Own Conclusions   23

23 When Ahithophel saw that his counsel was not followed, he saddled his ass, and went off home to his own city. And he set his house in order, and hanged himself; and he died, and was buried in the tomb of his father.

Once the clear thinker Ahithophel learns that Absalom has preferred Hushai's pretentious strategy to his own sound plan, the unerring logic of his mind drives him to despair. What can a wise man do when fools reject his wisdom and prefer folly? Since he knows that Absalom's cause is lost and since he is powerless to halt the approaching disaster, with typical logical precision he goes home, sets his affairs in order, and commits suicide. In the Old Testament suicide is "an impossible possibility," a sign that the person has reached complete darkness and godlessness. This is, in fact, the only case of suicide mentioned in the Old Testament, if we discount those rare cases in which a warrior kills himself to escape the enemy (Judg. 9:54; 1 Sam. 31:4-6; 1 Kings 16:18). Hence Ahithophel has been called the "Judas" of the Old Testament. He betrayed the anointed of the Lord and then took his own life, dying an accursed death.

THE REBELLION CRUSHED
AND ABSALOM KILLED   17:24 — 18:33

The fact that the military events in this section are so briefly described shows that our narrator's emphasis is not on them but on what Absalom's fall means for the crucial question of the day, the succession to David's throne.

David Is Prepared for the Approaching Battle   24-29

²⁴ Then David came to Mahanaim. And Absalom crossed the Jordan with all the men of Israel. ²⁵ Now Absalom had set Amasa over the army instead of Joab. Amasa was the son of a man named Ithra the Ishmaelite,ᵛ who had married Abigal the daughter of Nahash, sister of Zeruiah, Joab's mother. ²⁶ And Israel and Absalom encamped in the land of Gilead.

²⁷ When David came to Mahanaim, Shobi the son of Nahash from Rabbah of the Ammonites, and Machir the son of Ammiel from Lodebar, and Barzillai the Gileadite from Rogelim, ²⁸ brought beds, basins, and earthen vessels, wheat, barley, meal, parched grain, beans and lentils,ʷ ²⁹ honey and curds and sheep and cheese from the herd, for David and the people with him to eat; for they said, "The people are hungry and weary and thirsty in the wilderness."

ᵛ 1 Chron 2. 17: Heb *Israelite*   ʷ Heb *lentils and parched grain*

Thanks to Hushai's spectacular oratory and to the effective intelligence network, David and his veteran soldiers have plenty of time to make the city of Mahanaim their headquarters and to arrange sound military plans for meeting Absalom and the citizen army of Israel. Absalom, on the other hand, has at his disposal a less experienced, more cumbersome citizen army. It is commanded by his cousin Amasa, who is also a nephew of David and a cousin of Joab. He is, as we soon see, no match for Joab in military competence or statesmanship. David is not without other valuable support. Three wealthy Transjordanian rulers (Siho, Machir, and Barzillai) rally to his cause and come to his aid with large stores of welcome provisions and camp equipment.

David Gives Strange Battle Orders
Concerning the Rebel Absalom   *18:1-5*

[1] **Then David mustered the men who were with him, and set over them commanders of thousands and commanders of hundreds. [2] And David sent forth the army, one third under the command of Joab, one third under the command of Abishai the son of Zeruiah, Joab's brother, and one third under the command of Ittai the Gittite. And the king said to the men, "I myself will also go out with you." [3] But the men said, "You shall not go out. For if we flee, they will not care about us. If half of us die, they will not care about us. But you are worth ten thousand of us;** *x* **therefore it is better that you send us help from the city." [4] The king said to them, "Whatever seems best to you I will do." So the king stood at the side of the gate, while all the army marched out by hundreds and by thousands. [5] And the king ordered Joab and Abishai and Ittai, "Deal gently for my sake with**

x Gk Vg Symmachus: Heb *for now there are ten thousand such as we*

the young man Absalom." And all the people heard when the king gave orders to all the commanders about Absalom.

After organizing the newcomers into new units, David reviews the troops that march forth to the battle, himself remaining behind — at the army's insistence — in the city of Mahanaim with a small reserve force. David's final order to the three division commanders to deal lightly with the young man Absalom shows that what concerns him more than winning a victory for himself is the well-being of his son. This is not because Absalom is an especially lovable son, nor yet because of his paternal hopes for a brilliant and affable prince, but because he considers Absalom his heir and crown prince, through whom the promise of the enduring dynasty will be fulfilled.

The Battle of Mahanaim and the Death
of Absalom   *6-18*

⁶ So the army went out into the field against Israel; and the battle was fought in the forest of Ephraim. ⁷ And the men of Israel were defeated there by the servants of David, and the slaughter there was great on that day, twenty thousand men. ⁸ The battle spread over the face of all the country; and the forest devoured more people that day than the sword.

⁹ And Absalom chanced to meet the servants of David. Absalom was riding upon his mule, and the mule went under the thick branches of a great oak, and his head caught fast in the oak, and he was left hanging ʸ between heaven and earth, while the mule that was under him went on. ¹⁰ And a certain man

ʸ Gk Syr Tg: Heb *was put*

saw it, and told Joab, "Behold, I saw Absalom hanging in an oak." [11] Joab said to the man who told him, "What, you saw him! Why then did you not strike him there to the ground? I would have been glad to give you ten pieces of silver and a girdle." [12] But the man said to Joab, "Even if I felt in my hand the weight of a thousand pieces of silver, I would not put forth my hand against the king's son; for in our hearing the king commanded you and Abishai and Ittai, 'For my sake protect the young man Absalom.' [13] On the other hand, if I had dealt treacherously against his life [z] (and there is nothing hidden from the king), then you yourself would have stood aloof." [14] Joab said, "I will not waste time like this with you." And he took three darts in his hand, and thrust them into the heart of Absalom, while he was still alive in the oak. [15] And ten young men, Joab's armor-bearers, surrounded Absalom and struck him, and killed him.

[16] Then Joab blew the trumpet, and the troops came back from pursuing Israel; for Joab restrained them. [17] And they took Absalom, and threw him into a great pit in the forest, and raised over him a very great heap of stones; and all Israel fled every one to his own home. [18] Now Absalom in his lifetime had taken and set up for himself the pillar which is in the King's Valley, for he said, "I have no son to keep my name in remembrance"; he called the pillar after his own name, and it is called Absalom's monument to this day.

[z] Another reading is *at the risk of my life*

The site of the crucial battle is "the forest of Ephraim," the wooded and rocky terrain where the west-

Jordan tribe of Ephraim had done some colonizing in Transjordan. No wonder the battle soon "spreads over the face of all the country" and becomes a hand-to-hand melee, the special hazards of the forest proving more dangerous in the end than the enemy, as Absalom himself soon experiences when he flees from a chance encounter with some of David's bodyguard. We are not explicitly told that his fine head of hair, the crown of his physical beauty and the symbol of his pride and arrogance, is his undoing; we hear only that his head is caught in the thickset branches of the terebinth so firmly that he cannot free himself and is therefore left hanging between heaven and earth. An eyewitness reports this to Joab. A most revealing conversation ensues after the commander reproves the soldier for not having taken advantage of the situation to kill the helpless and dangerous traitor. The common soldier is unmoved by his superior's hot indignation and sharp words, especially when he considers the consequences the murder of Absalom would have for him. Unable to cope with such hardheaded single-mindedness, Joab breaks off the conversation, takes three darts in his hand, and thrusts them into the body of the helpless and exhausted prince. The subsequent attack upon Absalom by Joab's armor-bearers seems to be the same sort of humiliating treatment which we note in the following, when Absalom's body is cast into a pit and covered with a large mound of stones (cf. Josh. 7:26). Besides Absalom's large altarlike burial mound in the forest near Mahanaim we also hear of Absalom's funeral stele near Jerusalem, which the then childless Absalom had set up in his lifetime because he had no son to keep his memory alive. According to 14:27 "three sons and one daughter" had been born to him. While this is regarded by some as a variant tradition, it is quite possible that these children died in their childhood. In any case, this note serves to show that Absalom dies without an heir who might be considered a future successor to the throne.

Two Messengers Set Out to Bring David News
of the Battle 19-23

¹⁹ Then said Ahimaaz the son of Zadok, "Let me run, and carry tidings to the king that the LORD has delivered him from the power of his enemies." ²⁰ And Joab said to him, "You are not to carry tidings today; you may carry tidings another day, but today you shall carry no tidings, because the king's son is dead." ²¹ Then Joab said to the Cushite, "Go, tell the king what you have seen." The Cushite bowed before Joab, and ran. ²² Then Ahimaaz the son of Zadok said again to Joab, "Come what may, let me also run after the Cushite." And Joab said, "Why will you run, my son, seeing that you will have no reward for the tidings?" ²³ "Come what may," he said, "I will run." So he said to him, "Run." Then Ahimaaz ran by the way of the plain, and outran the Cushite.

With the death of Absalom the purpose of the war has been achieved. The only question that remains is how David will take the frightful news. Our narrator heightens the suspense by reporting, with great circumstantial detail, how Ahimaaz, the priest Zadok's fleet-footed son, volunteers to be the messenger of the victory communique. He doesn't seem to realize that in view of Absalom's death the message of victory will not be good news for David. Joab, however, very well knows what happened to certain other messengers who thought that they were bringing good news to David (2 Sam. 1:14 f.; 4:9 ff.). He does not want David's wrath to descend on this fine young man and therefore sends a Negro instead of him, thinking, perhaps, either that a black man would symbolize black news or that his death at the hands of the angry king would be less of a loss than that of Ahimaaz or even that the royal slave has little to fear since he is "a servant of the king." Ahimaaz, however, is not so easily dissuaded and in the end succeeds not only in obtaining Joab's belated permission (once the Negro has a good head start on him) but also in arriving at the goal just a bit before the Cushite (traveling on a longer, but more easily traveled route than the difficult one taken by the Negro).

The King on the Roof of the City Gate
at Mahanaim   *24-33*

[24] Now David was sitting between the two gates; and the watchman went up to the roof of the gate by the wall, and when he lifted up his eyes and looked, he saw a man running alone. [25] And the watchman called out and told the king. And the king said, "If he is alone, there are tidings in his mouth." And he came apace, and drew near. [26] And the watchman saw another man running, and the watchman called to the gate and said, "See, another man running alone!" The king said, "He also brings tidings." [27] And the watchman said, "I think the running of the foremost is like the running of Ahimaaz the son of Zadok." And the king said, "He is a good man, and comes with good tidings."

[28] Then Ahimaaz cried out to the king, "All is well." And he bowed before the king with his face to

the earth, and said, "Blessed be the LORD your God, who has delivered up the men who raised their hand against my lord the king." ²⁹ And the king said, "Is it well with the young man Absalom?" Ahimaaz answered, "When Joab sent your servant,^b I saw a great tumult, but I do not know what it was." ³⁰ And the king said, "Turn aside, and stand here." So he turned aside, and stood still.

³¹ And behold, the Cushite came; and the Cushite said, "Good tidings for my lord the king! For the LORD has delivered you this day from the power of all who rose up against you." ³² The king said to the Cushite, "Is it well with the young man Absalom?" And the Cushite answered, "May the enemies of my lord the king, and all who rise up against you for evil, be like that young man." ^{33 c} And the king was deeply moved, and went up to the chamber over the gate, and wept; and as he went, he said, "O my son Absalom, my son, my son Absàlom! Would I had died instead of you, O Absalom, my son, my son!"

^b Heb *the king's servant, your servant*   ^c Ch 19. 1 in Heb

After our narrator shifts the scene back to Mahanaim, the tempo of his narration is slowed down even more, so that the tension he builds up for his climax becomes truly overwhelming. Though finally both messengers arrive at the king's presence breathless almost at the same moment, our narrator succeeds in creating high drama of the account by having the watchman report each new bit of evidence separately and having the nearby king respond to each report, hoping that the message will prove to be good. The king responds to the first two news reports (that the runners come alone) with joy, interpreting this to mean that there has been no rout, otherwise many fugitives would appear scattered over the plain, running for protection. And when the watchman identifies the first runner as Ahimaaz, David is sure that the good character of the messenger presages a good message. When, however, the almost breathless Ahimaaz announces victory, the king disregards such information and presses on to what is much more crucial to him, the fate of the young man Absalom. Ahimaaz avoids reporting the bad news, leaving it to the second messenger to tell the truth. In direct and softened though it is, the Cushite gives the king an unmistakable answer: Absalom is dead! Having hoped against hope to the very last, the king now breaks out in uncontrollable grief. What causes the king's collapse is not the fact that he has lost a son who was a fratricide, a usurper, and rebel, but the son whom he considered the bearer of the promise. David honestly wishes he had died instead of Absalom. How will the promise ever be fulfilled?

DAVID'S RETURN FROM THE BATTLE
OF MAHANAIM
19

David Attempts to Run the State Without Joab   *1-15*

¹ It was told Joab, "Behold, the king is weeping and mourning for Absalom." ² So the victory that day was turned into mourning for all the people; for the people heard that day, "The king is grieving for his son." ³ And the people stole into the city that day as people steal in who are ashamed when they flee in battle. ⁴ The king covered his face, and the king cried with a loud voice, "O my son Absalom, O Absalom, my son, my son!" ⁵ Then Joab came into the house

to the king, and said, "You have today covered with shame the faces of all your servants, who have this day saved your life, and the lives of your sons and your daughters, and the lives of your wives and your concubines, ⁶ because you love those who hate you and hate those who love you. For you have made it clear today that commanders and servants are nothing to you; for today I perceive that if Absalom were alive and all of us were dead today, then you would be pleased. ⁷ Now therefore arise, go out and speak kindly to your servants; for I swear by the LORD, if you do not go, not a man will stay with you this night; and this will be worse for you than all the evil that has come upon you from your youth until now." ⁸ Then the king arose, and took his seat in the gate. And the people were all told, "Behold, the king is sitting in the gate"; and all the people came before the king.

Now Israel had fled every man to his own home. ⁹ And all the people were at strife throughout all the tribes of Israel, saying, "The king delivered us from the hand of our enemies, and saved us from the hand of the Philistines; and now he has fled out of the land from Absalom. ¹⁰ But Absalom, whom we anointed over us, is dead in battle. Now therefore why do you say nothing about bringing the king back?"

¹¹ And King David sent this message to Zadok and Abiathar the priests, "Say to the elders of Judah, 'Why should you be the last to bring the king back to his house, when the word of all Israel has come to the king? ᵈ ¹² You are my kinsmen, you are my bone and my flesh; why then should you be the last to bring back the king?' ¹³ And say to Amasa, 'Are you not my

ᵈ Gk: Heb *to the king, to his house*

bone and my flesh? God do so to me, and more also, if you are not commander of my army henceforth in place of Joab.'" ¹⁴ And he swayed the heart of all the men of Judah as one man; so that they sent word to the king, "Return, both you and all your servants." ¹⁵ So the king came back to the Jordan; and Judah came to Gilgal to meet the king and to bring the king over the Jordan.

David's lamentation-wish that he had died in Absalom's stead has not been a merely traditional lament formula. In the midst of a great political crisis he is truly concerned with only one thing: the loss of his son. No wonder his returning army is disappointed at hearing the dead traitor's name repeated again and again in lamentation from the chamber over the gate. Instead of being welcomed, the victorious soldiers must slink into Mahanaim like thieves, as if they had disgraced themselves on the field of battle. Again it is Joab who understands the situation and who speaks frankly and realistically to David about his obligation to the professional army, whose distinguished service alone had rescued him and his empire from ruin, and he correctly calls David's present attitude and actions political suicide. Thus he finally persuades the king to come down and preside over a belated triumphal entrance of the victorious troops into the city. Joab gives David another opportunity to show himself a great statesman, but David does not acknowledge his debt to Joab; in fact, we soon see that without Joab's aid David's plans go awry. David's plan is to manipulate the sectional rivalry between North (Israel) and South (Judah) for his own purposes. David is apprised of a strong desire in the North (Israel) to restore their allegiance to him. He there-

fore suggests—indirectly, through the Jerusalem priests
—to the South (Judah) that it step forth from the neutrality it had displayed during Absalom's revolt and
demonstrate its renewed allegiance to David by mustering its citizen army to escort the king back to Jerusalem.
If Judah hurries, it is suggested, it can beat Israel. To
conciliate the tribal militia, David permits them to keep
the traitorous commander who had led them in the revolt (Amasa) instead of assigning them to Joab, who had
been the group's original commander before the revolt.
This also is an unwise decision on David's part, not only
because Joab is a truly superior general but also because it shows that David little appreciated the fact
that at the revolt Joab had refused to be an accomplice
of the militia in the rebellion and had loyally gone into
exile with David and the professionals. Now out of
personal pique David punishes the loyal commander
because he dared cross him, while rewarding the traitorous commander with his post! Joab's stature in our
eyes rises even more when we see him accept his disgrace manfully, biding his time as a loyal servant of the
king. But it is evident that, without Joab, David is head-
ing for trouble. For the moment, however, David imagines that by calling forth the southern militia to counter-
balance the tremendous power of the northern militia
he will be able to establish some sort of equilibrium in
which he and his professionals will have the deciding
political power. At first David's independent political
maneuvers seem to prove successful. The Judeans do
come to the Jordan. Much more is involved than merely
the ceremonial honor of escorting the king across the
river, for the group that returns the king to his capital
will be his bodyguard, able to protect him and also to
influence him.

346

David Is Met by Benjaminite Defectors   *16-23*

¹⁶ And Shimei the son of Gera, the Benjaminite, from Bahurim, made haste to come down with the men of Judah to meet King David; ¹⁷ and with him were a thousand men from Benjamin. And Ziba the servant of the house of Saul, with his fifteen sons and his twenty servants, rushed down to the Jordan before the king, ¹⁸ and they crossed the ford *e* to bring over the king's household, and to do his pleasure. And Shimei the son of Gera fell down before the king, as he was about to cross the Jordan, ¹⁹ and said to the king, "Let not my lord hold me guilty or remember how your servant did wrong on the day my lord the king left Jerusalem; let not the king bear it in mind. ²⁰ For your servant knows that I have sinned; therefore, behold, I have come this day, the first of all the house of Joseph to come down to meet my lord the king." ²¹ Abishai the son of Zeruiah answered, "Shall not Shimei be put to death for this, because he cursed the LORD'S anointed?" ²² But David said, "What have I to do with you, you sons of Zeruiah, that you should this day be as an adversary to me? Shall any one be put to death in Israel this day? For do I not know that I am this day king over Israel?" ²³ And the king said to Shimei, "You shall not die." And the king gave him his oath.

e Cn: Heb *the ford crossed*

Our narrator's description of David's victorious return from Transjordan stands in fascinating contrast to his previous description of David's humiliating flight from Jerusalem; though the situation has changed, the same people are involved, some having to make a real about-face to meet the new circumstances. The Judean militiamen are by no means the only people who come to escort David home. Benjaminite partisans of the house of Saul are among the first to cross the river to throw themselves at the king's feet at his arrival on the river bank; Shimei comes with a muster of men for the king's service and Ziba with his large retinue of sons and servants, who rush into the very water itself to transport the women and children across the river. Shimei seems to be honest in his unqualified confession of guilt. At least he makes no attempt to conceal his earlier treason. But his shrewdness speaks through when he points out that he is the first one in Israel, in the house of Joseph, to reestablish allegiance, as if all Israel will now follow his example. It also seems that he expects that on this day of rejoicing no executions of traitors will take place (cf. 1 Sam. 11:13). Like a vindictive prosecuting attorney, Joab's brother Abishai calls for the death of the person who dared curse the anointed of the Lord. This, however, only aids Shimei's cause, since David sees Abishai's claim as of a piece with Joab's cruel refusal of mercy to Absalom, and in his present mood David will have nothing of such vindictiveness. This day he has again become king over Israel (v. 22); he guarantees Shimei's life with an oath.

David Decides the Case of Mephibosheth   24-30

24 And Mephibosheth the son of Saul came down to meet the king; he had neither dressed his feet, nor trimmed his beard, nor washed his clothes, from the day the king departed until the day he came back in safety. 25 And when he came from _f_ Jerusalem to meet the king, the king said to him, "Why did you not go

_f_ Heb to _g_ Gk Syr Vg: Heb _said, I will saddle an ass for myself_ with me, Mephibosheth?" [26] He answered, "My lord, O king, my servant deceived me; for your servant said to him, 'Saddle an ass for me,^{g} that I may ride upon it and go with the king.' For your servant is lame. [27] He has slandered your servant to my lord the king. But my lord the king is like the angel of God; do therefore what seems good to you. [28] For all my father's house were but men doomed to death before my lord the king; but you set your servant among those who eat at your table. What further right have I, then, to cry to the king?" [29] And the king said to him, "Why speak any more of your affairs? I have decided: you and Ziba shall divide the land." [30] And Mephibosheth said to the king, "Oh, let him take it all, since my lord the king has come safely home."

The king's magnanimity is also put to the test by the appearance of Mephibosheth, an alleged traitor. In response to the king's harsh reproof, Mephibosheth justifies himself, claiming that he was deceived by his servant Ziba. His unkempt appearance testifies to his long-standing sorrow and grief at David's exile. The only obstacle that kept him from going into exile with the king was his lameness, an obstacle that became insurmountable when his servant deprived him of his only means of transportation. Nevertheless, he leaves the decision up to the king, who is, he shrewdly reminds him, like the angel of God in judgment—a statement that contains much more than obsequious flattery, since it underscores David's responsibility to act justly as God's representative. David's verdict in this complicated case takes into account both Ziba's kindness and Mephibosheth's innocence. He decrees a division of Saul's property between the two. Mephibosheth's hearty response shows that he is happy with the king's decision; in fact, he would be happy even if the calculating Ziba got all of the property—just as long as the king is safely back home again.

A Delightful Farewell
to the Octogenarian Barzillai   *31-40*

   ³¹ Now Barzillai the Gileadite had come down from Rogelim; and he went on with the king to the Jordan, to escort him over the Jordan. ³² Barzillai was a very aged man, eighty years old; and he had provided the king with food while he stayed at Mahanaim; for he was a very wealthy man. ³³ And the king said to Barzillai, "Come over with me, and I will provide for you with me in Jerusalem." ³⁴ But Barzillai said to the king, "How many years have I still to live, that I should go up with the king to Jerusalem? ³⁵ I am this day eighty years old; can I discern what is pleasant and what is not? Can your servant taste what he eats or what he drinks? Can I still listen to the voice of singing men and singing women? Why then should your servant be an added burden to my lord the king? ³⁶ Your servant will go a little way over the Jordan with the king. Why should the king recompense me with such a reward? ³⁷ Pray let your servant return, that I may die in my own city, near the grave of my father and my mother. But here is your servant Chimham; let him go over with my lord the king; and do for him whatever seems good to you." ³⁸ And the king answered, "Chimham shall go over with me, and I will do for him whatever seems good to you; and all that you desire of me I will do for you." ³⁹ Then all the people went over the Jordan, and the king went over;

and the king kissed **Barzillai** and blessed him, and he returned to his own home. [40] The king went on to Gilgal, and Chimham went on with him; all the people of Judah, and also half the people of Israel, brought the king on his way.

Barzillai had helped David in his extremity, and David wishes to repay him for this by having him as his lifelong guest at court. But the aged man does not wish to change his simple patriarchal life in Transjordan for the sophisticated life of the court. He would rather spend his last days at home and be buried in his ancestors' tomb. He does, however, ask David to take his son in his place; then the old man returns home. (Cf. 1 Kings 2:7 ff.)

*Israel and Judah Quarrel About Escorting
the King* *41-43*

[41] Then all the men of Israel came to the king, and said to the king, "Why have our brethren the men of Judah stolen you away, and brought the king and his household over the Jordan, and all David's men with him?" [42] All the men of Judah answered the men of Israel, "Because the king is near of kin to us. Why then are you angry over this matter? Have we eaten at all at the king's expense? Or has he given us any gift?" [43] And the men of Israel answered the men of Judah, "We have ten shares in the king, and in David also we have more than you. Why then did you despise us? Were we not the first to speak of bringing back our king?" But the words of the men of Judah were fiercer than the words of the men of Israel.

Instead of the two factions (North and South) counterbalancing each other, as David planned, a new upset occurs. At first the Israelites complain that the Judeans have usurped their rights in coming down to escort the king. They seem to think that since Israel was the first section to renew its allegiance to David after the revolt, such privilege of escort is their sole prerogative. But now the Judeans, who conveniently remained in complacent neutrality during the revolt, have come and stolen the king away! The response of the elders of Judah only increases the suspicions of the northern tribes, for they appeal to David's kin relationship to them (see also v. 12). The Israelites counter by claiming that they are the larger party, that they have the right of the firstborn, and that they were the first to have the idea of bringing back "our king." The final response of Judah is not quoted, perhaps because it seems to have become mere shouting. David is unable to settle this quarrel. In fact, he has, in a way, fomented this quarrel which again threatens the empire. It is capable and realistic Joab who again restores order.

JOAB CRUSHES SHEBA'S REVOLT 20

Sheba Incites Israel's Second Revolt Against David *1-3*

¹ Now there happened to be there a worthless fellow, whose name was Sheba, the son of Bichri, a Benjaminite; and he blew the trumpet, and said,

"We have no portion in David,

and we have no inheritance in the son of Jesse;

every man to his tents, O Israel!"

² So all the men of Israel withdrew from David, and

followed Sheba the son of Bichri; but the men of Judah followed their king steadfastly from the Jordan to Jerusalem.

³ And David came to his house at Jerusalem; and the king took the ten concubines whom he had left to care for the house, and put them in a house under guard, and provided for them, but did not go in to them. So they were shut up until the day of their death, living as if in widowhood.

Sheba's rebellion begins and ends with a trumpet blast. The first blast, raised by Sheba himself, signals the secession of the northern tribes from David (v. 1); the second, raised by Joab, signals the restoration of the military situation to effective control. All of this is achieved without David's permission and yet actually for David's own good. (V. 22)

David's own unsuccessful attempt to play the North off against the South blew up in his face when the intertribal rivalry about who should have precedence in escorting the king back to the capital erupted in a heated argument. Now it is a Benjaminite, seemingly one of the descendants of Saul's house, who calls on the Northerners to abandon any further association with the Judean David and to resume their older tribal independence. The men of Israel hearken to the cry, deserting David's train and allowing his blood-relatives, the Judahites, to escort him back to Jerusalem.

Once back in the capital, David removes all vestiges of Absalom's revolt by isolating the 10 concubines on whom Absalom had demonstrated his possession of royal power. David puts these women, who had originally been left to guard his palace, under special guard, treating them, it seems, as widows of the dead

Absalom and therefore as taboo to every other man.
(Cf. 13:20)

*Deposed Joab Wrests Command
of the Army from David's Appointee*   *4-13*

⁴ Then the king said to Amasa, "Call the men
of Judah together to me within three days, and be
here yourself." ⁵ So Amasa went to summon Judah;
but he delayed beyond the set time which had been
appointed him. ⁶ And David said to Abishai, "Now
Sheba the son of Bichri will do us more harm than
Absalom; take your lord's servants and pursue him,
lest he get himself fortified cities, and cause us
trouble." *ʰ* ⁷ And there went out after Abishai, Joab *ⁱ*
and the Cherethites and the Pelethites, and all the
mighty men; they went out from Jerusalem to pursue
Sheba the son of Bichri. ⁸ When they were at the
great stone which is in Gibeon, Amasa came to meet
them. Now Joab was wearing a soldier's garment,
and over it was a girdle with a sword in its sheath
fastened upon his loins, and as he went forward it
fell out. ⁹ And Joab said to Amasa, "Is it well with
you, my brother?" And Joab took Amasa by the beard
with his right hand to kiss him. ¹⁰ But Amasa did
not observe the sword which was in Joab's hand;
so Joab struck him with it in the body, and shed his
bowels to the ground, without striking a second
blow; and he died.

Then Joab and Abishai his brother pursued
Sheba the son of Bichri. ¹¹ And one of Joab's men
took his stand by Amasa, and said, "Whoever favors
Joab, and whoever is for David, let him follow Joab."

ʰ Tg: Heb *snatch away our eyes*
ⁱ Cn Compare Gk: Heb *after him Joab's men*

¹² And Amasa lay wallowing in his blood in the high-way. And any one who came by, seeing him, stopped; ʲ and when the man saw that all the people stopped, he carried Amasa out of the highway into the field, and threw a garment over him. ¹³ When he was taken out of the highway, all the people went on after Joab to pursue Sheba the son of Bichri.

ʲ This clause is transposed from the end of the verse

David must act quickly to prevent Sheba's revolt from splitting the kingdom permanently. Instead of turning to the deposed Joab, who is out of favor, David turns to Amasa, the new commander of the militia, ordering him to mobilize the entire citizen army of Judah, only part of which had turned out, it seems, to escort him back to Jerusalem. By mobilizing this citizen army for the new campaign, David is seemingly proposing to reduce his dependence on his professional soldiers — an added reason for removing the disobedient Joab from the command of the militia and replacing him with the officer who had in fact led this force in the Absalom revolt, a man in whom the militiamen might be expected to have some confidence. In any case, David instructs Amasa to mobilize the citizen army of Judah and crush the rebellion. Actually, however, David's plan is unwise, since nothing could have served to aggravate the intertribal rivalry of North and South more than the use of the militia from his own tribe of Judah to put down a rebellion among the northern tribes. One can imagine that Joab, no longer David's commander-in-chief, was mightily exasperated with this move by the king. After all, such a move took this important campaign out of the hands of the professionals, whose loyalty to the king and the united empire

355

could not be compromised by any local tribal patriotism, and turned it over to the militiamen, who had proved to be notoriously susceptible to internal pressures.

As matters turn out, however, Amasa is unable to mobilize the force within the allotted three days, and since the situation threatens to get out of hand if it is not dealt with swiftly and decisively, David falls back on his professionals after all, calling on Joab's brother Abishai to crush the revolt and disperse the rebels before they become entrenched. Joab, we note, is given no position, and goes along, apparently without rank. At Gibeon, about 10 miles north of Jerusalem, Amasa overtakes David's men. It seems that Amasa really had done his utmost to gather the militia as quickly as possible; even now he seems to have hurried ahead of his Judean troops, who arrive on the scene a bit later (vv. 11-13). This, however, provides Joab with a perfect opportunity to deal with his archrival. But much more than Joab's personal position is at stake. Joab knows that Amasa dare not be leader of the campaign, lest tribal rivalry break out even more uncontrollably than before. Once before Joab had acted to preserve his own position against the rising rival Abner (3:27). Now Joab greets Amasa as a friend and brother, stretching out his right hand in the customary salutation of kinfolk to take hold of Amasa's beard and kiss him, while he meanwhile with his left hand takes hold of a concealed dagger. Though the text is obscure at this point, it seems that Joab had fastened the dagger in such a way that he had only to bend his body and it would fall free (cf. Judg. 3:16). Amasa's suspicions are not aroused. The experienced slayer of men is able to complete his work with one effective stroke. The deed done, the efficient Joab wastes not a moment in proceeding with

356

the military task at hand, assuming command without (even contrary to) David's command, while David's own appointee, the commander Amasa, lies on the highway, convulsing in the throes of death. For a moment this assassination threatens to cause new trouble as the militiamen arrive on the scene and see their commander wallowing in blood. A soldier is therefore stationed near the body to urge the passing soldiers to follow Joab. Even then people stop to look until finally the guard takes Amasa's body and puts it out into a field—with the result that all men, professionals and militiamen, go forward after Joab.

Joab Effectively Crushes the Revolt   *14-22*

¹⁴ And Sheba passed through all the tribes of Israel to Abel of Bethmaacah; *k* **and all the Bichrites** *l* **assembled, and followed him in. ¹⁵ And all the men who were with Joab came and besieged him in Abel of Bethmaacah; they cast up a mound against the city, and it stood against the rampart; and they were battering the wall, to throw it down. ¹⁶ Then a wise woman called from the city, "Hear! Hear! Tell Joab, 'Come here, that I may speak to you.'" ¹⁷ And he came near her; and the woman said, "Are you Joab?" He answered, "I am." Then she said to him, "Listen to the words of your maidservant." And he answered, "I am listening." ¹⁸ Then she said, "They were wont to say in old time, 'Let them but ask counsel at Abel'; and so they settled a matter. ¹⁹ I am one of those who are peaceable and faithful in Israel; you seek to destroy a city which is a mother in Israel; why will you swallow up the heritage of the LORD?" ²⁰ Joab answered, "Far be it from me, far be it, that I should**

---

k With 20. 15: Heb *and Beth-maacah*   *l* Heb *Berites*

swallow up or destroy! ²¹ That is not true. But a man
of the hill country of Ephraim, called Sheba the son
of Bichri, has lifted up his hand against King David;
give up him alone, and I will withdraw from the city."
And the woman said to Joab, "Behold, his head shall
be thrown to you over the wall." ²² Then the woman
went to all the people in her wisdom. And they cut off
the head of Sheba the son of Bichri, and threw it out
to Joab. So he blew the trumpet, and they dispersed
from the city, every man to his home. And Joab returned to Jerusalem to the king.

The rebel Sheba has very little success in gaining
supporters in the North except among his own Benjaminite clansmen. He establishes himself on the northernmost border in the provincial capital of Abel-Beth-
maacah, where he no doubt intends to establish his
authority. There Joab catches up with him and promptly
lays siege to the city, heaping up against the city's
outer wall an embankment of earth that serves as a ramp
for sappers. The work is so successful that in short
order the breaching of the wall is imminent.

At this juncture a wise woman appears on the main
wall and opens an interview with Joab. Citing a proverb
according to which good counsel is always to be found
in this city that guards Israel's ancient traditions and
often settles her quarrels with divine oracles, this wise
woman asks how David's commander can dare to destroy a city revered as "a mother in Israel" and thus
wipe out one of the divinely appointed allotments of
the Lord. Joab, of course, wants only the head of the
rebel leader who has caused the disturbance. And when
that is thrown over the wall to him, he immediately
calls a halt to the campaign and returns from the com-

pletely pacified North to Jerusalem. He has proved to
be David's irreplaceable deliverer. We hear nothing
of David's reaction to Joab's activity. Was the king
happy with it? Did he even swear protection to Joab
(cf. 1 Kings 2:5 f., 31 f.)? One thing is clear: David's empire is now stronger than ever before. But it is burdened
with bloodshed and disputes. We are well aware of the
weaknesses in its loose structure and especially of the
unresolved question about the succession to the throne.
The successor has proved to be neither Amnon, nor
Absalom, nor a descendant of Saul. Only the final
chapters of the narrative of the succession to David's
throne will show who it will be. (1 Kings 1−2)

List of David's Officials   *23-26*

²³ **Now Joab was in command of all the army of
Israel; and Benaiah the son of Jehoiada was in command of the Cherethites and the Pelethites; ²⁴ and
Adoram was in charge of the forced labor; and Jehoshaphat the son of Ahilud was the recorder; ²⁵ and
Sheva was secretary; and Zadok and Abiathar were
priests; ²⁶ and Ira the Jairite was also David's priest.**

The list of David's officials seems to appear a second
time at this point in the narrative, perhaps now in order
to signal Joab's reinstatement into his old position as
commander of all the army of Israel. In 8:15-18, at the
climax of the account of David's rise to power, an earlier
version of the list was a primary source of our knowledge of David's excellent administration. Here the same
list, repeated at the end of the account of the crisis,
shows how the empire has been restored to order.
There are a few significant changes (cf. commentary on
8:15-18). A new position is that of Adoram, who is in

charge of forced labor, a customary institution in the ancient Near East, one which was understandably hated (cf. 1 Kings 12:18). This addition may reflect the later situation in the last part of David's reign. Another change is that in place of the sons of David, mentioned previously as priests, we hear of Ira the Jairite, who perhaps became attached to David's court during his sojourn in Gilead.

The Appendix
of the Books of Samuel

2 Samuel 21 − 24

These four chapters interrupt the unfinished narrative
of the succession to David's throne (2 Sam. 9 − 1 Kings 2).
One theory holds that the once continuous account of
1 and 2 Samuel and 1 and 2 Kings may have been di-
vided at the end of 2 Sam. 20 into two separate scrolls
(one scroll would have become unwieldy); subsequently
the editor (who gradually gave final form to what is now
the present Books of Samuel) seems to have possessed
additional important materials about David that he did
not want to abandon. He therefore inserted such materials at the end of the cutoff into what grew to be our
present Appendix. It is probable that at the first stage
only the two similar stories of the plagues (21:1-14 and
24:1-25) stood side by side. Then this original pair seems
to have been split by the insertion between them of two
lists of heroic anecdotes, 21:15-21 (the four Philistine

giants) and 23:8-29 (David's mighty men). These two
lists, in turn, were separated by the insertion between
them of two poems: Ch. 22 (David's royal hymn of
thanksgiving) and 23:1-7 (the last words of David). In
this manner the Appendix seems to have developed.

GREAT FAMINE AND EXECUTION
OF SAUL'S DESCENDANTS   21:1-14

The Lord Reveals the Cause and the Cure
of the Famine   *21:1-9*

¹ Now there was a famine in the days of David
for three years, year after year; and David sought the
face of the LORD. And the LORD said, "There is
bloodguilt on Saul and on his house, because he put
the Gibeonites to death." ² So the king called the
Gibeonites.ᵐ Now the Gibeonites were not of the people of Israel, but of the remnant of the Amorites;
although the people of Israel had sworn to spare them,
Saul had sought to slay them in his zeal for the people of Israel and Judah. ³ And David said to the
Gibeonites, "What shall I do for you? And how shall
I make expiation, that you may bless the heritage
of the LORD?" ⁴ The Gibeonites said to him, "It is
not a matter of silver or gold between us and Saul
or his house; neither is it for us to put any man to
death in Israel." And he said, "What do you say that
I shall do for you?" ⁵ They said to the king, "The man
who consumed us and planned to destroy us, so that
we should have no place in all the territory of Israel,
⁶ let seven of his sons be given to us, so that we may
hang them up before the LORD at Gibeon on the

ᵐ Heb *the Gibeonites and said to them*

mountain of the LORD." [n] And the king said, "I will give them."

[7] But the king spared Mephibosheth, the son of Saul's son Jonathan, because of the oath of the LORD which was between them, between David and Jonathan the son of Saul. [8] The king took the two sons of Rizpah the daughter of Aiah, whom she bore to Saul, Armoni and Mephibosheth; and the five sons of Merab [o] the daughter of Saul, whom she bore to Adriel the son of Barzillai the Meholathite; [9] and he gave them into the hands of the Gibeonites, and they hanged them on the mountain before the LORD, and the seven of them perished together. They were put to death in the first days of harvest, at the beginning of barley harvest.

[n] Cn Compare Gk and 21.9: Heb *at Gibeah of Saul, the chosen of the* LORD
[o] Two Hebrew Mss Gk: Heb *Michal*

Chronologically this account would fit best before 9:1, where David asks whether any sons of Saul still remain. A famine caused by insufficient rain afflicts the land for three successive years. Disturbed in his conscience, the king consults the Lord, making, it seems, a pilgrimage to the high place of Gibeon, to obtain from the Lord of that famous sanctuary an oracle that would both explain the reason for the famine and suggest a cure. The response of the Lord (given presumably through His priest or prophet) refers to the fact that Saul's attempts to reduce the number of non-Israelites living in the heart of his kingdom had led him to break the sacred covenant made in the sight of the Lord between Gibeon and Israel when the latter entered Palestine under Joshua (Joshua 9). In his purge Saul had even gone so far as to shed the blood of these non-

Israelite Amorites. Hence curses instead of blessings rest upon "the heritage of the LORD." Though David suggests reparation by money from the guilty house, the Gibeonites refuse such monetary restitution and demand a full payment of blood, seemingly in accord with the stipulations of the original covenant. David assumes the responsibility of handing over to them seven of Saul's family. They are executed at the sanctuary in the presence of the Lord, whose anger at the broken covenant and shed blood is, it seems, appeased by the shed blood of the offending family. It is in a cultic act, then, that these seven are executed. It is also perhaps in keeping with express stipulations of the original covenant that the dead bodies of the transgressor's family are exposed—in this case for six months, from the beginning of the barley harvest in May until the beginning of the rains that end the drought in the autumn. (See Deut. 21:22-23.) We have only to recall the executions that followed World War II to recall similar justice in our culture. Until recently such a penal system of justice was almost universal.

A Bright Spot in a Grim Story   *10-14*

¹⁰ **Then Rizpah the daughter of Aiah took sackcloth, and spread it for herself on the rock, from the beginning of harvest until rain fell upon them from the heavens; and she did not allow the birds of the air to come upon them by day, or the beasts of the field by night. ¹¹ When David was told what Rizpah the daughter of Aiah, the concubine of Saul, had done, ¹² David went and took the bones of Saul and the bones of his son Jonathan from the men of Jabesh-gilead, who had stolen them from the public square of Beth-shan, where the Philistines had**

hanged them, on the day the Philistines killed Saul on Gilboa; [13] and he brought up from there the bones of Saul and the bones of his son Jonathan; and they gathered the bones of those who were hanged. [14] And they buried the bones of Saul and his son Jonathan in the land of Benjamin in Zela, in the tomb of Kish his father; and they did all that the king commanded. And after that God heeded supplications for the land.

Rizpah had been unable to prevent her sons and kinfolk from being executed or their bodies from being exposed until the expiation was completed and the rains fell again. Nevertheless, in great loyalty to the dead, she spreads her garment of sackcloth—itself a token of deep mourning—on the rock nearby as a sort of "sleeping bag" and guards the remains day and night, so that birds and beasts of prey may not dishonor them. King David is deeply moved by a report of her self-sacrificing loyalty. As soon as the rains fall, he therefore, gathers the remains and gives them honorable burial, together with the bones of Saul and Jonathan, which he brings from Jabesh-gilead, burying them all in the Benjaminite family grave.

EXPLOITS AGAINST THE PHILISTINES   21:15-22

In this section of the Appendix we have a stylized recital of anecdotes from the battles against the Philistines. Each time a giant, Goliath-like, Philistine champion is overcome by David and his men. This archival report might fit better at 5:17-25, at the beginning of David's reign. These verses seem to have been added here to the account of David's last campaign (Ch. 20) to give a more complete report of David's fighting.

Further Battles Against Giants 15-22

¹⁵ The Philistines had war again with Israel, and David went down together with his servants, and they fought against the Philistines; and David grew weary. ¹⁶ And Ishbibenob, one of the descendants of the giants, whose spear weighed three hundred shekels of bronze, and who was girded with a new sword, thought to kill David. ¹⁷ But Abishai the son of Zeruiah came to his aid, and attacked the Philistine and killed him. Then David's men adjured him, "You shall no more go out with us to battle, lest you quench the lamp of Israel."

¹⁸ After this there was again war with the Philistines at Gob; then Sibbecai the Hushathite slew Saph, who was one of the descendants of the giants. ¹⁹ And there was again war with the Philistines at Gob; and Elhanan the son of Jaareoregim, the Bethlehemite, slew Goliath the Gittite, the shaft of whose spear was like a weaver's beam. ²⁰ And there was again war at Gath, where there was a man of great stature, who had six fingers on each hand, and six toes on each foot, twenty-four in number; and he also was descended from the giants. ²¹ And when he taunted Israel, Jonathan the son of Shimei, David's brother, slew him. ²² These four were descended from the giants in Gath; and they fell by the hand of David and by the hand of his servants.

The first episode is somewhat more extended than the others. David's weariness is almost his undoing; it gives the mighty Goliath-like Philistine an opportunity to kill him. David's nephew, Abishai, however, intervenes in the duel and dispatches the Philistine.

After this narrow escape David's men insist that he dare never again enter such a duel, lest the lamp of Israel, which effectively guarantees the welfare of the entire community, be quenched.

At Gob (perhaps Gibbethon, a border town that blocked the Philistines' entry into Israelite hill country) Sabbecai, one of David's 30 "heroes," kills another Philistine giant. It is often claimed that Elhanan, the Bethlehemite who slays the giant Goliath, is the person who "really" slew the famous Goliath of Gath and that David subsequently got the credit for his soldier's deed. But, while some think that we are dealing with varying traditions of one and the same original event (cf. Introduction, 14 ff.), it is also possible that we are dealing with two separate events (the name Goliath being a general name given to several Philistine "sons of Rapha," giants) or that Elhanan is the personal name of the same man whose title name we know as David.

The last giant (unnamed) is a monster with abnormal toes and fingers who taunts Israel. His conqueror is David's nephew from Bethlehem. It is possible that all the heroes in this list come from Bethlehem. In any case these archive-like accounts differ in style from the narrative accounts of the rest of the book (see 1 Sam. 17). The editor of the Books of Samuel apparently did not want people to forget that the last remnants of the race of the giants were eliminated by David and his men.

THE LORD'S RESCUE
OF HIS ROYAL SERVANT   22

This psalm (cf. Ps. 18) brings a most illuminating theological commentary on the stories of David's military exploits. It follows the well-known pattern of an individual's psalm of praise, for after an initial summary (vv. 2-4) it brings two narrative accounts of God's deed (5-20 and 32-49) before the final praise (50-51). But this psalm lacks the usual call addressed to the bystanders to join in the praise, perhaps because it is a royal psalm to be recited by the king before a festival congregation in order to recount the Lord's saving deed. This also accounts for the inclusion of a very vivid theophany description of the Lord's coming (8-16) and an important royal declaration of loyalty to the covenant. (21-31)

Superscription and Introductory Summary   *22:1-4*

¹ And David spoke to the LORD the words of this song on the day when the LORD delivered him from the hand of all his enemies, and from the hand of Saul. ² He said,

"The LORD is my rock, and my fortress, and my
        deliverer,
³ my *p* God, my rock, in whom I take refuge,
    my shield and the horn of my salvation,
        my stronghold and my refuge,
        my savior; thou savest me from violence.
⁴ I call upon the LORD, who is worthy to be praised,
    and I am saved from my enemies.

p Gk Ps 18.2: Heb lacks *my*

In describing the Lord as the Protector of the oppressed, the king employs a number of word pictures derived from the Palestinian landscape (rock, fortress, stronghold, refuge) or from military life (deliverer, shield, horn of salvation). Despite the fact that David was often pursued and had to flee from one place to another, the Lord was his stronghold, his shield.

The First Account
of the Lord's Rescue   5-20

5 "For the waves of death encompassed me,
   the torrents of perdition assailed me;
6 the cords of Sheol entangled me,
   the snares of death confronted me.

7 "In my distress I called upon the LORD;
   to my God I called.
From his temple he heard my voice,
   and my cry came to his ears.

8 "Then the earth reeled and rocked;
   the foundations of the heavens trembled
   and quaked, because he was angry.
9 Smoke went up from his nostrils,
   and devouring fire from his mouth;
   glowing coals flamed forth from him.
10 He bowed the heavens, and came down;
   thick darkness was under his feet.
11 He rode on a cherub, and flew;
   he was seen upon the wings of the wind.
12 He made darkness around him
   his canopy, thick clouds, a gathering of water.
13 Out of the brightness before him
   coals of fire flamed forth.
14 The LORD thundered from heaven,
   and the Most High uttered his voice.
15 And he sent out arrows, and scattered them;
   lightning, and routed them.
16 Then the channels of the sea were seen,
   the foundations of the world were laid bare,
   at the rebuke of the LORD,
   at the blast of the breath of his nostrils.

¹⁷ "He reached from on high, he took me,
    he drew me out of many waters.
¹⁸ He delivered me from my strong enemy,
    from those who hated me;
    for they were too mighty for me.
¹⁹ They came upon me in the day of my calamity;
    but the LORD was my stay.
²⁰ He brought me forth into a broad place;
    he delivered me, because he delighted in me.

The king's trouble was that he had often been delivered up to death; we recall David's exposure to death at the hands of the Philistines, of Saul (cf. 1 Sam. 20:3), of rebellious Absalom and his followers, of other hostile nations. He could do nothing but cry to the Lord. From His dwelling place in the temple the Lord heard him; and so the deadly power of chaos did not triumph over him because the Lord intervened in His majestic God-hood, making a true epiphany (cf. Hab. 3:3-15). The Lord is pictured as coming from afar, soaring on an angelic chariot, accompanied by thunder and lightning-bolt arrows that cause heaven and earth to quake, His glorious splendor wrapped, however, in thick darkness. In anger He sends forth from His nostrils fire and smoke and routs the forces of chaos that wish to destroy His anointed. As we hear this highly poetic and religious account of God's rescue of the king, we recall that, according to the more prosaic account of David's struggles, he often did consult the Lord and received the Lord's answer (cf. 1 Sam. 23:1 f.; 30:7; 2 Sam. 2:1; 5:19-23) and His divine intervention. Even though no human eye beheld it, the Creator of heaven and earth moved heaven and earth to rescue His anointed servant.

*The King's Loyalty to the Lord
and the Lord's Loyalty to the King*　　　*21-31*

[21] "The **LORD** rewarded me according to my righteousness;
　according to the cleanness of my hands he recompensed me.
[22] For I have kept the ways of the **LORD**,
　and have not wickedly departed from my God.
[23] For all his ordinances were before me,
　and from his statutes I did not turn aside.
[24] I was blameless before him,
　and I kept myself from guilt.
[25] Therefore the **LORD** has recompensed me according to my righteousness,
　according to my cleanness in his sight.

[26] "With the loyal thou dost show thyself loyal;
　with the blameless man thou dost show thyself blameless;
[27] with the pure thou dost show thyself pure,
　and with the crooked thou dost show thyself perverse.
[28] Thou dost deliver a humble people,
　but thy eyes are upon the haughty to bring them down.
[29] Yea, thou art my lamp, O **LORD**,
　and my God lightens my darkness.
[30] Yea, by thee I can crush a troop,
　and by my God I can leap over a wall.
[31] This God—his way is perfect;
　the promise of the **LORD** proves true;
　he is a shield for all those who take refuge in him.

371

At first reading it might seem as if the king were here boasting of his own self-righteousness according to some self-chosen standard of his own. It is clear, however, that the king's declaration of innocence and righteousness in conformity with God's covenant is the sort of oath-declaration that was demanded in those days of all who would enter the Lord's holy presence (submitting to an ancient sort of lie-detector test). For example, Psalm 15 and Psalm 24:3-6 announce the conditions under which alone one might enter the holy sanctuary, the actual keeping of the stipulations of the Sinaitic covenant. Only the person who lived in the covenant dared be admitted into the Lord's holy presence, be he commoner or even king. Also, vv. 26-31 show that this declaration is the exact opposite of self-righteous boasting by the king. For in them God's righteousness is described as His activity of keeping the covenant with Israel, helping the humble and poor, and toppling the proud and haughty. This was also the God-given mission of the Lord's representative on Mount Zion, the Israelite king: he was to judge the poor and needy and thus uphold in Israel the Lord's covenant will. The king's righteousness therefore does not include sinlessness and absence of weakness; in fact, the king here identifies himself with the poor. When, for instance, David's sins were exposed by the Lord's prophet (2 Sam. 12:13), David confessed them and, instead of abandoning that covenant, continued to live in loyalty to it as the servant of the Lord. Thus David exercised the office of Israelite kingship, an office later to be fulfilled with the coming of the true King, Christ Jesus. Just as "the promise of the LORD" proved true for David, so it proved true for Jesus, who lived by every word that proceeded out of the mouth of God.

372

The Second Account of the Lord's Rescue   *32-49*

³² "For who is God, but the LORD?
    And who is a rock, except our God?
³³ This God is my strong refuge,
    and has made ʳ my ˢ way safe.
³⁴ He made my ˢ feet like hinds' feet,
    and set me secure on the heights.
³⁵ He trains my hands for war,
    so that my arms can bend a bow of bronze.
³⁶ Thou hast given me the shield of thy salvation,
    and thy help ᵗ made me great.
³⁷ Thou didst give a wide place for my steps under
        me,
    and my feet ᵘ did not slip;
³⁸ I pursued my enemies and destroyed them,
    and did not turn back until they were consumed.
³⁹ I consumed them; I thrust them through, so that
        they did not rise;
    they fell under my feet.
⁴⁰ For thou didst gird me with strength for the battle;
    thou didst make my assailants sink under me.
⁴¹ Thou didst make my enemies turn their backs to
        me,
    those who hated me, and I destroyed them.
⁴² They looked, but there was none to save;
    they cried to the LORD, but he did not answer
        them.
⁴³ I beat them fine as the dust of the earth,
    I crushed them and stamped them down like the
        mire of the streets.

ʳ Ps 18. 32: Heb *set free*   ˢ Another reading is *his*
ᵗ Or *gentleness*   ᵘ Heb *ankles*

373

⁴⁴ "Thou didst deliver me from strife with the peoples; ^{*v*}

thou didst keep me as the head of the nations;
people whom I had not known served me.

⁴⁵ Foreigners came cringing to me;

as soon as they heard of me, they obeyed me.

⁴⁶ Foreigners lost heart,

and came trembling ^{*w*} out of their fastnesses.

⁴⁷ "The LORD lives; and blessed be my rock,

and exalted be my God, the rock of my salvation,

⁴⁸ the God who gave me vengeance

and brought down peoples under me,

⁴⁹ who brought me out from my enemies;

thou didst exalt me above my adversaries,
thou didst deliver me from men of violence.

^{*v*} Gk: Heb *from strife with my people*
^{*w*} Ps 18. 45: Heb *girded themselves*

The continued account of the Lord's rescue turns to praise the Lord, who alone gave David victory over internal and external enemies. To be sure, David *was* a great military hero whom people admired; but behind him stood God. It was the Lord who taught him to bend the bow, to leap the walls, to surprise and crush his foes. It was the Lord who established David's great empire, making him "the head of the nations." As the Lord's anointed, the Davidic king is a type of Jesus Christ; he is the suffering one who does not appeal to his royal attributes or sacral prerogatives, as did heathen kings in their crises; rather, he subordinates himself to the covenant and to being the Lord's lowly servant. That is why the Lord exalts him over all nations. Some of the pattern of the Suffering Servant of Isaiah 53 shines through here. No wonder the psalm must end with special praise.

Final Praise   *50-51*

⁵⁰ "For this I will extol thee, O LORD, among the
    nations,
  and sing praises to thy name.
⁵¹ Great triumphs he gives ˣ to his king,
  and shows steadfast love to his anointed,
  to David, and his descendants for ever."

    ˣ Another reading is *He is a tower of salvation*

The king praises the Lord among the nations because of His steadfast loyal love to David and his dynasty. Again in these verses the king, the Lord's royal servant, is a type of the Son of David who entered into His glory only by suffering first. In this way our psalm, like the great Messianic promise of Nathan (2 Sam. 7), points not only to the deeper meaning of David's own military exploits but to the fulfillment in Christ Jesus.

DAVID'S "LAST WORDS"   23:1-7

After the royal psalm (Ch. 22) the Appendix brings us another song that celebrates the righteous rule of the Davidic king (like Ps. 72) and the covenant between the Lord and David's dynasty (like Psalms 2, 89, 132, 110). There is no reason to deny that this royal psalm goes back to king David himself. Its highly poetic vocabulary and thought have given rise to some textual variations in the course of its transmission (note the RSV variant readings), but its great Messianic message is entirely clear.

375

The Poet's Introduction   *23:1-3a*

¹ Now these are the last words of David:
The oracle of David, the son of Jesse,
    the oracle of the man who was raised on high,
the anointed of the God of Jacob,
    the sweet psalmist of Israel: *ʸ*

² "The Spirit of the LORD speaks by me,
    his word is upon my tongue.
³ The God of Israel has spoken,
    the Rock of Israel has said to me:

    ʸ Or *the favorite of the songs of Israel*

In the beginning strophe David characterizes himself not merely as the son of Jesse and the Lord's
anointed king, but more importantly as one endowed
with the Lord's Spirit, one who sings as His messenger
about the future of his royal dynasty and of his people.
(Cf. other "last words," Gen. 49 and Deut. 33.)

The Ideal Righteous Ruler   *3b-5*

When one rules justly over men,
    ruling in the fear of God,
⁴ he dawns on them like the morning light,
    like the sun shining forth upon a cloudless
        morning,
    like rain *ᶻ* that makes grass to sprout from the
        earth.
⁵ Yea, does not my house stand so with God?
    For he has made with me an everlasting covenant,
    ordered in all things and secure.
For will he not cause to prosper
    all my help and my desire?

    ᶻ Heb *from rain*

The Lord's oracle (which David prophetically proclaims) employs two interlocking word pictures to describe the ideal ruler; he is like (a) the rising sun on a cloudless morning, (b) a rain that has refreshed the green grass. Like them, the righteous and God-fearing ruler appears to quicken his people by a just and gracious rule. Such an ideal ruler is not part of a vague dream concerning a far-off millennium. The new era has already been inaugurated by the Lord through the eternal and steadfast covenant by which He has promised to send the righteous Ruler from this dynasty. What has now begun in David's own days will be fulfilled when the "Dayspring from on high" (Luke 1:78) appears to visit His people and complete all that has not yet reached its consummation.

The Wicked, Thorns to Be Cut Down and Burned   6-7

⁶ But godless men *ᵃ* are all like thorns that are thrown
      away;
   for they cannot be taken with the hand;
⁷ but the man who touches them
   arms himself with iron and the shaft of a spear,
   and they are utterly consumed with fire." *ᵇ*

   ᵃ Heb *worthlessness*   ᵇ Heb *fire in the sitting*

In contrast to this righteous ruler stand the wicked men who are so dangerous and thorny that people who wish to burn them even as fuel must take precautions as they gather them together "with iron and the shaft of a spear." Such were the people who opposed the rule of the Davidic king, in David's own days and in those of his dynastic successors; and such are all who oppose the rule of God that has been inaugurated by the resurrection of Jesus Christ from the dead.

DAVID'S WARRIORS 23:8-39

It is not surprising that the Appendix also brings a list of David's heroic professional soldiers, by whose aid he attained kingship over Judah and Israel and established and maintained his great empire. (See also 21:15-22; 1 Chron. 11:11-47.)

The Incomparable Three *8-17*

⁸ These are the names of the mighty men whom David had: Josheb-basshebeth a Tahchemonite; he was chief of the three; *ᶜ* he wielded his spear *ᵈ* against eight hundred whom he slew at one time.

⁹ And next to him among the three mighty men was Eleazar the son of Dodo, son of Ahohi. He was with David when they defied the Philistines who were gathered there for battle, and the men of Israel withdrew. ¹⁰ He rose and struck down the Philistines until his hand was weary, and his hand cleaved to the sword; and the LORD wrought a great victory that day; and the men returned after him only to strip the slain.

¹¹ And next to him was Shammah, the son of Agee the Hararite. The Philistines gathered together at Lehi, where there was a plot of ground full of lentils; and the men fled from the Philistines. ¹² But he took his stand in the midst of the plot, and defended it, and slew the Philistines; and the LORD wrought a great victory.

¹³ And three of the thirty chief men went down, and came about harvest time to David at the cave of Adullam, when a band of Philistines was encamped in the valley of Rephaim. ¹⁴ David was then in the

ᶜ Or *captains*   *ᵈ* 1 Chron 11. 11: Heb *obscure*

stronghold; and the garrison of the Philistines was then at Bethlehem. [15] And David said longingly, "O that some one would give me water to drink from the well of Bethlehem which is by the gate!" [16] Then the three mighty men broke through the camp of the Philistines, and drew water out of the well of Bethlehem which was by the gate, and took and brought it to David. But he would not drink of it; he poured it out to the LORD, [17] and said, "Far be it from me, O LORD, that I should do this. Shall I drink the blood of the men who went at the risk of their lives?" Therefore he would not drink it. These things did the three mighty men.

Instead of the celebrated Three turning out to be three heroes already well known from the Books of Samuel, for instance, the three sons of Zeruiah: Joab, Abishai, and Asahel (or perhaps in lieu of the early-slain Asahel the great fighter Benaiah), we find that three other, less-known warriors are given this highest honor: Josheb-basshebeth, Eleazar, and Shammah. Though all three of them were seemingly abandoned by the rest of the troops, they each saved a desperate situation by singlehandedly slaying heaps upon heaps of the enemy. Before writing off their exploits as pure fiction, modern readers ought to take into account parallel escapades reported in Scandinavian and other regional sagas, telling of heroes who go beserk as they fling themselves upon the enemy. After all, these heroes were fighting the Lord's battles in holy wars.

The special episode about the Three's breaking through enemy lines to get good cool water for David from his hometown spring shows how David's troops were ready to risk great danger to comply with his every wish. Moreover, David valued the water they brought him as the equal of their blood and would not therefore drink of it; rather, he poured it out as a libation to the Lord for having given him such loyal men.

Abishai, Benaiah, Asahel 18-24a

¹⁸ Now Abishai, the brother of Joab, the son of Zeruiah, was chief of the thirty.ᵉ And he wielded his spear against three hundred men and slew them, and won a name beside the three. ¹⁹ He was the most renowned of the thirty,ᶠ and became their commander; but he did not attain to the three.

²⁰ And Benaiah the son of Jehoiada was a valiant man ᵍ of Kabzeel, a doer of great deeds; he smote two ariels ʰ of Moab. He also went down and slew a lion in a pit on a day when snow had fallen. ²¹ And he slew an Egyptian, a handsome man. The Egyptian had a spear in his hand; but Benaiah went down to him with a staff, and snatched the spear out of the Egyptian's hand, and slew him with his own spear. ²² These things did Benaiah the son of Jehoiada, and won a name beside the three mighty men. ²³ He was renowned among the thirty, but he did not attain to the three. And David set him over his bodyguard.

²⁴ Asahel the brother of Joab was one of the thirty;

ᵉ Two Hebrew Mss Syr: MT *three*
ᶠ 1 Chron 11. 25: Heb *Was he the most renowned of the three?*
ᵍ Another reading is *the son of Ish-hai*
ʰ The meaning of the word *ariel* is unknown

The anecdotes about Abishai and Benaiah (18-23) are quite different from those about the Three; they are not episodes in holy wars; nor are they given such high evaluation. Abishai is the only one of the famous three sons of David's sister Zeruiah whose exploits are described at this point. Joab is surprisingly not listed, though he is referred to as the brother of Abishai and Asahel and his armor-bearer is mentioned. More than that, he must be included in the list if it is to finally total 37, as the last verse declares; perhaps he was so well known as to need no special introduction here. Asahel (cf. 2 Sam. 2) is mentioned only briefly in what may well have originally been a longer note, something to the effect of saying, "Asahel, Joab's brother, also belonged to the Thirty. He was as swift of foot as a wild gazelle (2 Sam. 2:18) and was renowned among the Thirty, but he did not attain to the Three."

No wonder David took Abishai along on the daring night-raid into Saul's sleeping camp (1 Sam. 26:6) and later gave him command over one third of his troops (2 Sam. 18:2). Benaiah was the rough and ready fighter to whom Solomon later delegated the liquidation of some politically dangerous persons (1 Kings 2). Besides his remarkable victory over the heavily armed Egyptian giant, his exploits with lions were celebrated. Some scholars feel that the "ariels" of Moab whom he smote were Moabite heroes, but others, noting the context, hold that they refer to actual lions. These were not African lions; nevertheless, tracking a rapacious Palestinian lion into a cistern at snowfall and then grappling with it successfully was no mean achievement.

The List of the Thirty   *24b-39*

Elhanan the son of Dodo of Bethlehem, 25 Shammah of Harod, Elika of Harod, 26 Helez the Paltite, Ira the son of Ikkesh of Tekoa, 27 Abiezer, of Anathoth, Mebunnai the Hushathite, 28 Zalmon the Ahohite,

Maharai of Netophah, [29] Heleb the son of Baanah of
Netophah, Ittai the son of Ribai of Gibeah of the
Benjaminites, [30] Benaiah of Pirathon, Hiddai of the
brooks of Gaash, [31] Abialbon the Arbathite, Azmaveth
of Bahurim, [32] Eliahba of Shaalbon, the sons of
Jashen, Jonathan, [33] Shammah the Hararite, Ahiam
the son of Sharar the Hararite, [34] Eliphelet the son
of Ahasbai of Maacah, Eliam the son of Ahithophel
of Gilo, [35] Hezro [i] of Carmel, Paarai the Arbite, [36] Igal
the son of Nathan of Zobah, Bani the Gadite, [37] Zelek
the Ammonite, Naharai of Beeroth, the armor-bearer
of Joab the son of Zeruiah, [38] Ira the Ithrite, Gareb
the Ithrite, [39] Uriah the Hittite: thirty-seven in all.

[i] Another reading is *Hezrai*

This list is very old and may even reflect the course
of David's fortunes, for the first ten warriors in the list
(24b-29a) are men from the Judean territory where
David first began to gather a Robin Hood group about
himself. The next group in the list (29b-32a) includes
warriors from Benjamin and other regions farther
north. Those named in 33-35 point to the period when
David was fleeing from Saul and living in the southern
Judean wilderness and finally in Ziklag. In addition to
these 23 are mentioned the Three (8-11), the three sons
of Zeruiah (Abishai, Asahel, and Joab), and Benaiah.

Some scholars consider this group of the Thirty as
having been organized at the time of David's sojourn
in Ziklag, organized on a model that had originally developed in Egypt but had long since been introduced
in Palestine also. If those given above were the original
Thirty, then the seven who are listed in the final verses
(36-39) are later additions to that elite group. That
there should be additions and replacements is a plausi-

ble suggestion, since the roster of the men who made up the corps undoubtedly did not remain constant, especially since the entire military organization continued to grow and some of the original Thirty were perhaps promoted to other duties (so Benaiah became chief of David's royal bodyguard).

It is, however, also possible to take the Thirty as including a different segment of the list, namely, those in the list from Elhanan to Uriah (24b-38); in this case, the final number of the entire list (37) is attained by adding Joab, Abishai, Benaiah, Asahel (18-?4a) and the Three (8-12). It is perhaps significant that a shadow falls over the list with the final name, Uriah the Hittite, the soldier whom David slew. David is by no means the Perfect Leader; He is still to come.

MERCY IN THE MIDST OF JUDGMENT   24

We have little difficulty in understanding that this story's main interest is to show how the Lord's temple came to be built on the onetime Jebusite threshing floor of Araunah on Mount Zion. It was because on that spot the Lord appeared, in answer to David's intercession, to halt His angel from executing judgment on Jerusalem. But when we venture beyond a consideration of the story's central point, we confront a number of puzzles. The reason for this is that the inspired storyteller has purposely shifted the accent at a number of points in order to emphasize the profound underlying factors involved in this story about God's judgment. Hence the story does not follow what might seem the normal sequence of (1) the king's sinful deed calling forth (2) the Lord's judgment, a judgment which is then (3) averted by the king's repentance, intercession, and sacrifice. Rather, our story purposely emphasizes — by surprising variations from such an expected sequence — the profound themes of the Lord's irrational and incomprehensible judgment and of the repentant royal believer's similarly irrational and incomprehensible response.

The Military Census   24:1-9

[1] Again the anger of the LORD was kindled against Israel, and he incited David against them, saying, "Go, number Israel and Judah." [2] So the king said to Joab and the commanders of the army,[j] who were with him, "Go through all the tribes of Israel, from Dan to Beer-sheba, and number the people, that I may know the number of the people." [3] But Joab said to the king, "May the LORD your God add to the people a hundred times as many as they are, while the eyes of my lord the king still see it; but why does my lord the king delight in this thing?" [4] But the king's word prevailed against Joab and the commanders of the army. So Joab and the commanders of the army went out from the presence of the king to number the people of Israel. [5] They crossed the Jordan, and began from Aroer,[k] and from the city that is in the middle of the valley, toward Gad and on to Jazer. [6] Then they came to Gilead, and to Kadesh in the land of the Hittites;[l] and they came to Dan, and from Dan [m] they went around to Sidon, [7] and came to the fortress of Tyre and to all the cities of the Hivites and Canaanites; and they went out to the Negeb of Judah at Beer-sheba. [8] So when they had

[j] 1 Chron 21. 2 Gk: Heb *to Joab the commander of the army*
[k] Gk: Heb *encamped in Aroer*
[l] Gk: Heb *to the land of Tahtim-hodshi*
[m] Cn Compare Gk: Heb *they came to Dan-jaan and*

gone through all the land, they came to Jerusalem
at the end of nine months and twenty days. ⁹ And
Joab gave the sum of the numbering of the people
to the king: in Israel there were eight hundred thousand valiant men who drew the sword, and the men
of Judah were five hundred thousand.

We might wonder what is sinful about the king's
preparations for an efficient and sensible use of his
military resources. Our story makes it clear, however,
that this particular census represents David's abandonment of the sacred procedure of the holy war (cf.
pp. 105 f.), which called for volunteers, not for conscripts
in a standing army. Precisely what aspect of the census
was the particularly offensive aspect is not spelled out.
Perhaps David, in his modernization, failed to take the
Lord's rights into account (Ex. 30:13), or he attempted
to fathom the secrets of God (Ex. 32:32 f.) or in general
took too much pride in national strength of arms.

Our story does not, however, really begin with an
assertion of David's sin, but with the surprising statement that it was the Lord who, in anger against Israel,
incited David to undertake the census; it was the Lord
who prompted David (apparently through a direct
oracle to him) to do the very thing that resulted in the
avenging plague. Even Joab's most diplomatic attempt
to dissuade David is unavailing. (Did Joab fear the political repercussions of a reorganization of the military
system that might cut through traditional tribal rights?
Or did Joab reflect religious scruples, and did he wish
by his long benediction to erase the curse he feared
would attend the execution of the plan?)

In any case, David's purpose prevails, and Joab

and his military officers go forth from the capital city to carry out the plan. We should not evade the problem raised by v. 1 (for instance, by claiming that two differing accounts have here been combined into one story or by specious "explanations" that will not change the fact that this is the way our account describes it) even though we cannot fathom why God acted thus. The writer here does not attribute the temptation of David to Satan, as does 1 Chron. 21:1. Here in the Book of Samuel it is the Lord who acts, and even His messengers, Gad and the destroying angel, are not identified with the evil angel Satan. The king and his people stand under the wrath of God. That is the import of the chilling statement: "Again the anger of the LORD was kindled against Israel, and He incited David against them, saying, 'Go, number Israel and Judah.'" Only persons who, like David, know the terror of God's wrath that gives people over to destruction can be so bold as to speak of God in this stark manner. Finally, like the entire mystery of evil, this can be "understood" by Christians only in its full context, which means it is looked at in the light of its final end, Christ's gracious epiphany, which overrides all that has been sinful and turns it into blessing. In a sense the Lord makes such a gracious epiphany already in this story.

The route of the census takers is briefly but clearly outlined. They begin their review of available manpower at the southern boundary of the southernmost Transjordanian tribe, Reuben; then they proceed northward to Dan and Kadesh-Naphthali; thereupon they return through the West-Jordan heartland to the southernmost boundary at Beer-sheba. The entire available fighting force numbers 800,000 Israelites and 500,000 Judahites. (Cf. 1 Chron. 21:5 and pp. 93 f.)

King David's Surprising Choice
of the Punishment of Pestilence   *10-15*

[10] But David's heart smote him after he had numbered the people. And David said to the LORD, "I have sinned greatly in what I have done. But now, O LORD, I pray thee, take away the iniquity of thy servant; for I have done very foolishly." [11] And when David arose in the morning, the word of the LORD came to the prophet Gad, David's seer, saying, [12] "Go and say to David, 'Thus says the LORD, Three things I offer [n] you; choose one of them, that I may do it to you.'" [13] So Gad came to David and told him, and said to him, "Shall three [o] years of famine come to you in your land? Or will you flee three months before your foes while they pursue you? Or shall there be three days' pestilence in your land? Now consider, and decide what answer I shall return to him who sent me." [14] Then David said to Gad, "I am in great distress; let us fall into the hand of the LORD, for his mercy is great; but let me not fall into the hand of man."

[15] So the LORD sent a pestilence upon Israel from the morning until the appointed time; and there died of the people from Dan to Beer-sheba seventy thousand men.

[n] Or *hold over*   [o] 1 Chron 21. 12 Gk: Heb *seven*

Though we perhaps now expect the Lord's prophet to arouse the king to see his error (cf. 2 Sam. 12), we hear — again surprisingly enough — that it is David who first has an uneasy conscience about his action and who confesses his sin to the Lord and asks for forgiveness. Thereupon, apparently in response to David's prayer, the Lord sends His messenger, the prophet Gad, to the king. It is also surprising that instead of attacking the king, as Elijah once accosted King Ahab, with a scolding exposure of his sin, the prophet Gad gives the royal sinner the special privilege of choosing his punishment among three alternatives — and thus the possibility of turning evil into good. Then David, again most unexpectedly, chooses the most severe of the three punishments: the pestilence, considered in those days a particularly direct manifestation of divine judgment (cf. Ex. 12:23 f. and 2 Kings 19:35). After all, famine or defeat in war still offer the victim certain chances of escaping, since they are to a certain extent subject to human regulation and manipulation. Why does David choose pestilence? Because he wants to crash through the intervening veil of God's wrath into the very heart of His love. He wants to fall into God's hands!

Many interpreters feel that the fact that the intensity of each proposed punishment grows as its duration diminishes (three years, three months, three days) means that there was no real choice among these equally devastating punishments, one being as severe as the other. This interpretation makes a valid point, but it does not go far enough and does not do justice to the story's expressly stated point that David chooses that judgment in which he and his people are delivered up to the Lord, in contrast to those punishments that would mean falling into men's hands. And it is not only that God might be more merciful than heartless men; more significantly, David believes that by casting himself into the direct path of the angry God of judgment he will experience the great pity of God. That is why David is willing to stand under God's direct punishment and fall into His hand.

388

Thereupon the pestilence actually begins (there is not the slightest indication at this point that God takes David's change of heart into account). A reconstruction based on the Septuagint text is helpful here: "David made the choice of pestilence, and it was the season of the wheat harvest and the plague began among the people, and seven thousand of the people died." This version seems superior to the shorter Hebrew version and also avoids the knotty question of what might be meant by the expression "until the appointed time," which cannot mean "until the end of the three days," since the plague was halted before the end of that.

The Halting of the Plague   16-25

16 And when the angel stretched forth his hand toward Jerusalem to destroy it, the LORD repented of the evil, and said to the angel who was working destruction among the people, "It is enough; now stay your hand." And the angel of the LORD was by the threshing floor of Araunah the Jebusite. 17 Then David spoke to the LORD when he saw the angel who was smiting the people, and said, "Lo, I have sinned, and I have done wickedly; but these sheep, what have they done? Let thy hand, I pray thee, be against me and against my father's house."

18 And Gad came that day to David, and said to him, "Go up, rear an altar to the LORD on the threshing floor of Araunah the Jebusite." 19 So David went up at Gad's word, as the LORD commanded. 20 And when Araunah looked down, he saw the king and his servants coming on toward him; and Araunah went forth, and did obeisance to the king with his face to the ground. 21 And Araunah said, "Why has my lord the king come to his servant?" David said,

"To buy the threshing floor of you, in order to build an altar to the LORD, that the plague may be averted from the people." [22] Then Araunah said to David, "Let my lord the king take and offer up what seems good to him; here are the oxen for the burnt offering, and the threshing sledges and the yokes of the oxen for the wood. [23] All this, O king, Araunah gives to the king." And Araunah said to the king, "The LORD your God accept you." [24] But the king said to Araunah, "No, but I will buy it of you for a price; I will not offer burnt offerings to the LORD my God which cost me nothing." So David bought the threshing floor and the oxen for fifty shekels of silver. [25] And David built there an altar to the LORD, and offered burnt offerings and peace offerings. So the LORD heeded supplications for the land, and the plague was averted from Israel.

Again we do not hear what we expect (viz., that David sees the angel of the Lord smiting the people and then intercedes for them). The account of such intercession does indeed come (v. 17), but—again surprisingly enough—only after we have first heard (in v. 16) how the Lord repented of the evil and spoke to the destroying angel, "It is enough; now stay your hand." Again our story gives precedence to the Lord's activity, no matter how this may be chronologically related to David's intercession and the actual building of the altar. We are not told that David the intercessor was responsible for the Lord's change of heart; we are simply told that it was the Lord who halted the plague. And if we look more closely for an explanation of the Lord's action, the only hint in the text seems to be His love for Jerusalem, since it was "when the angel stretched forth his hand toward Jerusalem to destroy it" that the Lord acted. At the same time it is apparently David, the very person who had chosen the pestilence punishment, who is so upset by the suffering of his people, as he sees the angel smiting them, that he assumes the role of mediator and intercessor, praying, "I have sinned . . . but these sheep, what have they done?" Like Moses, who wanted himself blotted out of the Lord's book if only the people might be spared (Ex. 32:32), David prays that the plague strike him and his house (the Messianic dynasty!). David is by no means a vanquished warrior who has been beaten into passivity, but he is a genuine spiritual hero who wrestles with the Lord as Jacob did at the Jabbok (Gen. 32:22 ff.); he will not let the Lord go until He blesses him. David prays for the people and proves to be a type of our Lord, who likewise underwent the punishing judgment of God, nevertheless commending Himself to the Father, who had forsaken Him, and thus winning the crucial victory on the cross.

Another aspect of this part of the story is illuminated when the Prophet Gad arrives with the Lord's express command that an altar be erected to the north of the city on the hill that dominated the city of David, where the angel of destruction would have to pass on his way to the city. David tells the owner of the threshing floor on the top of that hill, Araunah, that he wishes to buy it from him, "that the plague may be averted from the people." David is not content with receiving the site and all the materials of sacrifice as a gift from the most obliging owner; David wants to acquire proper legal title to the land where the Lord would be worshiped. Also David's attitude toward sacrifice becomes clear, "I will not offer burnt offerings to the LORD my God which cost me nothing." Far from offering a routine sort of magic sacrifice, David presents the Lord with the best he has. In this way the altar erected on Araunah's threshing floor becomes the "germ" of the future temple. The story ends with the same hopeful note that concluded the story of the famine in Ch. 21, "The LORD heeded supplications for the land, and the plague was averted from Israel." Grace is triumphant!

For Further Reading

* Recommended for the general, nonspecialist student

I. COMMENTARIES ON THE BOOKS OF SAMUEL

Caird, George B., John C. Schroeder, and Ganse Little. *The Interpreter's Bible.* Nashville: Abingdon Press, 1953. II, 853–1176. Introductions, commentary, expositions.

* Hertzberg, Hans Wilhelm. *I & II Samuel: A Commentary.* The Old Testament Library. Trans. J. S. Bowden. Philadelphia: The Westminster Press, 1964. Excellent theological and literary analysis.

* McKane, William. *I & II Samuel.* London: SCM Press, 1963. Introduction and commentary on the English text, providing sound assistance. Torch Commentary Series.

* Robinson, Gordon. *Historians of Israel* (1). Nashville: Abingdon Press, 1962. Bible Guide series. Paperback. General assistance in learning the plan, purpose, and power of the books.

* Rust, Eric C. *The Layman's Bible Commentary*. Vol. 6, pp. 77–152. Richmond, Va.: John Knox Press, 1961. Helpful comment of a literary, historical, and theological nature.

II. BACKGROUND MATERIALS

Bright, John. *A History of Israel*. Philadelphia: The Westminster Press, 1959. A retelling of Israel's story by a sensible American historian. For students.

Buttrick, George A., ed. *The Interpreter's Dictionary of the Bible*. 4 vols. Nashville: Abingdon Press, 1962. An illustrated encyclopedia, explaining Biblical names, terms, and subjects. For the serious student.

Douglas, J. D., ed. *The New Bible Dictionary*. Grand Rapids, Mich.: Wm. B. Eerdmans Publishing Co., 1962. 2,300 articles of a brief, conservative discussion of most Biblical subjects. A handy reference.

Grollenberg, L. H. *Atlas of the Bible*. New York: Thomas Nelson and Sons, 1956. A historical atlas, weaving excellent geographical (animated maps, photographs), archaeological, historical, and literary insights into the Biblical story.

* Westermann, Claus. *A Thousand Years and a Day*. Trans. Stanley Rudman. Philadelphia: Muhlenberg Press, 1961. A superior type of "popularization" by an expert who writes for nonspecialists.

Wright, G. Ernest. *Biblical Archaeology*. Philadelphia: The Westminster Press, 1957. The Biblical story as illustrated by archaeology.

* Wright, G. E., and Reginald H. Fuller. *The Book of the Acts of God*. Anchor Paperback 222. New York: 1957. Popular retelling of the Biblical story with illumination from history and archaeology.

Index of Special Subjects

Various subjects are discussed at different places throughout this commentary in order to supply more adequate background in key areas. Since these discussions are not as readily accessible as are the subjects discussed in the Introduction, the place where each occurs is here listed, together with the passage where it is best illustrated.

Ark

Its significance as the Lord's throne (1 Sam. 4—6), pp. 47 f.
Its procession ritual (2 Sam. 6), pp. 260 f.

Covenant

Basic elements in an ancient covenant (1 Sam. 12), pp. 97 ff.
Covenant Lawsuit—The mediator of the covenant indicts the covenant breakers (1 Sam. 7), p. 66
Cycle of covenant breaking and restoration (1 Sam. 12:7-15), pp. 101 f.

Historiography

> Historicity of the accounts, Introduction, pp. 18 f.
> Various types of history
>> 1. Eyewitness or contemporary accounts (2 Sam. 9 – 20), pp. 279 f.
>> 2. Archives-like reports (2 Sam. 8), pp. 272 f.
>> 3. Literary dramatization of a covenant lawsuit (1 Sam. 7), p. 66
>> 4. Narrative shaped by liturgical celebration (2 Sam. 6), pp. 260 f.
>
> Methodology of Israelite historian: compilation of existing traditions (2 Sam. 8), pp. 272 f. (cf. Introduction, pp. 14 ff.)
> Discordant Traditions
>> 1. In general, cf. Introduction, pp. 14 ff.
>> 2. Typical path of a tradition from its oral origin to its ultimate place in the final edition of a written history-compilation (2 Sam. 1:17), pp. 233 f.
>> 3. Varying traditions (1 Sam. 11), pp. 89 f. (cf. also pp. 150 f., 158)
>
> Evidence of successive editings (2 Sam. 21 – 24), p. 361

Holy War

> General procedures (1 Sam. 13 – 14), pp. 105 ff. (also pp. 48 f., 125)
> The ban of the holy war (1 Sam. 15), pp. 123 ff.

Lot, The Sacred

> Procedures (1 Sam. 14:16-23), pp. 116 f. (cf. also pp. 86 f., 185)

Numbers

Use, variants in Septuagint versions, "thousand" *('eleph)* as "clan unit" (1 Sam. 11:8), pp. 93 f.

Poetry, Patterns of

Elegy (2 Sam. 1:17-27), pp. 233 f.
Hymn (descriptive praise) (1 Sam. 2:1-10), pp. 33 f.
Psalm of praise (narrative praise) (2 Sam. 22), pp. 367 ff.

Prophooy

Calling a prophet (1 Sam. 3), pp. 43 ff.
Doom pronouncement, its typical pattern (1 Sam. 2:27-36), pp. 39 f.
Messianic prophecies
    "The faithful priest" (1 Sam. 2:35), pp. 41 f.
    "The sure house of David" (2 Sam. 7), pp. 267 ff.
    "The Lord's servant" (2 Sam. 22), pp. 367 ff.
    "The last words of David" (2 Sam. 23:1-7), pp. 375 f.
Successive refocusings of prophecy (1 Sam. 2:35), pp. 41 f.

Text

Additions from Septuagint (1 Sam. 29:10), p. 218 (cf. also p. 292)
Appendices added (2 Sam. 21 – 24), pp. 361 f.
Copyist's slip (1 Sam. 13:15), p. 111
Portions omitted in Septuagint and Qumran versions (1 Sam. 17:55 – 18:5), p. 151